SOCIAL POLICY AND SOCIAL WORK

SECOND EDITION

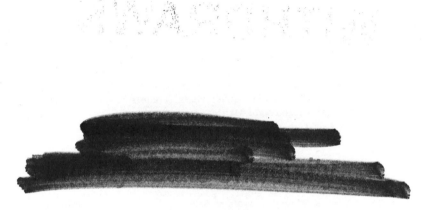

MODERN APPLICATIONS OF SOCIAL WORK

An Aldine de Gruyter Series of Texts and Monographs

SERIES EDITOR

James K. Whittaker

Paul Adams and Kristine E. Nelson (eds.), **Reinventing Human Services: Community and Family Centered Practice**

Ralph E. Anderson and Irl Carter, **Human Behavior in the Social Environment: A Social Systems Approach** (Fourth Edition)

Richard P. Barth, Mark Courtney, Jill Duerr Berrick, and Vicky Albert, **From Child Abuse to Permanency Planning: Child Welfare Services Pathways and Placements**

Kathleen Ell and Helen Northen, **Families and Health Care: Psychosocial Practice**

Marian Fatout, **Models for Change in Social Group Work**

Mark W. Fraser, Peter J. Pecora, and David A. Haapala, **Families in Crisis: The Impact of Intensive Family Preservation Services**

James Garbarino, **Children and Families in the Social Environment** (Second Edition)

James Garbarino, and Associates, **Special Children—Special Risks: The Maltreatment of Children with Disabilities**

James Garbarino, and Associates, **Troubled Youth, Troubled Families: Understanding Families At-Risk for Adolescent Maltreatment**

Roberta R. Greene, **Social Work with the Aged and Their Families**

Roberta R. Greene, **Human Behavior Theory: A Diversity Framework**

Roberta R. Greene and Paul H. Ephross, **Human Behavior Theory and Social Work Practice**

André Ivanoff, Betty J. Blythe, and Tony Tripodi, **Involuntary Clients in Social Work Practice: A Research-Based Approach**

Susan P. Kemp, James K. Whittaker, and Elizabeth M. Tracy, **Person-Environment Practice: The Sociology of Interpersonal Helping**

Paul K. H. Kim (ed.), **Serving the Elderly: Skills for Practice**

Jill Kinney, David A. Haapala, and Charlotte Booth, **Keeping Families Together: The Homebuilders Model**

Robert M. Moroney and Judy Krysik, **Social Policy and Social Work: Critical Essays on the Welfare State** (Second Edition)

Peter J. Pecora, Mark W. Fraser, Kristine Nelson, Jacqueline McCroskey, and William Meezan, **Evaluating Family-Based Services**

Peter J. Pecora, James K. Whittaker, Anthony N. Maluccio, Richard P. Barth, and Robert D. Plotnick, **The Child Welfare Challenge: Policy, Practice, and Research**

Robert L. Selman, Caroline L. Watts, and Lynn Hickey Schultz (eds.), **Fostering Friendship: Pair Therapy for Treatment and Prevention**

John R. Schuerman, Tina L. Rzepnicki, and Julia H. Littell, **Putting Families First: An Experiment in Family Preservation**

Madeline R. Stoner, **The Civil Rights of Homeless People: Law, Social Policy, and Social Work Practice**

Betsy S. Vourlekis and Roberta R. Greene (eds). **Social Work Case Management**

James K. Whittaker, and Associates, **Reaching High-Risk Families: Intensive Family Preservation in Human Services**

SOCIAL POLICY AND SOCIAL WORK
Critical Essays on the Welfare State

SECOND EDITION

Robert M. Moroney and Judy Krysik

ALDINE DE GRUYTER

New York

About the Authors

Robert M. Moroney is Professor of Social Policy and Planning at the School of Social Work, Arizona State University. Dr. Moroney is the author of eight books and over sixty articles and book chapters on various aspects of policy, planning and program evaluation. Dr. Moroney currently serves as a board member of the Rosalyn Carter Institute for Human Development.

Judy Krysik is an adjunct professor at the School of Social Work, Arizona State University where she teaches social policy and research.

ALDINE DE GRUYTER
A division of Walter de Gruyter, Inc.
200 Saw Mill River Road
Hawthorne, New York 10532

This publication is printed on acid free paper ⊚

Library of Congress Cataloging-in-Publication Data
Moroney, Robert, 1936–
    Social policy and social work : critical issues on the welfare
state / Robert M. Moroney and Judy Krysik. — 2nd ed.
        p.   cm. — (Modern applications of social work)
    Includes bibliographical references and index.
    ISBN 0-202-36113-6 (cloth : alk. paper). — ISBN 0-202-36114-4
(pbk. : alk. paper)
    1. Public welfare—United States.   2. Social service—United
States.   3. United States—Social policy.   I. Krysik, Judy.
II. Title.   III. Series.
HV95.M66   1998
361.973—dc21   97-46375
                                                    CIP

Manufactured in the United States of America
10 9 8 7 6 5 4 3 2 1

From R.M.M: in Memory of Matthew Iles
From J.L.K. to Alonso Peralta

Contents

Preface to the Second Edition

The decade of the 1990s has been a period of rapid change in our society, with the area of social policy being no exception. In the short time between the publication of the first edition of this book and this edition, we have seen radical changes in the relationship between the public and private sector and, within the public sector, between the federal government and state and local governments.

Privatization in areas that historically have been the responsibility of government, e.g., corrections, child welfare, and income maintenance, are now being transferred in part to the private sector. Moreover, this transfer has been to a growing for-profit sector, operating on the assumption that the private sector is more capable than the public sector and the for-profit sector superior to the voluntary sector. Notions of profit-taking, efficiency, and effectiveness are being seen as interchangeable. Furthermore, much of this is based on belief and not on fact. We do not know the benefits and costs of this new partnership.

Reforms in welfare, Medicare, and Medicaid and retrenchments in areas such as housing have been implemented that will have far-reaching affects on the fabric of our society and will reshape the welfare state begun in the 1930s. Historical ideas that have shaped our welfare system are being questioned. Ideas that have included entitlement and universal provision of services are being replaced with time-limited benefits to the vulnerable, means testing, and dual-service delivery systems for the poor and the nonpoor.

In this edition, we go beyond the argument in the original publication. There we discussed the perceived dichotomy between two major approaches to social welfare—the institutional and residual models—and argued that the former assumed shared responsibility and supported notions of communities, while the latter was concerned with the extension of rights to the individual. In this edition we have expanded the argument beyond the dichotomy, and by incorporating notions of citizenship, we now suggest that elements of both approaches can be integrated in such a way that the modified framework attempts to handle the critics from both sides.

We assume that changes will continue to occur after this book is published, but we still believe that the conceptual framework developed in the first edition and modified here will still be useful to analyze these changes as they unfold.

Robert M. Moroney
Judy Krysik
Tempe, Arizona

Preface to the First Edition

Taken separately, the ideas expressed in this book are not new. Other analysts have applied concepts associated with political economy, still others have introduced normative frameworks. This book attempts to integrate both frameworks.

Throughout this book, we argue that it is only possible to understand our system of social policies by understanding our particular political economy. The term "political economy" itself is not familiar to most people, and yet, until this century, political economy was a subject taught at most universities. Political economists were those who studied the relationship between the economic and political system of a particular country, a relationship characterized as one in which the primary goal of the state was to further the goals of the prevailing economic system. Given this, social policies were instruments used by the State to achieve these ends. It was only in this century that, in an attempt to remove the social sciences from any hint of being normative, the two were separated into two distinct disciplines: economics and political science.

What I find troublesome, however, is that, when asked if they have heard the term "political economy" most students I have taught over the past twenty years associate it with socialism and communism. They seem to be unaware that our capitalist society with its assumptions of free enterprise is a type of political economy, and it needs to be understood if we are to understand why we have the social policies we have. They are there for a reason.

Our purpose is not to suggest that capitalism is the "enemy" and the solution requires finding an alternative. While we do suggest that some forms of capitalism, such as those found in a number of European countries, offer a more balanced perspective on the relationship between economic and social objectives and define the functions of the State, industry, and the work force in less hostile and competitive terms, our major concern in this book is to identify where and under what conditions social policies intersect with economic policies. As we point out, capitalism is a system that inevitably produces cycles of growth followed by cycles of recession; cycles of inflation and cycles of high unemployment. A primary task of the welfare state, then, becomes one of humanizing these cycles, of buffering the periodic hardships suffered by some people and of providing an infrastructure for those who seem to be rejected by the economic system. It is a system in which there are winners and losers, and more often than not, we can predict who the winners and losers will be. This becomes critical when our beliefs about the free-enterprise system are not supported by empirical data, e.g., economic growth does not benefit all, the benefits only trickle down so far.

A second framework used in the analysis is one that attempts to tease out the underlying assumptions of our political economy as they relate to our understanding of human relationships and to balance these assumptions with alternative perspectives. We argue that an emphasis on individualism and freedom runs counter to notions of community and interdependence and that the trade-offs need to be exposed. Furthermore, we suggest that this belief in freedom and individualism has produced a somewhat divided society in which people with common needs are unwittingly pitted against each other as they compete for scarce resources.

Third, we develop the analysis by choosing six policy areas. Three of these deal with substantive areas such as (1) income maintenance, (2) housing, and (3) the personal social services. Three others deal with population groups (1) families and children, (2) the elderly, and (3) the poor. The reader will quickly see the many overlaps between the chapters. This was done purposely. Our choice of these six areas is not offered as an exhaustive list of the major policy issues. While we deal with Medicare and Medicaid in some depth in the chapter focusing on the elderly, the issue of health care could have been treated more comprehensively in a separate chapter. We chose these six to demonstrate that the frameworks used have relevance in analyzing substantive areas of target populations. One additional comment needs to be introduced. In dealing with each example of policy, we have taken time to trace the history of that policy. We recognize that many students today either believe that history has nothing to offer or that history began the day they were born. Furthermore, they argue, history is not exciting. We cannot argue that history is exciting (exciting is in the eye of the beholder) but we can argue that to ignore history is to arrive at an incomplete and at times an inaccurate understanding of a particular policy area.

Finally a few words on the subtitle of this book: *Critical Essays on the Welfare State*. There are two parts to this: (1) critical essays and (2) essays on the welfare state. These two phrases are used in acknowledgment of the contributions of two theorists, Habermas and Titmuss.

Jurgen Habermas, the current leader of the Frankfort School of Critical Theory has forcefully argued the need to integrate empirical analysis with a concern for normative questions. For Habermas, analysis needs to be grounded in acceptable methodological rigor, but it also must go beyond the limits imposed by logical positivists. The analyst cannot be "detached" and value free when he or she deals with policy issues. Rather, it is appropriate for the analyst to go beyond description and explanation and to provide insight or understanding into the "why" of policies, especially if those policies strengthen or maintain inequalities in that society. He urges the analyst to probe and uncover contradictions so that corrective action might become part of the decision-making discussion.

Titmuss, on the other hand, is more widely known and has long been an advocate for universal services and the building of communities through social policies. Many of the seminal ideas he introduced in his 1958 publication, *Essays on the Welfare State,* are found throughout this analysis and are as useful today as they were then.

Robert M. Moroney,
Tempe, AZ

CHAPTER

1

The Field of Policy

The purpose of this chapter is to introduce and then explore the concept of policy as a process of decision-making. Rather than attempting to offer a precise definition of policy at the outset, we begin instead with the concept of decision-making and then describe policy analysis in terms of four significant "decision" questions:

- What *should* be done when confronted with a situation that has been labeled a problem?
- What *can* be done?
- What *must* be done?
- *By whom* should it be done?

The relevance of these four questions as a general guide to policy formulation and analysis is discussed in the context of the Social Security Act.

We then examine a number of key issues—always found in policy debates in this country—which are concerned with rationales for government intervention: under what conditions and for what purposes should government become involved in the lives of its citizens? Explicit in our treatment of social policy is the importance of political economy as it shapes social policy. We argue that it is unreasonable to analyze policy without (1) acknowledging the interrelationship between political and economic processes, and (2) recognizing that the political economy of a society, whether it be some form of capitalism or socialism, will determine that society's social policies. Political economy, as used in this book, recognizes that the primary role of the state is to support the existing economic system and that social policies are instruments used by the state to achieve economic objectives. We will argue throughout our analysis that unless this notion of interrelationship is understood, it is not possible to understand our existing policies, e.g., income maintenance, housing, personal social services, and mental health.

1

DECISION-MAKING AND CHOICE

Policy is primarily concerned with decision-making and choosing among alternative courses of action. Choices have to be made among competing claims for resources, each of which may be reasonable or at least perceived as reasonable by some group. Policy might involve the question of allocating resources between, e.g., defense, transportation, and social programs. It might be concerned with choosing between specific military systems or choosing between health programs for children or for the aged. To complicate this decision-making or choice process even further, we are also faced with issues involving the future. Shall we continue to consume existing natural resources at a rate that will leave little for future generations or shall we ration their use now so that adequate resources will be available for our children and grandchildren? Shall we continue to allow the national debt to increase (with its impact on the federal deficit) so that our children's and their children's future is heavily mortgaged before they are even born? An overriding concern in all of these situations is a term used by economists: *opportunity costs*. Simply stated, this means that once a decision is made to support one goal or claim, e.g., health programs for the aged, we have, de facto, made a decision to forgo supporting other valued goals or claims.

Choices also have to be made between proposed implementation strategies once a goal has been established. These would include:

- issues of financing and reimbursement, e.g., sources of revenue and formulas for sharing costs;
- whether to use market mechanisms or public provision, or some combination of both;
- appropriateness of administrative mechanisms for a particular policy; and
- level(s) of government involvement and appropriateness of roles.

Policy formulation, then, involves a *process* of decision-making that results in selecting a course of action. It is a dynamic activity that is open to modification when conditions change. The products of policy (e.g., a law, a set of regulations, or a judicial statement) are also subject to modification over time for the same reasons. Policy, therefore, is a fairly stable but potentially changeable statement of a desired *end* or goal. The development of policy involves the identification of alternative strategies or *means* to achieve these goals, and the identification and application of criteria judged useful in choosing among the strategies. Policy is also concerned with the *implementation* of the chosen strategy and, finally, the *evaluation* of its impact. Because policy contains statements of goals and values, depends on procedures to analyze alternatives, and is concerned with implementation strategies and evaluation of results, it consequently includes both normative and technical aspects.

Policy formulation begins with the following:

- the definition of the problem;
- the presentation of relevant information;
- a critical appraisal of the dynamics of the underlying issue; and
- tracing through the implications of various courses of action.

Analysis, the cornerstone of the policy process, begins with description. This descriptive function raises a variety of questions from a range of sources and, to the extent possible, ensures a balanced perspective. Analysis clarifies and sharpens the discussion. This does not mean, however, that the analysis is value-neutral or value-free.

Policymakers *label* a condition or situation a "problem" to be corrected or, in some instances, a source of future problems. We are using the term "problem" in a specific way: as a condition that needs addressing, one on which action will be taken. This labeling is based in part on the analysis and in part on the beliefs and values of the policymaker. At this point in the process we have shifted from a purely descriptive/analytic set of activities to one that integrates both descriptive and normative aspects or dimensions—one that addresses the question of *what should be done*.

When sufficient consensus is reached by the policymakers and political preferences have emerged, short- and long-range strategies need to be developed. These are often shaped by the existing state of knowledge and technology, the availability of resources, and political feasibility. The questions now shifts from What should be done? to What *can* be done?

Since many so-called experts disagree on ways to solve complex social problems, we are usually faced with choosing among alternative solutions. Procedures are required to carefully weigh each proposal—procedures that are grounded in competing and often contradictory values, emphasizing for example:

- individual freedom
- efficiency
- effectiveness
- equality
- equity
- comparative justice

As will be argued throughout this book, these and other values cannot be simultaneously *maximized*—a concept used by economists, which in essence means you can only realize one value at the expense of the others.

Finally, policy is concerned with implementation issues. These include questions of coverage, financing, administrative structures, personnel requirements, and the roles of the public and private sector.

The policy process, then, is a blend of fact and preference. The participants in this process include policymakers, policy analysts, policy implementors, policy influencers or special-interest groups advocating specific policies, and the recipients of the policy. While roles often become merged, or at least blurred, these are the actors (Rein 1970; Moroney 1976, 1986a; Baumheimer and Schorr 1977).

The above description of the general policy process can be thought of as a response to the four fundamental questions: What should be done? What can be done? What must be done? By whom should it be done? The following example takes this framework and applies it to the Social Security Act of 1935.

THE SOCIAL SECURITY ACT OF 1935: AN EXAMPLE

What Should Be Done?

This question is normative in that it seeks to identify the goal we hope to achieve. We often assume that the (elected) policymaker has the responsibility to answer the question in that he or she, having been elected, is seen as the person who in theory has offered his or her ideas, proposals, or even vision to an electorate, and in being elected has had these affirmed by "the people." The policymaker is given a mandate and is held accountable through an elaborate system of political checks and balances, the ultimate being the reelection process. In turn, elected officials appoint administrators who not only have a responsibility to implement policies, but in reality will also make policies.

For example, in 1935, Congress passed the Social Security Act, legislation emphasizing that the economic security of the people of the United States was an important national goal. No comparable public statement had existed before. Historically, American social policy has been shaped by a belief in laissez-faire economics. Initially, this position assumed that the positive force of the free-enterprise system far outweighed the potential negative impact of government intervention in the economy or in the lives of people. In fact, state intervention was thought to be legitimate only if its purpose was to strengthen and support the free market's continuing operation.

In time, society began to recognize the need to humanize the economic system—to develop a buffer by providing corrective measures for individuals who were shunted aside by the market system. These attempts to balance individual and collective welfare with the free-enterprise system were grounded in the long-standing Poor Law tradition. People were divided into two groups: (1) a minority, or residual group, who needed assistance to survive, and (2) the majority, who could take care of their own needs without government intervention.

Almost all social policy prior to the Social Security Act purposely ignored the well-being of this majority in the belief that they would always be self-sufficient. When these individuals did experience difficulty, the cause of their problems was believed to be either a moral flaw in their character or some other personal deficit (Wilensky and Lebeaux 1965).

The Social Security Act was a departure from this view insofar as it acknowledged that modernization and industrialization had created risks and consequences that potentially affected *all people* and not just a small percentage of the population (Wilensky and Lebeaux 1965; Hobbs, Dokecki, Dempsey, and Moroney 1984). When we believed that only small numbers of people were involved we could and did, in Ryan's (1976) term, "blame the victim." However, when these numbers increased (as they did during the depression), this belief became untenable. Not only did the numbers of unemployed people increase dramatically—4 million in 1930, 8 million in 1931, 12 million in 1932, 18 million in 1933—but these people had formerly been productive and still wanted to work. To argue that these people were the cause of their own unemployment was not only irrational but was politically untenable.

Beginning with the Social Security Act, enacted over 60 years ago, we have responded to the question What should be done? by identifying basic goods and services citizens should have as rights:

- economic security;
- employment (the Federal Employment Act of 1946 expressed the goal of full employment for everyone able to work);
- housing [the Housing Act of 1949 (P.L. 81-171) stated that all Americans have "the right to decent housing, in decent surroundings of their choosing"];
- health (the Comprehensive Health Planning Act of 1967 stated that Americans have the right to the highest quality of health care services available);
- education for handicapped children (P.L. 94-142 of 1975 insured the provision of a free, appropriate public education for all).

What Can Be Done?

The translation of these broad goals into actual programs proved to be much more elusive. While politically tenable, goals are stated in such a general fashion that they cannot serve as working objectives (Baumheimer and Schorr 1977). Specific proposals are shaped by the availability of resources and competing demands for those resources, knowledge and technology, political acceptability, and administrative capability. Comprehensive approaches give way to piecemeal solutions. Concern about a situation is, of course, a necessary prerequisite, but unless viable strategies are available, this concern has limited value.

Today, social welfare analysts have identified a number of mechanisms that government might use to achieve the economic security of its citizens. The government can, for example:

- act as employer, e.g., through public works projects;
- stimulate the development of jobs through the tax system;
- subsidize jobs for the hard-core unemployed as it did in the automobile industry during the 1960s;
- stimulate economic growth at the national and state levels under the assumption that such growth would eventually "trickle down" to all people;
- provide services aimed at bridging the gap between work force supply and employment demand, e.g., education, job training, and job placement; and
- transfer funds directly to those who are "economically insecure," e.g., social insurance, unemployment insurance, family allowances, public assistance, or negative income tax programs.

It is important to note, however, that each of the strategies emerges from a different set of assumptions about the nature of the problem. Moreover, proponents of one solution argue that certain strategies are counterproductive to other strategies, e.g., economic growth is negatively affected when direct transfers are substantial or when expenditures for social programs reach a certain level.

While our "knowledge" today has produced a range of possible theories leading to multiple proposals to achieve economic security, such was not the case in the depression. By 1932 the economy was paralyzed, public confidence was shaken, and the clamor for increased government action was growing. One problem facing the policy analysts and decision-makers of the day was that there were few precedents on which to fall back. Furthermore, the number and types of alternatives were limited to those that emphasized the need to strengthen the existing free-enterprise system.

Two major strategies were eventually enacted: (1) social insurance and (2) social assistance. Social insurance provided benefits to the aged who could not work (a federally administered plan of compulsory old-age annuities; OASI, old-age social insurance) and to those who were temporarily unemployed through no fault of their own (a federal-state program of unemployment insurance; UI).

Social insurance was viable for two reasons: (1) It was *politically acceptable* because, in theory, benefits were given to people who had made prior payments. Given this, it was argued, the program was built on sound actuarial principles. Recipients did not feel stigmatized since they were entitled to the benefits. (2) The policy formulators had a number of existing social insurance models to draw upon. *They were not creating a new, untested system.* In the 1880s Bismarck had initiated a set of social insurance programs in the newly unified Germany, and early in the twentieth century, Lloyd George, the prime minister of England, developed an insurance system in England.

The second major strategy—social assistance—was, in effect, an extension of the Poor Law with its emphasis on the dole and "work relief," although great pains were taken to argue that the Poor Law was being replaced. The English Poor Laws (often referred to as the "Elizabethan Poor Laws") had been brought to the American colonies by the early settlers and became the basis for the modern public assistance programs. The Poor Laws established public responsibility for the care of the "worthy" poor. Under these laws, responsibility was placed on local communities to care for those residents who were aged, sick, handicapped, or the children of widows and orphans. They were labeled "worthy" in the sense they were not held accountable for their poverty.

The Social Security Act of 1935, recognizing that some persons would not be covered by social insurance, established three categories of social assistance: Old Age Assistance (OAA), Aid to the Blind (AB), and Aid to Dependent Children (ADC). Unlike the social insurance programs under which people received benefits as their right, beneficiaries under the social assistance programs were required to pass a means test proving that they were old, blind, or a dependent child *and* poor, i.e., their income was below some predetermined level.

Work relief was another Poor Law program with deep historical roots. After 200 years of trying to deter vagrancy and indiscriminate almsgiving through harsh measures (e.g., imprisonment, flogging, maiming, and even death for the "incorrigibles"), Parliament, over a 100-year period, (1495–1597) passed a series of new Poor Law statutes that clearly delineated between the "impotent" or "worthy poor" and the "sturdy beggar" or "ablebodied" poor. This latter group was forced to work on local government projects—forced in the sense that if they refused to work, they were remanded to local houses of correction. Throughout the seventeenth and eighteenth centuries these "work-fare" programs were modified, culminating in the watershed reform of 1834, known as the Victorian Poor Laws.

Whereas the social assistance income maintenance programs focused on the worthy poor (i.e., those unable to work through no fault of their own), the employment programs targeted the ablebodied poor, who could and should work. Work, it was believed, not only provided the individual with the means to buy needed goods and services and thus stimulate economic growth, it not only supported and maintained the economy by guaranteeing a viable work force, it also had spiritual and psychological value for the individual. Therefore, people who could work, should work. While the particular forms of work relief changed in the thirties from coercive to voluntary, and while the work itself became more meaningful, the basic assumptions remained the same. The Roosevelt administration decided early in 1933 to create jobs for the ablebodied. Through programs such as the Federal Emergency Relief Act (FERA), the Civilian Conservation Corps (CCC), the Public Works Administration (PWA), and the Civil Works Administration (CWA), government created millions of jobs.

While radical in terms of national government involvement, both the income support program (social assistance) and employment programs had a historical basis. While certain demeaning aspects of the Poor Law were replaced with a more humane system, this country's response to the depression was not a rejection of that Poor Law. The earlier laissez-faire system was humanized through significant modifications, but the philosophy of that system was incorporated into the New Deal. This was a political necessity at that time and these century-old underpinnings provide us with insights into current income maintenance programs.

The stated national goal of economic security for *all* was translated into income support for the aged, the blind, and children without fathers, and jobs for the ablebodied. If an individual was in economic need but did not fall into one of these categories, that individual received no assistance. Decisions were made as to which portion of the population would be covered and which would be excluded. The specific strategies chosen were, moreover, shaped by political and ideological factors. The approach continued to emphasize the value of (1) independent, strong, competitive individuals and families and (2) a state concerned primarily with economic principles.

When the state did intervene, it would do so reluctantly and minimally, consistent with the well-being of the economy and only secondarily with humanitarian concerns. Social policy in the 1930s continued to emphasize the provision of a minimum standard of living and (with the exception of the social insurance program) a reactive, crisis-oriented provision of goods and services. It was guided by economic concepts, with social services functioning as "the ambulance at the bottom of the cliff, rather than the fence at the top that prevented people from falling over" (Marsh 1970:13). For example, unemployment insurance does not prevent unemployment, health insurance does not prevent illness, and social assistance does not foster independence and self-reliance. In previous times we spoke of subsistence levels and a basic minimum. Today, we speak of a safety net—one whose holes expand and contract not as a response to shifting human need but as a response to the needs of the economy at that time. Unfortunately, there tends to be an inverse relationship between the two sets of needs, i.e., when the economy contracts or stagnates, human needs increase; when the economy heats up and expands, more people are able to care for themselves.

What Must Be Done?

The decision that something must be done provides a stimulus for action. During 1931–1932, for example, talk of revolution and civil unrest was widespread. Hunger riots were common, and many unemployed and homeless persons were being arrested, some by their own choice. The Soviet Union advertised for skilled workers to construct its dams and over 100,000 Americans applied. Perhaps the single most important event was the Bonus March of 1932, when World War I veterans came to Washington demanding the bonus they had been promised by a grateful Congress after the war was won. President Hoover's response was to call in the army under General Douglas MacArthur, which burned the veterans' tent encampments and physically forced the veterans to leave the city. The image of mounted soldiers riding through scores of veterans wearing their uniforms and medals horrified the nation.

The Hoover administration experienced a number of equally devastating public relations fiascos. States, having exhausted their own resources, requested the federal government to become more directly involved in supporting their "public relief" efforts. In some instances this meant direct financial support to the unemployed; in other cases, low-interest loans; and in a small number of instances, money to buy seed for farmers who otherwise would not be able to plant their crops.

President Hoover refused their requests, arguing that such involvement was unconstitutional. His position was that similar federal involvement had been tested earlier when President Pierce vetoed a bill to establish federally supported institutions for the mentally ill. In his veto Pierce stated:

If Congress is to make such provision for such objects, the fountains of charity will be dried up at home, and several states instead of bestowing their own means in the social wants of their own people, may themselves through strong temptation, which appeals to the States as individuals, become humble supplicants for the bounty of the federal government, reversing their true relation to the Union. (Trattner 1974:62)

During this same period, the president approved the awarding of millions of dollars to a small number of banks experiencing financial difficulties. President Hoover publicly argued that, while direct aid to individuals was not constitutional, the direct support of banks was. These actions, and many others, were instrumental in his losing the election in 1932. As a result of that election, Roosevelt perceived that he had been given a mandate to deal with these problems. Even the Supreme Court supported the administration's becoming directly involved in assisting people, by declaring in 1937 that the Social Security Act was constitutional. Reacting to President Pierce's earlier veto the Court concluded:

[N]eeds that were narrow or parochial a century ago may be interwoven in our day with the well-being of the nation. (Helvering v. Davis, 301 U.S. 619, 641, 57, Sup. Ct. 904, 908, 81 L. Ed. 1307)

Another aspect of the question of what must be done concerned the level of effort to be implemented. As discussed above, not all people would be covered. Benefits would be given primarily to the elderly, the blind, children without fathers, and those who were temporarily unemployed. This, however, is only one part of the issue. The other decision concerned the amount they would receive. Table 1.1 shows the average monthly benefit under each program in 1940, (as well as 1993 for comparative purposes), and the percentage of the median income that the benefit constituted.

Table 1.1. Average Monthly Benefits: Social Security, 1940 and 1993[a]

	Average benefit ($)		Percentage of median family income[b]	
Program[c]	1940	1993	1940	1993
OASI	22.60	567.26	22	18
UI	42.24	692.00	41	22
OAA (SSI)	20.25	317.41	19	10
AB (SSI)	25.35	317.41	25	10
ADC (AFDC)	32.40	373.00	32	12

[a]With the exception of ADC, all beneficiaries are individuals. ADC beneficiaries are families.
[b]Program names for 1993 are in parentheses.
[c]Median monthly family income was $102.42 in 1940 and $3,158.75 in 1993.

All grants were well below the average monthly income for an employed worker ($102.42). Economic security, by definition, involved the provision of benefits to achieve and maintain subsistence, i.e., the minimum necessary to meet basic needs, and not wage replacement.

Who Should Do It?

This fourth question deals specifically with the appropriate roles of government and the private sector. Should responsibility for meeting the basic needs of people reside in the private or the public sector, and if the latter, at which level of government? If the former, should this be through the not-for-profit of the for-profit sector? Should needs be met directly by providing goods and services or indirectly through market mechanisms? The Social Security Act is an excellent example of a mixed strategy:

- The compulsory retirement program (OASI) was financed through payroll taxes contributed to by both employer and employee and administered by the federal government.
- Under the employment insurance (UI) program, employers were taxed by the federal government, which then channeled these funds to states to administer.
- The social assistance programs (OAA, AB, ADC) were to be financed by both the federal and state governments and administered by the state.
- The service components of the act (public health, child welfare, etc.) were also financed by both levels of governments and administered by the state.

In some instances, services were provided by government (e.g., medical care services for children, adoption services, surplus food), but in the income programs, which assumed that recipients were capable of purchasing what they needed in the market, individuals received money. To understand this mixed strategy, we now need to examine our views toward government and identify those preconditions necessary for intervention.

RATIONALES FOR GOVERNMENT INTERVENTION

All of the rationales on which the government might justify its intervention in social and economic life are based on three general assumptions:

The first assumption states that an economic system characterized by perfectly competitive markets provides socially optimal results, i.e., products of the highest quality will be provided at reasonable prices when people (consumers) want them. A market may be defined as a group of people who are in contact with one another for the purpose of buying and selling some commodity. Given this, the appropriate role of government is to refrain from entering those markets. The one exception is when a market(s) does not yield those optimal results predicted by the model of perfect competition (Adam Smith's "invisible hand").

The second assumption suggests that certain goods and services are the rights of all people by the nature of their citizenship. Such goods and services, called "merit wants," are usually specified in basic social documents, such as the Constitution, or may be legislatively mandated. An example would be trial by a jury of one's peers.

The third assumption rests on the concept of *public goods*. At the heart of this concept is the distinction between collective and individual action and between public and private action. But what persuades members of a society that values individualism to seek a collective solution to a problem rather than to rely on their own individual action?

The need for collective action arises when individuals believe that they cannot achieve their objectives individually, that problems transcend individual solutions. Collective action is justified when some segment of the public wants and is prepared to pay for goods and services other than what the unhampered market will produce. Collective goods, however, need not be public goods, e.g., a voluntary church-sponsored food cooperative.

In its purest form, the public goods rationale for government intervention is invoked when the consumption of particular goods and services by a substantial proportion of the population does not prevent or preclude their consumption by the rest of the population. For example, when the government allocates resources for national defense, each citizen (in theory) can consume all of the security obtained from the expenditures without preventing others also from consuming the same amount of security. Local police and fire departments as well as governmental support of an art gallery can be similarly justified. One person's use and enjoyment of the facility does not use it up; others can use and enjoy it equally. The only constraint is the timing of consumption by each person, i.e., everyone cannot use the art gallery or the fire and police services at the same time.

Beyond these three arguments, two other rationales are often introduced: (1) externalities and (2) market imperfections.

1. Externalities and the Public Interest. The externality rationale is used when, in forcing individuals either to do something or to stop doing what they are doing, society as a whole benefits. Government is justified in intervening in the market even if individual members of the society may receive different benefits and even if some individuals may feel that the intervention is not warranted from their perspective.

It is assumed in these instances that the private market system will not produce the optimal quantity of the particular good because markets reflect the private benefits that accrue to each individual. Since "rational" individuals seek to maximize their own personal utility (well-being), they may not consider the utility of society or may consider that actions to improve the well-being of society may be at too great a personal expense.

Historically, services such as education and public health immunizations are justified on externality grounds. In both instances, individuals and society benefit from individual consumption of the services. In the first case, society as a whole achieves a general level of literacy; in the second, target diseases are eradicated, thereby improving the general health and productivity of the population. Moreover, all citizens pay for these services even if they are not using them, e.g., adults without children are taxed for schools.

> If the community, or at any rate, a sizable part of it has an interest in a particular utility accruing to an individual, then it would clearly be unreasonable to allow the creation of the more general utility to depend solely on that individual; he might not value the state activity highly enough to make the sacrifice of paying the required fee or charge, or else ignorance may cause him or poverty force him to do without the service. Herein lies the chief justification of the modern demands for free or very cheap processes of law, education, medical care, certain public health measures, etc. (Wicksell 1958:15)

The above are examples of "positive" externalities—a situation in which many people will benefit if actions are taken, even if coercion is used. Parents have to demonstrate that their children have received the required immunizations before they are allowed to begin school; children are required to attend school for so many years or until they reach the prescribed age; all working people are required to participate in the Social Security system whether or not they have alternative pension plans.

We also find "negative" externality arguments used to justify government intervention. While positive externalities force people to take action, the negative externality argument is used to force people to stop doing what they are doing. For example, a steel mill is forced to stop polluting the air because the pollution is negatively affecting residents of neighboring towns. This would be justified even if the residents of the town where the plant is located were to vote to maintain the existing system, arguing that pollution is a reasonable price to pay for guaranteed jobs. We often see negative externalities referred to as "neighborhood effects" in the literature.

2. *Market Imperfections.* Efficient (i.e., perfect) markets presuppose adequate information so that consumers can make informed decisions, timely adjustments (when a need arises, providers will respond quickly), sufficient competition, and modest transaction costs. The absence of any of these may legitimize government intervention in these imperfect markets. Government intervention may take a number of forms, some of which are more preferable than others under our specific political economy. If government is to become involved at all, that involvement should be as unintrusive as possible. The following interventions are listed in a hierarchal order, from most to least preferred:

- The provision of an extensive information and referral service so that people needing or wanting a service can find that service (e.g., a long-term-care clearinghouse that would inform families of available private nursing homes in a community). This assumes that adequate resources exist.
- Furthermore, if there are time lags in the private sector, i.e., there is a private market but it is incapable of meeting existing need because of a shortage of facilities or skilled personnel, government can intervene by stimulating supply side factors (e.g., low-cost construction loans and/or financial assistance for training programs).
- Regulations and licensing (e.g., a state might set standards, license and monitor nursing homes).
- Pay for the provision of a service (e.g., contract with private providers to pay for low income patients).
- The actual provision of a service (e.g., a county might administer its own system of public nursing homes).

As discussed earlier, the 1935 Social Security Act was a major departure from earlier social welfare measures in that it resulted in a much broader role for government. Moreover, each of the major provisions of the act was justified by one or more of the above rationales.

The income programs [social insurance (OASI), unemployment insurance (UI), and social assistance (OAA, AB, ADC)] were seen as necessary governmental responses because the economic system was not providing the socially optimal results predicted by the market. The benefits cannot, however, be defined as merit wants within a strict definition of the term, i.e., benefits provided as right of citizenship; nor do they meet the strict criteria of public goods in the sense that one person's consumption does not lessen the quantity of the good. They have been justified with an externality rationale: that it is in the public interest to provide these benefits. Moreover, by providing income benefits rather than goods and services, government preference was clearly for the least intrusive intervention—the giving of money so that individual recipients could enter existing markets to obtain desired or necessary goods.

The service programs under the act incorporated a similar justification. Public health and child welfare services were seen as necessary because of a nonresponsive market and also were justified under the externality rationale. These programs provided benefits not only to the individuals and families receiving them, but also to society as a whole. The decision was also made to provide services and goods (unlike the income programs that provided the means to purchase goods and services) and thus to directly influence patterns of consumption.

ROLES OF GOVERNMENT

The issue of governmental involvement goes beyond the issues discussed in the previous section. Once a decision has been made that government will become involved, the next issue of concern to be addressed is which level of government. America's political tradition historically has stressed decentralized decision-making, with wide discretion left to the states by constitutional reservation and political inclination.

The federal government has utilized the politically expedient grants-in-aid approach—one that is less intrusive than others—resulting in the states being given a significant role. This supports the strong historical preference for state and local administration of domestic programs. While some benefits such as social security and other income transfer programs are provided by the federal government directly, the great bulk of public services in health, education, housing, highway construction, public protection, parks and recreation, and social services are provided by state and local government, although all of these areas are partially funded by the federal government. As Heller has suggested:

> A very large part of what we do through Government is done through state and local units. They are the ones to whom we usually turn as we seek to maintain or upgrade our educational efforts, improve our physical and mental health, redevelop our decaying urban areas, build better and safer highways, overcome air and water pollution and equip our suburbs with water systems, sewers, roads, parks, schools and the like. The list is striking partly because each item on it represents either an essential function or a reasonable aspiration of a great and growing society; partly because each item falls squarely within the traditional sphere of state-local operations;

and partly because so many items on the list are suffused with a national interest that transcends state and local lives and demands federal action and support. (1967:121–22)

This pattern is deeply rooted in the historical development of this country. In the colonial period, before the advent of state and national governments, public services were the responsibility of local government, i.e., the township in New England, the county in the Southern Colonies, and a mixture of both patterns in New York and Pennsylvania. Throughout the nineteenth century, federal involvement was virtually nonexistent. Major exceptions at the federal level included medical care for merchant seamen, lepers, and Native Americans. The rationales for these three groups differed somewhat:

1.   Merchant seamen did not meet local residency requirements—did not pay local taxes—and therefore were not eligible for medical care (the existing market was imperfect). The nation needed a strong merchant navy for protection from external powers and to establish international trade relationships (the externality argument).
Given this, the federal government was justified in establishing a network of hospitals from Boston to New Orleans to serve this population group. Eventually, this network became the foundation of the U.S. Public Health Service.
2.   Leprosy was such a low-incidence condition requiring costly and highly specialized medical services that local and even state markets were not efficient providers (the existing market was imperfect). Leprosy was also an infectious disease and therefore the public interest required lepers to be quarantined (the externality argument). Based on these rationales the federal government established a specialized hospital for the treatment of leprosy at Carville, Louisiana.
3.   Medical care markets were nonexistent on reservations established by the federal government and market forces were not likely to respond (the existing market was imperfect and unintrusive measures were unlikely to prove effective). By law, Native Americans in the nineteenth century were not citizens of the state in which their reservation was located and therefore were not the responsibility of the state. This argument parallels that used in the case of the merchant seamen. Given this, the federal government was justified in establishing the Indian Health Service.

State involvement was equally small. The major exceptions were in the areas of mental illness and certain communicable diseases such as tuberculosis. The rationale used was similar to that used at the federal level in the case of lepers—low incidence and protection of the public interest.

Categorical Grants: A Growing Federal Role

Federal participation did, of course, increase significantly in the twentieth century. In the 1920s federal grants-in-aid were available for vocational education, vocational rehabilitation, and maternal and child health programs. During the depression, a dozen major grant programs were enacted. These were justified with the argument that the resources of state and local governments were inadequate to provide necessary public services since they were unable to raise sufficient revenue. Furthermore, it was argued that state and local taxes were not only inflexible and regressive but also that citizens would not receive equal treatment since some states were poorer than others.

These grant-in-aid programs, also referred to as *categorical programs,* established national goals, goals that transcended the right of state and local governments to decide on what services should be provided. National goals implied that citizens had rights that only the federal government could guarantee.

Through these programs, the federal government in effect told the states that they would receive federal funds but could only use them for specific types of programs. In fact, the federal government required that the states establish mandated organizational structures, deliver prescribed services, and accept certain federally determined eligibility standards.

Block Grants: The New Relationship

While the creation of those programs did effectively deal with the specific problems of targeted populations, the later movement toward block grants may be seen as a reaction to some of the problems created by categorical funding, that is, as they evolved the programs were no longer seen as person-focused, individualistic, or flexible, but rather program-focused, rule-driven, rigid, and not coordinated with other services.

Beginning in the mid-1960s, a number of block grants were developed in housing and community development. While cities were given these funds to combat urban problems (in this sense they were still categorical), they were also given considerable latitude in how they were to spend the money. In the early 1970s, Title XX of the Social Security Act was passed and block grants moved from the status of demonstration and experimentation to that of preferred federal government policy.

In the 1980s, the federal government expanded the block grant programs. Categorical programs increasingly gave way to this new approach. These included major block grants in the area of mental health and social services. In the 1990s, Congress has proposed an even greater expansion of block grants in the areas of child welfare, welfare reform, and medical care.

While states are offered these funds with fewer strings attached than under previous categorical programs, the federal government has also imposed ceilings on their share of the financing. The goal of greater state control of how the funds were to be spent has been tempered with the equally important federal goal of cost containment.

A RETRENCHMENT ON THE PART OF THE FEDERAL GOVERNMENT

In their book *Reinventing Government*, Osborne and Gaebler (1992) discuss the advantages of market-oriented government as involving the changing of systems (government services, competition, customer choice, accountability for results, and public enterprise). They note, however, that markets can create inequitable outcomes (e.g., poor people with limited access to health care). Because of this, Osborne and Gaebler stress the need to improve communities:

> To complement the efficiency and effectiveness of market mechanisms, we need the warmth and caring of families and neighborhoods and communities. As entrepreneurial governments move away from administrative bureaucracies, they need to embrace both markets *and* community. (p. 309)

Two significant attempts to move in this direction are the growth of *purchase of service contracting (POSC)* and *managed care*. The federal government first authorized state welfare departments to purchase services from other state agencies through amendments to the Social Security Act passed in 1962. In this early attempt at welfare reform, the federal government not only encouraged states to purchase services from other agencies, but also increased their match of funds from 50% to 75%. The policy left social services open-ended, and significantly expanded the eligible population. Through the 1967 amendments to the Social Security Act, Congress encouraged the states not only to expand their POSC but to purchase these services from private agencies.

Thirty years later, POSC not only has expanded, it has become the preferred vehicle for delivering many of the human services to the point that most private, not-for-profit agencies are dependent on these contracts for their survival (Eggers & Ng 1993; McMurtry et al. 1991). Under this program, agencies agree to provide a specific number of units of services to designated client populations. State agencies, beyond deciding on what services are to be delivered and to whom, have the responsibility to monitor the contracts, that is, they are concerned that the services are actually delivered and that they meet established quality standards. However, little if any attention to date has been given to evaluating the effectiveness of these services as to whether recipients are better off because of the services they received.

At the same time that the private agencies came to depend more heavily on these contracts, Congress began to cut back on the amount of federal dollars allocated for these services—as part of the block grant strategy: the new partnership was driven by what has become known as the "block, cap, and cut" approach to human services.

Kettner and Martin (1996) in their assessment of the impact of POSC on the private sector, found in their sample of 98 agencies drawn from all 50 states that, while 82% of the agencies reported that demand was increasing from clients who could not pay anything toward the costs of the services and over 90% of the agencies reported that demand was increasing from clients who could pay something but not all of the costs of the services, 45% of the agencies were forced to accept fewer clients, more clients were placed on waiting lists, 63% were forced to increase staff workloads, and 42% had to terminate programs in light of reduced funding.

Kettner and Martin also cite the findings of Knapp et al. (1990) suggesting that POSC has the potential for "fragmentation, discontinuity, complexity, low quality outputs, poorly targeted services, productive inefficiencies, and inappropriate replication, sectarianism and paternalism" (p. 24), and Gronbjerg, who found that "private, nonprofit agencies devote most of their efforts to serving middle and upper-middle income groups" (1990:24).

Managed care, which emerged in the 1980s, is a more recent innovation in the human services field. Block grants and POSC on one level provide more responsibility and flexibility to the states to determine what services will be offered and allow for new partnerships between the public and private sectors. On another level they have been the major instruments of cutbacks in the amount of resources available to the states. Managed care, on the other hand, has turned the human service system around, especially in the health and mental health fields. Flexibility has given way to a highly structured and rigid set of policies and procedures that determine the type and amount of services that providers will be allowed to deliver. Managed care is basically concerned with cost containment, and the organizations who reimburse providers are in a position to determine how much they will pay.

Under managed care, professional judgment and discretion have been diminished to the point where the needs of clients are only a part of the decision-making calculus. The concept of allowable costs has become more significant in determining what will be done. While different in many ways from the strategy of using Diagnostic Related Groupings (DRGs) introduced in the mid 1980s, one similarity is their reliance on relating the provision of services to a predetermined idea of what a typical client with a typical problem (diagnosis) will need. Furthermore, if providers exceed this level of services, the third-party payer will not reimburse them for these "additional" services.

And finally, the federal government, through the Government Performance and Results Act of 1993 (P.L. 103-61) and the administration's proposed Performance Act, will require government at all levels to establish *performance measures* for all federally funded programs falling under what will be known as Performance Partnership Grants (PPGs). While the operationalization of this new emphasis is still being worked out, some elements are taking shape, especially in the area of the process to be used to determine acceptable performance measurements.

The performance measurement movement is proposed as a management tool, not to be used to determine cutbacks and contain costs as its primary goal, but to "clarify what we want to achieve, document the contribution that we can make to achieving our goals, and document what we are getting for our investment" (U.S. Department of Health and Human Services, DHHS, 1997).

To develop these measures:

> important stakeholders, . . . from organizations representing potential grant recipients . . . selected not only for their personal expertise or perspective, but also because they have shown an ability to foster participation by interested stakeholders who are not able to attend the meetings (DHHS 1997)

will be asked, in advance of the meetings, to identify what results they would identify as important to their individual programs. This information, in turn, will be the basis for discussions at the regional meetings. The output from the regional meetings—lists of desired program results—will then be reviewed by various federal agencies who will evaluate them from a technical perspective (e.g., whether they are measurable or feasible).

The third phase of the process involves asking those who participated in the regional meetings to comment on the technical report and make additional recommendations to the Department of Health and Human Services (DHHS). Phases four and five involve the development of operational state plans to achieve the agreed-upon objectives and the actualization of meaningful partnerships among the affected stakeholders.

Table 1.2. Public Social Welfare Expenditures as Percentage of Gross Domestic Product[a]

	1950	1960	1970	1980	1990	1993
Social insurance	1.9	3.8	5.3	8.5	9.0	10.2
Public aid	0.9	0.8	1.6	2.7	2.6	3.4
Health	0.8	0.9	0.9	1.0	1.1	1.2
Education	2.5	3.5	5.0	4.5	4.5	5.1
Total	8.9	10.3	14.2	18.1	18.5	21.1

[a] Total includes other categories such as housing, veterans, etc.
Sources: Adapted from *Social Security Bulletin,* Annual Statistical Supplement, 1996. Washington DC: USGPO.

By 1993, the role of government in general and that of the federal government in particular had grown considerably. Social welfare expenditures as a percentage of the gross national product (GNP) have more than doubled since 1950 (see Table 1.2), with the largest increases occurring in the entitlement program: social security.

Given these increases, in conjunction with the federal deficit and the rising national debt, the mood in the country now seems to seriously question whether we should continue the federal government's functions as defined over the past 60 years, functions that include the establishment of broad national goals and the targeting of "at risk" recipient groups for specific health and social services (see Table 1.3).

In 1996, the federal government spent $241 billion to pay interest on the debt. This represented almost 15% of the federal budget for that year. Whereas this interest accounted for 7% of the budget throughout the decade of the 1960s and 10% of the budget throughout the decade of the 1970s, it averaged 18% in the 1980s. There are signs that the situation is improving—the deficit has shrunk significantly—but the debt continues to grow.

This concern with the deficit and the national debt seems to support the more historical position (i.e., predepression) of supporting state and

Table 1.3. Increases in the National Debt

	Federal Deficit	National Debt
1980	$74 billion	$800 billion
1985	$212 billion	$1.8 trillion
1990	$221 billion	$3.35 trillion
1996	$55 billion	$5.8 trillion

local governments' responsibilities to meet the health and social needs of their citizens.

The "new" role of the federal government emphasizes fewer federal restrictions, cutbacks on categorical programs that restrict the use of federal funds, and an increase in the number and amount of less-restrictive block grants. These shifts, however, raise a number of critical questions:

- Why would states expand their efforts and be willing to spend more on social programs when previously they were unwilling to do so?
- Are we retreating to the position that the federal government's responsibility should be restricted to national defense and other international issues?
- Are we arguing that *all*, or at least most, social and economic problems can be more effectively dealt with at the state and/or local level and that regional and national solutions are neither needed nor relevant?

Most proposals, moreover, in offering more autonomy and more responsibility to the states, are also capping the amounts of federal funds that will be available for these programs—caps that could be used to eliminate the use of federal funds for these purposes as a means of solving the federal deficit problem.

SUMMARY

This chapter has defined public policy as a process of making choices among competing demands, especially when there are scarce resources. In making these choices, decision-makers either implicitly or explicitly rely on values. The policy process has been identified as a set of activities addressing four basic questions. While the first question (What should be done?) is clearly normative, the other three also have value dimensions. Rationales for government interventions were then introduced followed by a discussion of locus of authority and responsibility. These issues are key to the understanding of the specific social policies analyzed in later chapters. The next chapter continues to develop the overall conceptual framework to be used in analyzing specific policies. It begins with a discussion of the major and conflicting functions carried out by the dominant schools of policy analysis and concludes with the identification of fundamental concepts that analysts and policymakers must deal with.

2

Policy Analysis

The purpose of this chapter is to explore the professional activity referred to as policy analysis. While the discussion in the preceding chapter dealt with the umbrella concept of social policy, here we emphasize analysis. Two competing approaches to policy analysis are critiqued. The first approach is grounded in and limited to technical analysis, while the second assumes a broader perspective, one that systematically incorporates values into the analysis. The implications of each approach are addressed, with a discussion of the role of the policy analyst. Questions are raised about the adequacy of these traditional approaches to social policy analysis as we enter the twenty-first century. The chapter concludes with a synthesis of the two approaches and a discussion of the role of the policy analyst in fostering participation in the policy process. While theoretical and somewhat abstract, this chapter presents the framework for the remainder of the book by introducing a series of concepts useful in analyzing this country's social policies, several of which are dealt with specifically in later chapters.

POLICY ANALYSIS AND RESEARCH

Policy analysis, as a field of professional practice, is relatively new. Lasswell (1970) first proposed the concept of the "policy sciences." For Lasswell, the purpose of the policy sciences is to augment, by scientific methods of decision-making and data from the behavioral sciences, the processes that humans use in making judgments and decisions. This approach to informing decision-making is grounded in logical positivism and scientism, and recognizes only two forms of legitimate knowledge: the empirical or natural sciences, and the formal disciplines such as logic and mathematics.

Although policy analysis grew out of the rational approach, it is not synonymous with research. More often than not, the policy analyst relies on available data and existing research rather than on collecting new data. What tends to distinguish policy analysis from traditional research is the way questions are formulated and the specific purpose of the analysis. Policy analysis sets out to produce information that legislators, administrators, and other interested parties can easily translate into action, while traditional research attempts to provide a better understanding of social phenomena. Policy analysis, then, relies heavily on research, while research can stand by itself.

Policy analysis, to be useful, must be responsive to the needs of policymakers, who are often operating under considerable time constraints. Analysts who inform a decision-maker that the specific information requested will not be available for several years will soon lose their audience. Similarly, analysts who inform policymakers that research findings must be treated as tentative and in need of further verification contribute little to the policy process. While the best possible information may not exist, the analyst must reexamine what is available and through a synthesizing process generate reasonable policy options and recommendations.

The perceived nonresponsive attitude on the part of traditional behavioral and social science researchers is probably the major reason that policy analysis has become a new and somewhat parallel activity. Over the past 25 years, significant numbers of public policy curricula have come into existence and have attracted large numbers of undergraduate and graduate students. Today, policy centers draw considerable support from government agencies and private foundations and are found in most major universities.

In the remainder of this chapter, a range of frameworks for policy analysis is discussed. Two distinct approaches to policy analysis are explored in some detail. The first approach emphasizes the process of policy analysis by focusing on the technical aspects of decision-making, while the second emphasizes the purpose or ends to be achieved by the policy. These approaches are then synthesized in an attempt to move beyond an either-or approach by blending aspects of each as they might have an impact on the level of citizen participation in the decision-making process.

APPROACH 1: EMPHASIS ON PROCESS

The process model of policy analysis seeks to provide decision-makers with the kind of information they need in order to make decisions more rationally with respect to their stated goal. Within this framework, policy formulation assumes that decisions are made rationally, with the analyst functioning in a technical capacity. Analysis is introduced only when the general goal has been specified. The analyst accepts the "goodness" of the general policy statement, implicitly saying to the decision-maker, "Tell me what you want and I'll tell you how it can be achieved." The analyst does not determine the goal and does not have responsibility for selecting among alternative means of achieving the goal. Rather, analytic activity is limited to evaluate the generation of alternatives and the application of various criteria to those alternatives. Traditionally, these criteria have tended to be grounded in economic analysis, with specific emphasis on efficiency and cost-effectiveness. The role of the analyst is limited to analysis that will aide the decision-maker to choose among alternatives.

An example of this approach was the analysts' role in the welfare reform proposal introduced in Congress in 1969 (commonly known as the Family Assistance Plan). This proposal embodied the administration's basic incentive mechanism for shifting recipient families from a welfare program to a workfare program. To support the workfare program and to facilitate the employment of Aid to Families with Dependent Children (AFDC) mothers, day care would be expanded and supported with up to 90% federal reimbursement. The analyst, as technician, approached this issue with day care as a given, rather than one strategy or alternative among many, and identified alternative ways to deliver the service to the target population. Variables such as the size of day-care facilities, types of services, and staffing ratios became the basis for a modified cost-benefit analysis. The results of the analysis were then given to a decision-maker, who would choose among the alternative day-care strategies.

Ironically, efforts to facilitate employment for the purpose of downsizing AFDC rolls are as fashionable today as they were in 1969. Today the task of the policy analyst is to provide advice on how to create jobs, regardless of whether the jobs will pay at a level to achieve self-sufficiency, or whether quality and affordable child care or a public transportation system is available that would facilitate employment.

This form of structured rationality in the decision-making process has had strong support in the literature. Dror describes the basic function of social policy analysis as "identifying and documenting various alternatives within a range of decision possibilities" (1970:136). Dror's seminal work is still one of the major influences in the practice of policy analysis. He suggests that the policy sciences "constitute a new and additional approach to the uses of systematic knowledge and structured rationality for the conscious shaping of society" (ibid.:137) and represent an integration of pure and applied research. Dror's approach builds on three fundamental components:

- a systems view, i.e., examining problems and alternatives in such a way that all relevant variables and probable results are taken into account;
- searching for an optimal (single best) solution within a "broad benefit cost frame without being limited to environmental changes" (ibid.:141);
- identification of the preferable alternative "with the help of a large set of techniques ranging from mathematical models to human gaming and from canvassing of expert's opinions to sensitivity testing" (ibid.).

In sum, Dror argues that policy analysis, based in the management sciences and systems analysis, can provide the decision-maker with the means to choose among proposed courses of action once a goal has been articulated. He assumes that "rationality and intellectualism" are the only appropriate foundations for policy analysis. Even more important is his belief that knowledge provides the authority to plan and act.

Under the process approach of policy analysis, the role of the analyst is that of technician. The technician, in an effort to be objective, is removed from dealing with the adequacy of the ends, or the purpose of the policy. Any creativity introduced by the analyst is in response to the creative rearrangement of the data. This creativity, however, is limited to generating means to achieve the ends as proposed by the decision-maker.

Unlike Dror, Lasswell does not see policy as a linear process. Rather he describes the activity more in terms of iterations, a moving "back and forth between images of the whole and particular details of time, place and figure" (1970:13). Finally, though Dror and Laswell tend to view the analyst as technician, Dror allows for "organized day dreaming" and Laswell speaks of the "creative flash," i.e., the examination of factual data in a way that leads to creative rearrangements of the data and eventually to novel solutions. This creativity, however, only deals with generating means and not ends. Furthermore, while the various phases of analysis are rational and scientific, the creative process is seen by these policy scientists as "irrational" and prescientific in nature.

Dror's position on the role of the analyst as technician is consistent with the dominant view expressed in the early planning literature. As early as 1910 we find that reformers concerned with the inefficiency and corruption of existing political mechanisms were agitating for new processes of decision-making, processes that would facilitate representation of "the community as a whole" or "interests at large and not specific interests" (Banfield and Wilson 1963). It was thought that utilizing techniques of scientific or rational management would produce a more democratic government. The key element in this movement toward a rational method of decision-making was the notion of public interest:

> There is a public interest that can be applied to all issues of local government. The public interest is that course of action which best serves the public as a whole. Private interest . . . must take a back seat to the public interest. . . . "[P]olitics" involves the serving of private interests and, therefore, should be kept out of government. (Ranney 1969:46)

This new paradigm of rationality, grounded in science and technology introduced before World War I, was more fully developed during the early 1950s by Banfield. The decision-maker:

1.   considers all of the possible alternatives,
2.   identifies and evaluates all of the consequences that would follow from the adoption of each alternative, and
3.   selects the alternative that will more likely achieve the desired ends.

The rational model seeks to provide those who are influential in the political process, e.g., the mayors, managers, and heads of municipal departments, the kind of information they need in order to make decisions more rationally with respect to their "most valued ends." Implicitly, these valued ends are seen to be in the public interest. The role of the analyst is limited to analysis that will aid the decision-maker to choose among alternatives, and to do so the analyst must suppress his or her own personal values.

CRITICISM OF THE PROCESS APPROACH

Despite its great intellectual appeal, rational decision theory has not been able to resolve a number of problems. Freidmann and Hudson (1974) identify three difficulties with this approach. The first is the problem of knowledge and information. Rational decision-making, as noted earlier, requires consideration of all the alternatives and an evaluation of all of the consequences that would follow from the adoption of each alternative. However, most decision analysis in the public policy arena involves nonrepetitive situations, which in turn affects our capability to predict consequences. Moreover, such analysis requires an information system with accurate, relevant, and comprehensive data. Such a system, however, has been difficult to realize. Freidmann and Hudson also point out that human intelligence is such that only a limited number of variables can be taken into account, that continuous social change is the norm and not the exception, and that this turbulent environment only allows for the development of partial and limited social models for estimating the impact of decisions.

A second limitation or obstacle is our inability to derive a community welfare function, i.e., "a collection of tradeoffs among a community's preference for different objectives" (p. 11). Without this function, the analyst has no independent and objective basis for evaluating alternatives. The notion of a community welfare function was derived from the works of Jeremy Bentham and John Stuart Mill and has roots in utilitarianism. "Good" decisions were those that maximized the utility (well-being) for the greatest number. If we aggregate individual and group preferences, we should be able to derive the community welfare function and thus choose the alternative that is in the public interest. While the concept is reasonable, the technical means to do this have not been found (Arrow 1951).

The third problem raised by Freidmann and Hudson is concerned with implementation:

> Decision theorists work on the assumption that once a decision is made, it will be carried out with a minimum of friction. Again, this belief stems from the notion that within bureaucratic organizations decisions are, in effect, commands and that commands are invariably obeyed. But empirical studies of organizational behavior have concluded that coordination not only may be difficult to achieve but may in some cases be altogether impossible. (1974:11)

It is often noted that policy formulation is only about 10% of the challenge to realizing change, and implementation the other 90%. As Thomas Corbett (1995) points out in his discussion of changing the culture of welfare, the challenge of policy implementation occurs at different levels: at the point of contact between the client and the system, at the point of responsibility for the organization of the local system, and among state and federal executive agencies responsible for establishing procedures and motivating implementation.

A fourth criticism of the process approach was raised by Mannheim (1940) almost 60 years ago. He argued that planners were preoccupied with "functional rationality" at the expense of "substantial rationality." Functional rationality is concerned with relating means to given ends, while substantial rationality deals with the appropriateness of the ends themselves. The analyst who operates within the process approach of policy formulation assumes that his or her role is purely technical and that questions of substantial rationality belong only in the domain of the decision-maker. Mannheim used Germany of the 1930s as an example of functional rationality in its extreme. The analyst's function was not to question the decisions of those in power, but it was solely one of implementing the "final solution," the official Nazi code name for the extermination of Jews.

The process approach is not only limiting, but in many ways dysfunctional, in that it emphasizes means and tends to bypass the issue of ends. Because it is convenient to do so, we assume that a fundamental consensus on societal goals exists. Policy analysis within this framework is primarily concerned with technical or administrative issues of social engineering. In reality, this fundamental consensus does not exist and the tendency to sidestep the existing ideological conflict has resulted in formulating policies that are at cross-purposes with other policies. Under the process approach, policy design has come to be viewed as a choice among neutral alternatives, and analysis an activity that helps decision-makers achieve an optimal solution for some predetermined goal. Analysis tends to be concentrated on how services will be financed, organized, and administered and all too rarely on the nature, aims, and value of the services.

A number of policy committees, commissions, and individual scholars in recent years have stressed procedure and have not attempted to relate these procedures to a set of desired outcomes. Arguments are made in terms of who has what responsibility: Does the public or does the private sector? If the public sector, at what level of government? Should needs be met through the direct provision of services or indirectly through market mechanisms? If the latter, should the strategy be focused on income maintenance programs such as the negative income tax, on a family allowance program, on a modified public assistance program, or on vouchers earmarked for certain categories of goods, e.g., housing, food, day care, or education? Whether this growing emphasis on procedures reflects a discouragement with the alleged failure of previous large-scale programs, a distrust of government, or a lack of confidence in being able to deal successfully with complex social problems, it does reflect a reluctance to sort out values, and to define relationships between means and ends. This criticism is in no way meant to suggest that procedures are unimportant. The issues related to financing, organization, and administration of services are critical, but they should be reviewed in the context of the purpose of the services. It should be underscored that administrative and technical issues related to process are, in fact, not neutral or value-free. In the absence of an identified purpose or outcome, means are inevitably chosen on efficiency criteria, with primary consideration given to cost-effectiveness in achieving narrowly defined objectives that may serve cross-purposes.

The approach discussed in the next section suggests that the parameters of policy analysis be enlarged, not in terms of additional techniques, but more in terms of the scope of the analysis. This approach, we suggest, attempts to combine functional and substantial rationality, to systematically integrate facts and values. It begins with a concern for purpose or outcome and not means.

APPROACH 2: EMPHASIS ON PURPOSE

Titmuss defines social policy as the "study of the range of social needs and the functions, in conditions of social scarcity, of human organizations traditionally called social service or social welfare systems to meet those needs" (1968:20). He argues that the analyst must be concerned with the ends and not just the means of policy. When we direct our attention toward social policy objectives, we are usually concerned with their moral justification. To put this another way, how do supporters of a social policy aimed at a particular objective justify its pursuit? What alternative objectives can be morally justified? For Titmuss, values not only influence policy decisions, but they are the motivating force for advocating a particular course of action. Titmuss suggests the following:

> Social policy models . . . with all their apparent remoteness from reality, can serve a purpose in providing us with an ideological framework which may stimulate us to ask the significant questions and to expose the significant choices. (1971:136)

Rein agrees with Titmuss's view that (a) social policy is concerned with choosing among multiple, conflicting, and yet desirable goals; (b) no scientific rules exist to make these choices; and (c) values provide the criteria by which we judge the desirability of a course of action. Given the probability of conflicting ideologies, there is never one true analysis, but potentially a number of different analyses, each to be judged good or bad within the framework of its value assumptions.

Social policy then is concerned with social need and can be defined in terms of social purposes. It involves societal mechanisms to bring about social change, and values permeate the entire policy process. Values influence the selection of a specific policy issue and how it will be defined. They are the basis for setting policy goals and objectives, for selecting criteria for comparing policy options to achieve these goals and objectives, and for evaluating policies once they are implemented.

Rein (1976) amplifies the point by suggesting that the study of social policy involves the interaction between values (found in statements of purpose/goals), operating principles (means or instruments to achieve these purposes), and outcomes. To put it another way, social policy is an articulation of the ideology between means and ends. Values concern both ends and means of public intervention involving normative propositions and assumptions about what public policy is and what it should be. Theory provides insight into factors possibly related to policy issues, assisting us in interpreting how the world operates and how it might work in the future. Finally, research provides factual information relative to values, either repudiating or confirming existing beliefs about how people, institutions, and society function. Insofar as values are central to the policy domain and influence decision-making, they must become central to policy analysis. Analysts using the purpose approach do not suggest, however, that policy analysts can develop an objective-value calculus that rationalizes different value sets and goals.

Since values have a subjective aspect and are inherently controversial, they cannot be addressed exclusively within a positivistic framework. Purists in the behavioral and social sciences have therefore been reluctant to explore the role of values in policy analysis, since—they argue—values are outside the purview of the scientist unless they are the object of inquiry, i.e., they are seen as dependent variables (Nagel 1956).

In some respects, their reluctance is warranted in that two extreme but complementary errors have been committed in the intellectual history of value studies (Dewey 1939). One is the value-arbitrary error, which holds that all values are equally good, a view that, says Dewey, "if it were systematically acted upon would produce disordered behavior to the point of complete chaos" (p. 69). The other is value-absolute error, which asserts that the ultimate standards of valuation are a priori ends-in- themselves: "This theory, in its endeavor to escape from the frying pan of disordered valuations, jumps into the fire of absolutism" (ibid.: 70).

Perhaps this caution is why Rein (1970) has argued that no single academic or professional discipline can be expected to provide the insight necessary for developing the most appropriate framework for analyzing social problems and identifying effective policies and programs. The analyst, in fact, must "trespass on academic and professional domains in which he [she] may have no special competence" (p. xii). The analyst's unique contribution then becomes one of identifying and understanding approaches used in the different disciplines (e.g., economics, political science, history, philosophy) and the professional fields (e.g., public health, social work, education, law) and then synthesizing them into a meaningful whole. The role of the analyst is to make the values clear, expose value choices that confront society, and probe and push the value assumptions underlying the development of policy.

As noted earlier, there can be no single calculus just as there cannot be a single "true" or correct analysis. The values that inform policy analysis are the values that society or groups in that society espouse, and there are inherent conflicts implicit in these. Take, for example, the expressed goals of liberty, equality, and community. While all three may be desirable organizing principles for social policy formulation, they cannot all be maximized at once. In fact, more of one will inevitably result in less of the others. An emphasis on absolute liberty will lead to an individualistic and competitive society. An emphasis on equality calls for a more just society, a society committed to reducing age-old inequities in the redistribution of resources and in access to opportunity. An emphasis on community underscores the importance of social interaction, interdependency, and exchanges—the existence of common need and risk, the necessity for shared responsibility.

The issue becomes one of determining which value is to be given primacy. If we begin with a communitarian first principle, absolute liberty is not possible in that social responsibilities are a sine qua non. The same happens, of course, if we begin with liberty, with its emphasis on individualism, or equality, with its emphasis on redistribution.

Titmuss (1968) argues for the former while Milton Friedman (1962) supports the latter. Friedman is opposed to those who would suggest we begin with a concern for equality or community. In his view, we must start with extending freedom and choice, that anything else is paternalistic, and in the long run counterproductive to the economic and social well-being of a society. This extension of freedom is best achieved through a competitive market, which will not only be responsive but will achieve a proper balance between government, the private sector, and individuals. These competitive mechanisms, in time, will increase national wealth, and in turn provide society with the means to achieve social objectives. Social objectives can only be achieved by first realizing economic objectives. Friedman builds his approach to social policy on an economic definition of the human person, one who interacts with others in bilateral, impersonal transactions:

> Under ordinary circumstances, the exchange is impersonal . . . requiring no special effort or attention from either buyer or seller. Once the exchange has taken place, there is no residual or accumulation of unfulfilled obligations, and thus no inherent dynamic to extend the relationships beyond the time contractually specified. (Pruger 1973:290)

Individuals thus have the responsibility to act only in their own interests, and the idea of collective responsibility or welfare is nonexistent.

Titmuss, on the other hand, can be characterized as a communitarian, i.e., he believes that by nature we are social beings with responsibility for others. In his view, industrialization and modernization, with their emphasis on economic values, have brought about community breakdown and alienation. Specifically, he argues that past and present approaches to social welfare are consistent with Friedman's postulation in that they emphasize a "we-they" relationship that has produced a divided society. "We," the nonpoor, provide for a residual proportion of society because "they" are incapable of providing for themselves. This divisiveness is often reflected in separate service delivery systems that involve psychological stigmatization for the poor. Both positions are value laden, and depending on which foundation one accepts, some options will be acceptable and others will be rejected. They involve different views of society, the state, individuals, and families.

Moreover, while their positions may appear to be abstract and philosophical, both have had significant influence in the political arena: Milton Friedman on the conservative wing of the Republican party in the United States and Richard Titmuss on the Labour party in the United Kingdom.

Friedman, in beginning with the principle of freedom, and the position that the free-enterprise system (competitive capitalism) is the only way to ensure freedom, argues that government efforts to improve the quality of life of individuals and families are undesirable and inevitably harmful. In essence he is arguing the position discussed in Chapter 1 under rationales for government intervention, that intervention invariably becomes interference and eventually leads to an ineffective family unit. To put this another way, when you take responsibilities away from people, you make them irresponsible. If government is to intervene, it should do so reactively, i.e., only when there is clearly defined pathology. Furthermore, if government is to have a role, it should be decentralized; local government is preferred over state government and state over national government, since centralized decision-making leads to coercion and a weakening of individual freedom.

Titmuss, in beginning with the principle of community, on the other hand, argues that families have been weakened and are experiencing stress in an industrialized society characterized by periodic shifts in a less than perfect market economy. He also accepts the notion of pathology, but argues that the basic problems reside in the structures and institutions of society and not in the individual. Therefore, government at the national level (only at this level does the state have the ability to acquire and distribute resources as well as guarantee fairness to all citizens) should proactively work to reduce these risks. This is, of course, the argument used by the Roosevelt administration during the depression. With this as background, it is understandable that Friedman has actively fought against compulsory social insurance (OASDI), public housing, minimum wages, and national health insurance, while Titmuss has supported these policies. Friedman would have individuals and families develop their own insurance (retirement and health) plans, find the housing they can afford in the marketplace, and be free to choose work at whatever wages are offered. If government is to get involved, it should only do so with the poor and "those whom we designate as not responsible," e.g., children and the mentally ill. Titmuss disagrees and argues that risks should be shared and services available to all citizens because they are bonded by their citizenship.

We introduced Titmuss and Friedman to identify polar positions on the role of the state and corresponding social policies. Both are radical in their prescriptions. Both are arguing for a society that does not exist, i.e., Friedman for competitive capitalism and Titmuss for a pure socialist state. With few exceptions, most people find themselves some place in between and probably to the near right or left of center. For example, neoconservatives such as Glazer (1983) and Kristol (1978, 1983) argue that many of the human services have created dependency (and thus have reduced individual freedom) and that to continue on our present course would help neither the recipients of the services nor the economic system. However, unlike others who are more conservative, they do not argue for drastic retrenchment of social expenditures. Rather, they propose a shifting of these resources from direct services to indirect services, from social services to benefits that permit the recipient to enter the market to purchase services. Theoretically, this would allow families to develop their own capabilities because it allows for choice. Examples of policies neoconservatives might support would include national health insurance, housing vouchers, and negative–income tax programs. Liberals (i.e., New Deal, Great Society liberals) support these policies but also defend the value of social services and direct governmental provision of these services. What becomes apparent, however, is that unlike Friedman and Titmuss, neither the neoconservatives nor the liberals have a comprehensive theory underlying their positions—a theory of the state. When we view Friedman and Titmuss in terms of their first principles (freedom or community), both are logical and consistent in their recommendations.

The next section extends this discussion and focuses on the formulation and analysis of social policy using the purpose approach. The purpose of this section is to take the seemingly contradictory values of freedom and community and explore how one might operationalize an abstract goal and eventually generate criteria for formulating and analyzing policy alternatives.

FIRST PRINCIPLES: AN APPLICATION

R. Friedman (1968) agrees that social policies can be classified by purpose and that, depending on the purpose, specific forms of policy design are likely to be implemented. He offers a framework that begins to operationalize concepts useful in the formulation and analysis of social policy.

Social-welfare policies, according to Friedman, can be initially distinguished into those that are "pure-welfare" and those that are "social-insurance." Table 2.1 has been developed from Friedman's analysis and identifies several criteria that differentiate the two approaches, differences that affect how and under what conditions goods and services are provided to different groups of people.

Table 2.1. Models of Social Welfare

Criteria	Social-insurance model	Pure-welfare model
Purpose	Proactive	Reactive
Concept of fault	No fault	Individual deficit
Eligibility	Entitlement	Charity
Public perception	Deserving	Unworthy
Administration	Centralized	Decentralized
Mode of distribution	Cash	In-kind

THE CONCEPT OF PURPOSE

The pure-welfare model tends to emphasize a remedial function, while the social-insurance model focuses on prevention. Three classes of prevention have been identified in the literature (Haddix, Teutsch, Shaffer, and Dunet 1996). Primary prevention targets risk factors to prevent problems before they occur, for instance, laws that regulate the sale of tobacco to children. Secondary prevention activities target problems through early identification and treatment, whereas tertiary prevention is aimed at existing problems in order to ameliorate their progression and maximize the functioning of those affected. In contrast, the unwritten edict of the pure-welfare model is "if it's not broke, don't fix it." Under the pure-welfare model, problems are viewed as personal, and government intervention is acceptable only as a last resort.

THE CONCEPT OF FAULT

Social policies implicitly divide the population into one of two groups: (1) those who are experiencing problems or deprivation through no fault of their own and (2) those who are to blame for their situation. This division was introduced in Chapter 1 in the discussion of the Social Security Act. The concept of fault has serious consequences related to levels of benefit. In those instances where the condition (problem, need, etc.) is not perceived to be the fault of the individual (e.g., old age and retirement are inevitable, veterans do not start wars, people lose their jobs because of uncontrollable events), benefits tend to be restitutionary. The beneficiaries have fallen from an economic or social position they once had and the program attempts to restore them to a previous position. Given this, benefits would vary according to the individual's status. For example, retirement benefits under the Social Security Act are measured by contributions and contributions are a function of wages. The more you earn, the more you contribute, the more you will receive, at least up to a point. The same is true for unemployment insurance. In principle, benefits are wage related, with minimum and maximum benefits set by federal and state law.

Underlying other policies, however, is the concept of personal fault, whereby a person is perceived to be experiencing deprivation by choice, i.e., he or she is not blameless. With this as a beginning point, people should not be encouraged to choose deprivation, i.e., if the state provides benefits that are too attractive, adults will not participate in employment. In these instances, benefits are not restitutionary but maintenance. To provide an incentive to self-sufficiency, the maintenance level must be set at a bare minimum. Under the AFDC provision of the Social Security Act, each state determines that minimum, and, depending on family size, each family receives the same benefit. Moreover, in practice the benefit levels are only a percentage of what the state has established as necessary to meet basic needs. For example, in 1992 the maximum monthly AFDC benefit level for a family of three, living in Arizona, was only 36% of Arizona's need standard, i.e., the minimum amount necessary to sustain a family (Committee on Ways and Means 1992).

THE CONCEPT OF ELIGIBILITY

Programs can also be classified by whether eligibility is or is not a matter of right. In R. Friedman's definition of right, if a beneficiary follows the rules for claiming a benefit and meets the legal definition of a beneficiary, he or she must be given the benefit. He further points out that, in theory, the supply of the benefits must equal the number of beneficiaries. Finally, programs that define eligibility in terms of rights tend to provide goods and services to the middle-class population. Unemployment compensation, old-age pensions, and Medicare, all of which are provisions of the Social Security Act, are examples of benefits as rights. A recipient is required only to demonstrate that he or she is unemployed or elderly and has contributed to the program. No one, in theory, can be turned away because the supply of benefits has been exhausted. Moreover, these programs do not have the appearance of charity.

Other programs target the poor and use some form of means test to determine eligibility. Beneficiaries must not only demonstrate need, but must prove that they are poor. Also, officials must investigate and verify eligibility on a case-by-case basis. When provision is based on rights, beneficiaries do not have to prove that they are poor, nor do they have to exhaust their own resources before they receive benefits. In means-tested programs, they do. The means test is associated with programs that benefit people of inferior social position and usually result in stigmatization. This, in turn, serves as a deterrent by making receipt of the benefit unpleasant. Furthermore, these beneficiaries are vulnerable in times of fiscal retrenchment: programs for the poor are the first and simplest to cut.

Whereas programs tend to be universal when benefits are defined as rights, in means-tested programs they are selective in provision. We introduced this concept earlier when discussing the targeting of certain groups for goods and services. In that context, we suggested that many policies are reactive and deal with a residual population. *Selective* can also be used in another sense. Universal programs, by definition, provide benefits to all who meet eligibility requirements. In some selective programs, the eligible recipient is not guaranteed the benefit, i.e., the program is not entitlement-based. Public housing is a good example. The supply of public housing units is always smaller than the number of eligible families, and program administrators must choose among beneficiaries. Furthermore, unlike universal programs, program administrators can deny anyone the opportunity to review their decision.

PUBLIC PERCEPTION

Friedman further distinguishes between benefits that are earned and those that are unearned. Retirement pensions and unemployment insurance under the Social Security Act are earned, in the sense that the employee has paid into the system. AFDC and Supplementary Security Income (SSI), on the other hand, are considered charity, benefits that are not earned. The above earned benefits, however, are not in the strict actuarial sense "earned." It is more a sense of earning in psychological and political terms. People feel they have earned the benefit and there is no social stigma attached to receiving it. In fact, many old-age insurance beneficiaries receive far more than they contribute. This has led to concern over the viability of the OASI program, a problem that has been exacerbated by the increased life expectancy of men and women.

Unearned benefits, such as AFDC, carry a stigma, and the process of determining eligibility and monitoring the status of these families is basically to keep them from receiving the benefits. Rather than viewing recipients as people who are entitled to the maximum benefit allowed, AFDC mothers are seen as chiselers, attempting to defraud the system. Moreover, Friedman argues that employees, in those programs where the recipient is viewed as having earned the benefit, tend to be helpful and polite while poor people are often kept waiting for service at a clinic or for a social worker's time.

ADMINISTRATION:
CENTRALIZED VERSUS DECENTRALIZED

In Chapter 1, we introduced the concept of federalism and pointed out that social policy involves all three levels of government: federal, state, and local. Prior to the twentieth century, state and local governments carried the major responsibility for public welfare, with the federal government minimally involved. Today, some programs are federal, some state, some local, and still others are a combination of levels. Friedman would place these on a continuum from highly centralized (federal) to highly decentralized (local).

With this as a beginning point, he argues that highly centralized programs tend to target the middle class, are highly bureaucratized with rules and regulations clearly spelled out, and finally are run by "clerks" who routinely carry out the policy. Decentralized programs, on the other hand, allow for professional discretion in dealing with recipients. Friedman's analysis is intriguing in that the latter approach (professional discretion and flexibility) would on the surface appear more attractive than government by clerks, but his conclusion is just the opposite:

> If government reduces itself to a roomful of clerks with merely ministerial duty, program initiative passes to the beneficiaries themselves. It is they who decide. . . . For those who comply with rigid rules and who can know and master the rules, it is far more manageable than the free discretion of the professional. Hence, the middle class tends to demand, paradoxically, that programs be as bureaucratized as possible. (1968:59)

The federal retirement program (OASDI) is such a program. AFDC (now known as TANF—Temporary Assistance for Needy Families), on the other hand, is more decentralized, administered by professionals, and allows for some discretion in application. Friedman concludes, however, that the poor tend to be victimized by such flexibility. An example of this was the refusal by many state welfare departments in the late 1960s to make available to welfare rights organizations the manuals that welfare workers used to determine eligibility and benefits.

MODE OF DISTRIBUTION: CASH VERSUS IN-KIND

Some programs provide benefits in cash while others provide benefits in kind. Cash payments give the beneficiary freedom to choose, to enter the market to purchase goods and services. In theory, cash benefits introduce the least amount of government control. It is interesting that both preventive and residual, restitutionary and basic premium programs provide benefits in cash, e.g., OASDI, UI, AFDC, and SSI. However, public opinion tends to run counter to cash grants for the poor. We question whether they are capable purchasers and continually experiment with reducing benefits by providing in-kind services such as food (commodity programs), or at least by controlling their purchasing through vouchers such as food stamps, which do not allow the purchase of nonfood items and housing allowances. Some welfare departments, moreover, have experimented with direct payments to landlords and utility companies when recipients have fallen behind in their payments. Programs that define benefits as rights usually provide cash (a major exception is Medicare); but the rationale is to protect a defenseless recipient against an uncontrollable market); those that define benefits as charity are more likely to provide them in-kind.

FIRST PRINCIPLES REVISITED

We have introduced Friedman's analysis of social policy to demonstrate the relevancy of the first principles discussed in an earlier section. The middle column in Table 2.1 describes a system that according to Titmuss would strengthen a sense of community and reduce inequality. It does not polarize the population, but assumes common risk, common need, and citizenship as the basis for eligibility. Wilensky and Lebeaux (1965) have referred to this as the "institutional approach" to social welfare. The column on the right correlates well with Milton Friedman's position—the extension of freedom. Benefits should be made available only when problems have occurred and should be proposed as temporary measures until the individual or family can function independently—the "residual approach." Whereas Titmuss argues that "we" are the objects of social policy, Friedman argues that "they" are the object. The six criteria are excellent examples of operationalizing first principles. The role of the policy analyst in the purpose approach, therefore, is to make value choices explicit and to advocate for policies that are consistent with certain primary values—freedom, equality, community.

CRITICISMS OF THE PURPOSE APPROACH

Bulmer (1981) offers a cogent and provocative analysis of the strengths and limitations of both the process and purpose approaches to policy analysis. He traces our rejection of the purpose approach with its concern for value explication to the rise of the social sciences following World War I. In the tradition of the logical positivists, Park, a leading exponent of the new sociology "advocated the detached scientific study of social phenomenon untrammeled by political or philosophical ends" (Bulmer 1981:36). He felt that the "world was full of crusaders" and that the role of the social scientist should be that of the "calm, detached scientist." The social scientist did have a contribution to make to policy formulation, but this contribution was to be achieved through the application of theory and methods, not through "moral and prescriptive explorations." These early social scientists believed that to go beyond theory and methods leading to understanding would result in a weakening of the professional status of the social sciences. To maintain their credibility as scientists, the sociologist, economist, and political scientist had to demonstrate that their personal values did not shape their work.

According to Bulmer, proponents of the purpose approach are "strong on application, moderate on empirical research and extremely weak on theory" (ibid.:39). In practice, their approach is less a science and more a "humanistic social science with strong links to history, philosophy, and ethics" (ibid.). Bulmer cites Pinker, who argues that this approach "begins with fact finding and ends in moral rhetoric, still lacking those explanatory theories that might show the process as a whole and reveal the relations of the separate problems to one another" (ibid.). Pinker criticizes Titmuss for presenting his arguments in a way that ensures the moral superiority of the institutional model of social welfare. We also find the link between the institutional model of social welfare and the first principle of community to be tenuous. Titmuss fails to demonstrate the relationship between the institutional model of social welfare and the development of citizenship and moral behavior, characteristics central to community.

If we say, as the purpose approach does, that the consideration of values in relation to the ends of social policy is important, and yet we cannot justify the choice between first principles such as equality, community, and freedom on any basis beyond moral superiority, then we must question the adequacy of this approach. Bulmer's answer to this criticism is "not to discard the moral dimension altogether, but to combine it with an adequate theoretical and methodological structure" (ibid.:41), which we attempt to do in the next section through a synthesis of the two approaches.

COMBINING THE TWO APPROACHES

The idea of social policy as a tool to create a moral community has strong theoretical support in the literature from several disciplines. Schottland defines social policy as a "statement of social goals and strategy, a settled course of action dealing with the relations of people with each other, the mutual relations of people with their government" (cited in Gil 1973:5). Boulding argues that the "objective of social policy is to build the identity of a person around some community" with which he or she is associated (1967). Macbeath suggests that "social policies are concerned with the right ordering of the network of relationships between men and women who live together in societies, or with the principle which should govern the activities of individuals and groups so far as they affect the lives and interests of other people" (1957:3). In his work on equality, Tawney (1964) identifies fraternity and fellowship as prime concerns for social policy. Others, such as Gil (1973) and Ponsioen (1962), view social policy in similar terms, i.e., promoting moral transactions and social relations.

These ideas also have a foundation in traditional sociology. As a social scientist, Nisbet argues that most of the earlier sociologists were concerned with the idea and reality of a moral community. These social theorists include Comte, LePlay, Tonnies, de Coulanges, Weber, Durkheim, Simmel, and—from a radically different perspective—Marx. While each of these writers criticizes the excessive individualism, impersonality, acquisitiveness, and rational calculating of capitalism, they do not agree with each other on the cause or solution. Marx, for example, suggests that the loss of community is a consequence of capitalism, while Tonnies treats capitalism as the consequence of a loss of community. Both Marx and Durkheim are critical of societies

> in which economic activities and values have become separated from and commanding over all other spheres of collective life. The most intense social activity in modern industrial societies, economic activity, was the least social. (Horton 1964:286)

All tend to argue that the notion of a moral community is critical, and that without this we will be faced with high levels of anomie and alienation. Unfortunately, their solutions are not very feasible. The enemies they address are the extension of bureaucratic forms of domination and their effect upon the quality of social life (Weber), capitalist modes of production (Marx), and the industrialization of society insofar as it has eroded social solidarity and moral relationships (Durkheim).

Boulding develops the idea of social relations as the primary object of social policy more fully when he suggests that social policy should be concerned with building an "integrative system," a system "that includes those aspects of social life that are characterized not so much by exchange in which a quid is got for a quo as by unilateral transfers that are justified by some kind of appeal to a status or legitimacy, identity or community" (1967:5). He suggests that a major purpose of social policy is to assist individuals and families in becoming members of communities. Why? Boulding's argument rests clearly on those concerns raised by earlier theorists. Alienated people cause problems and those integrated into a community solve problems:

> One thing is clear: we must look upon the total dynamic process of society as essentially a process in human learning. . . . It is even clearer that the development of social integration is a learning process. We have to be taught to love just as we have to be taught to hate. Practically nothing in human life comes naturally. It is from vague and formless biological drives and the extraordinary learning potential of the human nervous system that the intricate structure of our personalities, our identities, our values and our communities are molded. (ibid.:9)

If we argue, as we have up to this point, that the purpose of social policy is to enhance a sense of community, and we have presented a theoretical rationale for this position, then we must ask ourselves: Do existing social policies enhance community? This question is critical in that we agree with Gil (1973) that social policies are not merely potential solutions of social problems but can be the underlying cause of existing problems. We illustrate this point with Titmuss's (1971) study of blood transfusion systems. From his examination of 27 countries, Titmuss concluded that those societies that rely solely on the voluntary giving of blood foster a sense of altruism, while those that rely on paid or contract donors foster self-interest and individual gain. He argues, therefore, that social policy is not simply a utilitarian system of redistribution, but a facilitator of society's moral sense. The "gift relationship," as Titmuss labeled his study, "serves as an illustration of how social policy, in one of its potential roles, can help actualize the social and moral potentialities of all citizens" (ibid.:238). Policies not only reflect values, they can also shape values and enforce behavior.

While Titmuss and Friedman were presented in the preceding section as polar opposites, here we look for their commonalities. Both are concerned with social policy as it impacts moral transactions and notions of exchange or reciprocal relations. Friedman, in promoting a laissez-faire role for government, is concerned that transferring responsibility for social well-being from the individual to the state will invariably lead to an ineffective family and community unit. Nisbet agrees with this position: "There are countless persons today for whom the massive changes of the past century have meant a dislocation of the contexts of function: the extended family, neighborhood, apprenticeship, social class, and parish" (1967:xiii). Thus, their concern for freedom from government interaction is really based on a concern for preserving a sense of community.

Titmuss (1968) and Rein (1970), on the other hand, view the provision of benefits, with its basis for eligibility in citizenship, as necessary to bring about and maintain social and community relations in a modern industrial society. All three view social policy as a means of promoting moral transactions, Titmuss and Rein through government provision and Friedman through a laissez-faire role of government. The fault we find with their arguments, however, is that they advocate a particular model of social welfare, i.e., institutional or residual, and then treat these models as if they were synonymous with the first principles, i.e., community and freedom. In effect, this reifies concepts associated with the welfare state and promotes the evaluation of labels as opposed to the evaluation of outcomes.

The trend of classifying welfare states gained popularity in the 1970s (Titmuss 1971; Wilensky 1975; Mishra 1981). While typologies can increase our understanding of welfare state variation, evaluations of ideal types can detract from critical discourse on social goals. While these typologies are useful in making distinctions, they tend to emphasize differences at the expense of overlooking the similarities between types and the heterogeneity within each type. Social welfare in the United States, for instance, represents a broad range of policy approaches: social insurance, direct provision of cash and in-kind benefits, subsidies, and action through local authorities. Examining this mix of government strategies we see elements of both the institutional and residual models of social welfare. We can examine policies representing both of these approaches against our first principle enhancing community.

If institutional welfare programs enhance a sense of community then we would expect to see wide-based public support for them. However, this is not always the case. The Social Security system is a good example. Criticisms of the OASI program come from feminists, minorities, and more recently from its beneficiaries. As Ginsburg writes: "The social security system not only reflects but strengthens the subordinate position of women as domestic workers inside the family and wage workers outside the family" (1979:26). Social Security continues the pattern of workplace discrimination into retirement by awarding men higher average monthly payments than women and whites more than minorities. Women are also penalized in the Social Security system because of their part-time and sporadic employment histories due to childbearing and caretaking. More recently, the mandatory nature of the OASI program has been criticized by those who feel that individuals would be financially better off if they were free to save and invest their surplus income, free from government-mandated involvement.

Similarly, we can evaluate the ability of the residual model of social welfare to enhance community. Almost 10 million U.S. children do not have medical insurance, an estimated 5 five million of whom have a parent employed full-time, year round, but cannot afford health insurance. The Medicaid program is available to the children of low-income families and yet many who are eligible are not receiving the benefit. Why? The rules of eligibility for Medicaid are exceedingly complicated and not well understood. The application process usually means a mandatory visit to the local welfare office. In some families, younger children are eligible and their older siblings excluded. Furthermore, rules differ from state to state. The program generally sends out new insurance cards every month and parents must notify the program immediately of any change in income. Medicaid also carries the stigma associated with welfare.

In evaluating the OASI and Medicaid programs, we could apply the criteria in Table 2.1 and classify the first as social insurance and the second pure welfare, and then associate the first principles of community with the former and freedom with the latter. By expanding our analyses, however, we see by example how both the institutional and residual models of social welfare can be viewed as divisive, creating "we" versus "they" relationships. The criteria in Table 2.1 provide a useful organizing framework for examining policy alternatives; however, they are limited in terms of evaluation.

The evaluation of social policy based on a traditional classification social welfare models fails to encourage debate about the effects of redistribution, provision, etc. Titmuss alludes to this danger:

> Have the democracies recognized sufficiently the need to cultivate deliberately those forces and institutions whose purposes include social self-criticism and the destruction of myth? . . . Perhaps it is its relative newness which accounts for the misconceptions and confusion which surround the term welfare state. Its use during the last twenty years implies that some human societies can be classified as welfare states while others cannot, what then distinguishes such a state and by what criteria is it judged? (1971:100)

ROLE OF THE POLICY ANALYST: TOWARD THE TWENTY-FIRST CENTURY

Our current understanding of the first principles of freedom, equality, and community have been drawn by eighteenth- and nineteenth-century philosophers and may no longer adequately define our world. What is, by definition, equality? Does equality mean equality before the law, equal opportunity, or equal living conditions? To be useful, these concepts must continually be redefined. Christian Bay discusses the outmoded conceptualization of freedom as it relates to liberal individualism:

> Our celebrated liberal individualism in the western world coincides, as we all know, with vast and growing disparities in individual access to rights and liberties, and even to the means of survival. . . . Could it be that the 'individual' who is celebrated in the West is, whether by skill, inheritance, good connections, or luck, understood to be a member of an elite upper class, whose privileges require that others be underprivileged? Or could we imagine, and work toward, a whole world of liberal individualists, with equal access to the means or conditions for developing their own individualities? (1988:161)

Similarly, if we examine the notion of community, we see not only citizenship, but the idea of broad participation embedded in many of the definitions. Nisbet for example, describes community as "the product of people working together on problems, of autonomous and collective fulfillment of internal objectives, and of the experience of living under codes of authority which have been set in large degree by the persons involved" (1967:xvi).

James Midgley (1986) speaks of participation as not only one of the goals of community development, but as an integral part of the process. Community development, according to Midgley, is facilitated if people participate fully in making decisions that affect their welfare and in implementing these decisions. Participation creates a sense of community that gives meaning to human existence and fosters social integration.

This view of community, as both process and purpose, has been influenced by the Third World community development movement of the 1950s, the current school of critical theory advanced by Habermas, feminist, and social justice theorists, and new models of research that reject the elite position of positivism.

Habermas believed that social science should serve an "emancipatory interest." That is, social science, should foster improvement of human existence through increased awareness and participation on the part of individuals as political actors. Critical policy analysis serves not to advocate a particular philosophical position or to argue the strongest possible case. Critical policy analysis seeks to blend the empirical with the normative to stimulate rich and intense debate from diverse sources.

Bobrow and Dryzek (1987) describe the role of the policy analyst as raising the level of the debate and providing informed contributions. They see many of the important policy questions as "transcientific" in nature and therefore unamenable to the technical or scientific approach. Within this frame of reference, the role of the analyst is not merely that of technician. The idea of the analyst as technician was developed at a time when there was a small monopoly on data and there was only one acceptable method of knowledge creation: logical positivism. Recent developments in research and information technology have lessened the mystique and broadened the accessibility of research. Today, our capacity to rapidly transmit information around the world is tremendous and permits the possibility of greater transparency and accountability. Thus, the role of the analyst may not be to interpret the data, but to provide it. The burden of what constitutes evidence for social policy has also changed. Case studies, action research, and qualitative methods of data analysis constitute acceptable forms of knowledge development.

As limited as the role of technician is the role of advocate, attached to a certain value position. A participatory approach recognizes that all values are not compatible, and that in an increasingly diverse society all values are not equally valued. There is no formula for choosing among values, and yet the process of choice is extremely important. If we think of social policy as a process of making allocations in conditions of scarceness, we know that not everyone will get what they want, let alone what they need. While there are differences in what people want, and there are limits on resources, there are similarities in how people want to be treated. How these value conflicts will be resolved presents a challenge to the policy analyst of the twenty-first century. Concern evolves around how mechanisms for meaningful community participation can be established. At this point, the synthesized approach may be accused of greater idealism than operational clarity.

The problem of policy implementation was raised in the discussion of the process approach. Successful implementation of social policy relies largely on voluntary compliance. The power of authority is limited. One factor that leads to voluntary compliance is the perception of fairness in the process: procedural justice. A participatory approach acknowledges the importance of values and seeks involvement, so that what is done in the notion of "the public interest" is a matter of intense public debate. Meaningful participation infuses a sense of fairness, smooths implementation, and fosters a sense of belonging and integration. On the other hand, a lack of meaningful participation sends a message that people are not valued and that the procedures are unfair. Inclusionist tactics can provide an anchor during conflict, be the basis of cooperation and coordination, and stimulate enthusiasm and energy. The language of social policy has typically been exclusionary. For instance, the term "one-parent" or "single-parent" family suggests that gender does not matter, and ignores the fact that the majority of one-parent families are headed by females and lack a "male" wage. The manner in which language is used in social policy tends to obscure important distinctions. The consequences of such exclusionist tactics are alienation and dissension, and examples of their manifestation are the creation of subcultures and the desire for self-government and separate societies. As the population becomes increasingly diverse, and as global interaction becomes more common and crucial to the economy, the negative impact of continued exclusion of major sectors of society through social policy is likely to intensify.

SUMMARY

As we conclude this chapter, the one thing we are certain of is that policy analysis is, as it should be, continually being redefined. This chapter has introduced two traditional approaches to policy analysis, process and purpose, and it argues that neither is sufficient for the analysis of social policy as we enter the twenty-first century. The process approach is criticized for the neutrality of the analyst and its reluctance to welcome the ideological debate on values. The purpose approach is criticized for its lack of attention to process in determining what values will be pursued. What we have done, in effect, is synthesize the two approaches to emphasize the relationship between process and outcome. While the approach on process has been the dominant approach to policy analysis in this country, recent shifts in philosophy such as a focus on the teaching of morals and values and the promotion of civil education in kindergarten through high school indicate a philosophical change that will support this new role for the policy analyst. Greater acceptance of alternative methods of knowledge creation beyond positivism and new developments in information technology have increased the range of people able and willing to participate in the policymaking process.

The remainder of the book attempts to demonstrate the value of a synthesized approach. Concepts from this and the previous chapter are applied in a number of policy areas. They include appropriate roles of government, the role of the private sector, our understanding of human behavior as it is shaped by economic rationales, and the critical tensions between first principles such as freedom, equality, and community in attempting to achieve social objectives through social policies. While the above may not be brought together in a tight and synoptic framework in the chapters that follow, the ideas in the first two chapters are the keys to such an understanding.

To make this manageable, we have chosen seven applications. Furthermore, we have divided these eight into two major sections. The first offers four examples of the application of this approach to substantive areas: income maintenance (Chapter 3), health and medical care (Chapter 4), housing (Chapter 5), and employment (Chapter 8). The second section focuses on three target populations: families and care of the dependent (Chapter 6), the aged (Chapter 7), and the poor (Chapter 9). We chose these topics because they are critical areas of social policy. The purpose of these essays is not to offer an exhaustive treatment of all issues. We are more concerned with the application and relevance of the approach outlined in the first two chapters. Finally, in Chapter 10, we offer a review and synthesis of the critical issues we are still faced with in these areas and possible directions we might take as we approach the year 2000.

CHAPTER

3

Income Maintenance

In Chapter 1 we suggested that within our capitalist society the roles and functions of the state were more narrowly prescribed than in other forms of political economy. Three basic arguments for exception to the agreed-upon minimalist role were introduced and discussed: (1) the public goods argument, (2) the externality argument, and (3) specific market imperfections

Accepting these basic rationales, this nation over the past 60 years has evolved (though some would argue rather reluctantly) into its unique form of a modern welfare state:

> A welfare state is a state in which organized power is deliberately used (through politics and administration) in an effort to modify the play of market forces in at least three directions—first by guaranteeing individuals and families a minimum income, irrespective of the market value of their work or property; second, by narrowing the extent of insecurity by enabling individuals and families to meet "social contingencies" . . . which lead otherwise to individual and family crises; and third, by ensuring that all citizens without distinction of status or class are offered the best standards available in relation to a certain agreed range of social services. (Briggs 1967:29)

While Briggs does not offer a philosophical rationale for the above, he is clear as to what the intervention involves. First, a welfare state has a responsibility to provide to everyone some agreed-upon minimum income regardless of their work status. Second, the state has a responsibility to buffer various risks to economic security in an industrial society. These risks would include sickness, old age, and unemployment. Finally, Briggs would argue for a more egalitarian society, or at least a society that does not establish separate social service delivery systems for the poor and the nonpoor.

The first two dimensions of the modern welfare state are associated with what we have come to label "income maintenance" or "income transfer" policies and programs. Income maintenance is a major pillar of the welfare state, a foundation upon which other social policies are built. As Beveridge so eloquently argued, the basic threats to all modern societies are (1) want, (2) disease, (3) ignorance, (4) squalor and (5) idleness (Beveridge 1942:para 8). He argued that while health care, education, housing, and employment were essential to achieving and preserving the well-being of individuals and families, these efforts would be dissipated unless they were integrated with an adequate system of income maintenance.

Furthermore, recent national surveys suggest that most Americans believe that these functions are legitimate and worthwhile. The difficulties come when specific policies are evaluated or proposed, since these goals have to be balanced with other equally important goals. As Ozawa (1982) points out, we are constantly attempting to develop an income maintenance system that is based on "a coherent incentive system so as to preserve the work incentive, and yet, at the same time, allow the nation to care and provide adequately for vulnerable groups of individuals, i.e., children, the elderly and the disabled" (p. viii). This is the dilemma we face. How do we create a desirable balance between economic goals and social goals?

This is the age-old issue that continues to shape the welfare debate and to raise that debate to an emotional level that often transcends the reality of available data. In other words, "income maintenance" is not a technical problem to be solved, though it has technical dimensions. It is, first and foremost, a moral problem that pulls and pushes us between values that cannot be maximized simultaneously—but values that we have been conditioned to believe in and hold dearly since our childhood.

THEORETICAL CONSIDERATIONS

Income Maintenance and Political Economy

The search for such a calculus has become a major issue since many believe that the well-being of all individuals in our complex modern society depends on the economic system, its success in producing wealth and the ways in which this wealth is shared. In simpler terms, the question can be reduced at the societal level to one that asks how much income we can afford to transfer so that economic growth will not be adversely affected. At the microlevel it becomes even more of an issue, because it begins to question whether giving financial support to an individual or family will have negative effects, i.e., will it prove to be a disincentive to work—which in turn would have adverse effects on the economic system?

This is, of course, the overarching question facing all political economies regardless of ideology. While the language used—create a balance between and among desirable objectives—might suggest a sense of "equal" value or worth between economic and social objectives, such is not the case. Political economy is a term used to underscore the interrelationship between the political and the economic systems of a given country. This interrelationship, however, is not an equal partnership: the primary purpose of the political system is to further the goals of the existing economic system. Social policies, including income maintenance policies, are created to function as instruments used by the political system to achieve specific economic objectives. In our country, this system is referred to as a market economy that has been shaped to reflect the demands of advanced capitalism. It is only through applying this framework that we are in a position to understand why our social policies are secondary to and dependent upon economic policies. In fact, it is fair to say that our social policies have meaning only within the framework of political economy.

Income Maintenance: An Instrument
of Economic Policy

In Chapter 1, we introduced the notion that policy is concerned with decision-making and choosing among alternative courses of action. Choices have to be made among competing claims for resources, all of which may be desirable or at least desirable to some group. We also introduced into this discussion the reality that we can never maximize these competing claims simultaneously because of insufficient resources. In Chapter 2, we complicated an already complex issue by arguing that in some instances we are also faced with making choices between conflicting values or aspirations, e.g., the first principles of liberty, equality, and community, all of which are desirable but cannot be maximized at the same time.

Earlier in this chapter we introduced Briggs's position that a modern welfare state is one that interacts with, or even modifies, the economic system so that the basic needs and security of individuals and their families are met. O'Neill agrees with this position:

> It is the duty of the community through the power of the state to modify deliberately the normal play of economic forces in a market economy in order to assist the needs of the underprivileged groups and individuals by

providing every citizen with a basic real income adequate for subsistence, irrespective of the market value of his work. (1967:72)

While this view would appear to be reasonable given the unpredictability of modern life, whatever consensus we thought existed usually breaks down when we begin to operationalize the concept into policies and programs.

A major concern is that acceptable options must "create a desirable balance among the goals of high employment and positive economic growth and the broader social goals of choice and equality of opportunity" (Lampman 1984:7). What, then, constitutes "a desirable balance"? What are we capable of introducing into the economy that will moderate cyclical swings of production and employment?

Historically, we have come to accept a certain level of unemployment as inevitable if inflation is to be contained. In fact, "full employment" has been defined over the past 40 years to include unemployment rates that ranged from a low of 4% in the Johnson administration to a high of almost 10% in the Reagan administration.

To put it another way, the two goals of full employment and price stability have been seen to be in conflict. The more closely we achieve one, the further we move from the other. As inflation increased to an unacceptable level, we allowed unemployment to increase as a deflationary strategy. As prices stabilized, we implemented strategies to increase employment. This dynamic and cyclical phenomenon is known as the "Phillips curve" (Phillips 1958).

Another part of the debate is concerned with both Briggs's and O'Neill's position that individuals and families be provided with an income "adequate for subsistence irrespective of the market value of that work." While today this debate is concerned with minimum wage policies and their perceived "negative" impacts on the American economy and our ability to remain competitive with other nations, the debate has a number of historical antecedents that have implications of a different kind for today.

Morris (1986) points out that as far back as 594 B.C., the Greek city states distributed corn at reduced prices from public granaries to supplement low income, a practice continued for centuries in the Roman Empire. Similar policies were enacted in England between 1495 and 1597 through various Poor Law statutes when the price for bread and other staples rose sharply. Perhaps the most important (at least in terms of understanding current income maintenance policies) were the reforms that occurred in England toward the end of the eighteenth century, especially those known as the Speenhamland system. This system offered, in effect, both a guaranteed minimum wage and the guarantee of work. In reality, it was a strategy to adjust real income to the needs of the worker and not to the prevailing wage structure. When employers argued that lower profits required their lowering wages (the market value of the work) government intervened by subsidizing those wages, thus guaranteeing a minimum level determined to be adequate for meeting basic needs. The subsidy, as elaborate as it was, was basically tied to the price of bread.

Shortly after the Speenhamland system was introduced, political economists (or perhaps more accurately, philosophers concerned with political economy) such as Bentham, Malthus, Ricardo, John Stuart Mill, and Pareto, attacked it as a system that interfered with the natural workings of the market and those "laws" that determined these workings, e.g.:

- There is a fixed amount of funds available for wages regardless of the number of people who want work (Mill).
- There exists only a limited amount of money available for wages. When public assistance is subtracted from this pool, there remains that much less for wages (Smith).
- To increase wages you must decrease the number of workers (Mill).
- Income distribution is determined by the natural law and this distribution will always be uneven (Pareto)
- Labor is bound to a wage that can never rise above subsistence (the Iron Law of Wages) (Ricardo).
- Subsidized wages or wages above subsistence levels will encourage premature marriage and increase the birth rate to the point that population will outstrip resources (Malthus).

All agreed that to provide wages above market value and to guarantee these wages despite market fluctuations (i.e., to remove this issue from concerns about production, exchange, distribution, and price structure) would (1) stimulate employers to reduce wages since government would make up the difference; (2) remove from the employee any incentive to work since a living wage was guaranteed and not tied to productivity; and (3) result in dramatically lower levels of production.

These beliefs (there were few empirical studies to test these "laws" and "hypotheses") were accepted and the earlier Elizabethan Poor Law gave way to the Victorian Poor Law enacted in 1834—a law that has had a lasting impact on many aspects of our current income maintenance policies.

The political economists of the nineteenth century were not the "detached" social scientists of the twentieth century. Bentham, for example treated political economy as a theological phenomenon and held that individual or even community deviations from accepted economic "laws" were problems of moral turpitude and should be treated as "sins."

Bentham's position became the theoretical underpinning for the new Poor Law since it embodied positive economic functions and negative welfare functions (true welfare was to be found in the economic market). Bentham argued that the "economic virtues of industry, sobriety and thrift were to be accorded a prominent place and raised to the level of spiritual values" (Poynter 1969).

Moreover, to stimulate this "industry," Bentham argued that poverty had to be defined as more than a social fact (i.e., the lack of money, etc., necessary to meet basic needs); it also had to be viewed as a form of spiritual bankruptcy. To put it in simpler terms: if the problem was defined as a lack of resources leading to dependency, the solution was to give the poor person resources. The individual was not blamed for his or her condition because the problem was a structural problem involving economic cycles. But this interpretation leads to Speenhamland-type solutions!

If, however, the problem could be redefined as first and foremost a problem of dependency that led to poverty (over time we shifted the definition of dependency from one involving "moral pathology" to a condition involving "character flaws" or other forms of deficits) the solution would require the dependent person to change. While the first definition concludes that poverty (a lack of resources) causes dependency; the new definition suggests that people are poor because they are dependent. Bentham successfully combined the explanation of the problem with the solution or treatment of the problem.

To complete the transformation, Bentham argued that the term "poverty" (connoting a condition or social fact) should be replaced with the term "pauper" (connoting a weakness in the individual). A pauper, then, was seen as someone with serious character flaws or moral deficits and pauperism was regarded as failure of character. In essence, Bentham was stating that God (and a wrathful God at that) was a capitalist and salvation was to be achieved only through an acceptance of the new work ethic—one that would transform farmers into obedient factory workers who would show up on time, work a full day, and accept without question the mind-dulling routinized tasks of the new factory system. Finally, Bentham's reformulation of the earlier Poor Law included the long-lasting prescription that anyone receiving "alms," the "dole," or "relief" should receive less than the lowest paid worker. Otherwise, there would be no incentive for workers to continue working, or for those receiving support to seek employment. This concept—less eligibility—was also a psychological device in that it reminded people of what they did *not* want. As a policy, its purpose was to separate the genuinely poor from those who were lazy.

Spencer took Smith, Bentham, and Ricardo, mixed them with his version of Darwin's position on the "survival of the fittest," and concluded that human behavior also responds to natural laws and should not be the object of government intervention. To involve government would impede the evolutionary process and would lead to adverse consequences regardless of intentions. If one group is supported, another is weakened since the first benefits at the expense of the other. As Coll (1970:62) demonstrates, Spencer's ideas became the theoretical underpinning for the emerging Charity Organization Society, which over time emphasized personal failure as the major cause of poverty and assumed that no one would work unless every aspect of their life was constantly investigated, that close supervision was required, and that the lowest level of relief should be given.

Until the depression this was the prevailing ideology, but by then it proved to be untenable. The remainder of the chapter will (1) introduce various rationales for income maintenance programs, (2) describe our existing policies, and (3) critique them against these different rationales.

Rationales for Income Maintenance Programs

There have been at least three major rationales offered to justify previous, current, and proposed income maintenance programs. These rationales, however, are neither exclusionary nor are they contradictory and are often used in some combination to argue for a particular policy:

- to buffer the risks associated with temporary or permanent unemployment;
- to stabilize the labor force and prevent the possibility of civil unrest;
- to promote a more egalitarian society through the redistribution of wealth.

These rationales, however, are neither exclusionary nor contradictory and are often used in some combination to argue for a particular policy.

1. Buffer the Risks Associated with Temporary or Permanent Unemployment. This rationale is the most explicit of the rationales and dominates debates on income maintenance policies. It has been argued that the purpose of income maintenance policies is clearly stated in the words themselves, i.e., the "maintenance of income" during periods when a person is not working, whether these periods are temporary or permanent. Traditionally, we have identified five (5) major threats to economic security of workers and their families:

- retirement because of age;
- inability to work because of industrial accidents;
- permanent disability or temporary illness;
- death of the "breadwinner(s)";
- unemployment caused by economic fluctuation.

Other formulations include phrases such as "the provision of economic security when employment is interrupted" and "the replacement of lost income." Under this rationale, we usually find three distinct formulations of the major purpose of these transfers: (1) to replace wages, (2) to prevent poverty, (3) to meet basic needs. If income maintenance programs are to replace wages, then the amount of income to be transferred to an individual should be equal to the amount earned while he or she worked or to some percentage of that amount. If the programs are to prevent poverty, the amount of income to be transferred should be the difference between actual income and the agreed-upon poverty level. Finally, if the programs are structured to provide a minimum subsistence level, the task is to document what amount is required to meet basic needs. All of these would, moreover, have to have an anti-inflationary mechanism in place that would increase the amount of the transfer as the cost of living increased.

2. *Stabilize the Labor Force and Prevent the Possibility of Civil Unrest.* Earlier in this chapter, we pointed out that under advanced capitalism the two goals of full employment and price stability have historically been in conflict and that the more closely we achieved one, the further we moved away from achieving the other. Periodic unemployment for some and more permanent unemployment and underemployment for others have become facts of life in our society. Our economy is such that (1) cycles of growth are always followed by cycles of decline; (2) inflation historically increases as unemployment declines; and (3) structural and frictional factors "cause" higher unemployment rates in certain labor markets, regional disparities, and the channeling of women and minorities into secondary labor markets with low-paying, dead-end jobs. Given this, some analysts argue that income maintenance policies are concerned with labor market effects, and that their primary purpose is to provide disincentives to welfare when an expanding labor force is needed (i.e., eligibility is more difficult to achieve) but income support when the labor force contracts (i.e., eligibility requirements are loosened).

3. *Promote a More Egalitarian Society through the Redistribution of Wealth.* Since the days of the New Deal and the Great Depression, we have been told that because of changes in fiscal policies, income maintenance policies, and the expansion of health and social services, our society

is becoming more and more "equal." Equality is, however, an extremely elusive term. Marshall held that equality of status is more important that equality of income. Others such as Keynes (1931, 1936, 1973), Beveridge (1943, 1944), and Galbraith (1984) have argued that "equality of opportunity" should be given the highest priority and that efforts to produce a more equal society through the redistribution of income and wealth would be inefficient. On the other hand, the Fabians, including Titmuss (1958, 1968), Tawney (1961, 1964), and Crosland (1970), define equality as some combination of opportunity *and* outcome. And finally, there are those such as Gil (1973), Harrington (1975), and Rein (1970) who most emphatically argue for equality of outcome as our major priority.

When one deals with income maintenance, the primary focus of the analysis is usually equality of outcome, with attention to documenting shifts in the distribution of income within that society. Specifically, we measure the shares of total income received by specific income—the lowest fifth, the second fifth, and so on—and then plot them over time to determine whether income inequality has increased or decreased (Plotnick 1987).

MAJOR INCOME MAINTENANCE PROGRAMS

Pre–Social Security Efforts

The picture dealing with the Victorian Poor Law painted in a previous section of this chapter is harsh but accurate. In the early decades of the nineteenth century, a major social agency—the New York Society for the Prevention of Pauperism—listed the following as the leading causes of poverty:

- ignorance,
- idleness,
- intemperance,
- imprudent and hasty marriages,
- lotteries and pawnbrokers,
- houses of ill-fame,
- too many charities.

Agreeing with their colleagues and implementing Bentham's view of appropriate forms of "relief" (e.g., "less eligibility"), another major agency of the time—the New York Association for Improving the Conditions of the Poor—stated in its training manual for new workers:

The evils of improvidence can never be diminished except by removing the
cause, and this can only be done by elevating the moral character of the
poor, and by teaching them to depend upon themselves. . . . The rule is *that*
the willingly dependent upon alms should not live so comfortably with them as the
humblest independent laborer without them. (Coll:1970:34; emphasis added)

Existing income maintenance programs were not only punitive during
this period but were the purview of the private sector. Government at all
levels had very little involvement.

Furthermore, while there were cyclical periods of depression in the
earlier days of this country's industrialization, jobs for the unskilled and
the uneducated were more readily available. As Ozawa points out, "the
economy which did not depend on high or advanced technology could
produce endless jobs for the unskilled and the poor" (1982:7).

By the turn of the century, in a period that today we refer to as the
Progressive era, reformers such as Jane Addams, Lillian Wald, and Jacob
Riis began to argue that the existing economic system did not operate as
the theorists had hypothesized and that many people were unable to
meet their needs. Still, these critics believed that capitalism was superior
to any other form of political economy. Given this, they recognized the
right and responsibility of the state "to interfere and to compulsorily
modify and supplement its (i.e., market) operations" (Marshall 1972:31).

The "reformers" initiated a number of efforts that attempted to minimize these economic risks through collective measures in the public sector. Classical liberalism (competition, individualism, and laissez-faire)
was rejected since "the realities of the economic market were making a
nonsense of the normative theories of political economy" (Pinker 1973:75).
And, finally, as Ozawa (1982) suggests, more and more we came to recognize that the welfare of each individual depends on the economic welfare
of all and that we need to pool our resources if we are to deal with the
risks we all will potentially experience.

In the area of income maintenance, two major programs dominated the
first two decades of the twentieth century. In 1911, the first state worker's
compensation law (or industrial accident insurance) was passed. Prior to
the passage of this legislation, workers seeking compensation for work-
related injuries (or their families seeking compensation for work-related
deaths) were required to prove fault (usually negligence) on the part of
employers in a court of law. In demonstrating fault, the injured worker
had to "prove" that the accident was not caused by or related to (1) his or
her own negligence, (2) the negligence of a fellow worker, or (3) the
ordinary risks associated with employment. Given these legal barriers,
few workers attempted to collect compensation, and of those who did,
few were successful. Worker's compensation laws removed these require-

ments and the concept of "fault" no longer was a consideration. By 1917, 40 states and territories had enacted similar legislation and by 1929 only 4 states did not have worker's compensation programs. By 1988, 87% of labor force participants were covered.

During this period, a number of states began to provide means-tested, cash assistance to some categories of the poor—usually the old, the handicapped, and young children whose fathers had died. Perhaps the most common program found in the states was "Mother's Aid," a program initially implemented in Missouri and Illinois in 1911. By 1935 all but two states had implemented this program. However, as Rothman points out, such support was not far removed from the earlier practices of the Poor Law:

> [W]idows did not receive their allowances as a matter of right the way a pensioner did. She had to apply, demonstrate her qualifications, her economic need and her moral worth and then trust to the decision of the welfare board. At their pleasure and by their reckoning she then obtained or did not obtain help. (1979:78)

By 1935, 26 states had also passed "old age pension" programs and 23 states had developed programs for the needy blind.

The Great Depression of the 1930s both changed and accelerated the nature and extent of public intervention, especially in terms of the federal government. In the early days of the New Deal, the Roosevelt administration emphasized economic recovery, i.e., intervention in the overall structure of the market system. Accepting the argument of the British economist John Maynard Keynes, who rejected the idea of a self-regulating market and suggested that excessive savings and low levels of investment would decrease demand for goods and services, which in turn would increase unemployment, the government set out to prime a stagnant economy. The Keynesian solution was government spending even if this were to result in deficit financing, and lower taxes on consumers to increase purchasing power (Keynes [1936] 1973).

Thus was born the myriad of the "alphabet programs": National Industrial Recovery Act (NIRA), Public Works Administration (PWA), National Recovery Administration (NRA), Civilian Conservation Corps (CCC), Federal Emergency Recovery Act (FERA), Works Progress Administration (WPA), and others, too numerous to list.

One program, the Civil Works Administration (CWA) established in 1934, produced jobs for over 4 million persons in a matter of months. Although it was terminated in less than a year, it made a significant contribution: "Over 400,000 projects were started; 500,000 miles of road were built or repaired; 40,000 schools were built or improved; 500 new airports were established; parks, sewers, firebreaks, irrigation ditches, forestry trails and public buildings were started or improved" (Schottland 1963:33).

Social Security: A Shift in Federal Responsibilities

As the depression deepened, the federal government expanded its role beyond that of stimulating the economy and the employment market and for the first time in history began to deal more directly with the immediate economic needs of individuals and families. These efforts culminated in 1935 with the passage of the Social Security Act—an act that once and for all moved this society into the era of the modern welfare state. While initially the legislation was threatened on the issue of its constitutionality (i.e., is the federal government empowered to directly aid citizens or does this power reside in the individual states?), the Supreme Court eventually supported the administration and in 1937 ruled that it was constitutional for the federal government to go beyond its traditional role—including its role in the area of income maintenance.

To understand the magnitude of this action, we need only look at the data in Table 3.1. Public social welfare expenditures reached almost $1.3 trillion in 1993 (U.S. Bureau of the Census 1996). Five of these programs, providing income to various groups who met eligibility requirements, were responsible for 57% of these expenditures. Moreover, expenditures in these areas were over $720 billion in 1993, compared to $18 billion in

Table 3.1. Major Income Maintenance Programs ($ in Millions)

Year	OASDI	UI	WC	PA[a]	SSI
1960	11,080	2,867	860	4,101	
1965	18,094	2,283	1,214	5,875	
1970	31,570	4,184	1,981	14,443	
1975	66,586	18,188	4,568	27,409	5,877
1980	120,272	18,756	9,632	45,064	7,857
1985	186,082	13,538	15,170	66,170	11,107
1990	382,289	28,805	41,703	133,646	19,646
1993	449,277	40,271	43,376	160,695	26,501

Source: Social Security Bulletin, Statistical Abstract of the United States. 1996. Washington, DC: USGPO.

[a] PA Includes Old Age Assistance (OAA), Aid to the Blind (AB), Aid to the Permanently and Totally Disabled (APTD) through 1973, Aid to Families with Dependent Children (AFDC), and General Assistance (GA).

1960 (see Table 3.1). Of these five federally administered or federally supported programs, four came into being with the passage of the Social Security Act of 1935 (the exception being Workers Compensation, which preceded the act).

OASDI has always been the largest of the programs and since 1965 has represented approximately half of all federal income maintenance expenditures. Three of the other programs show a steady increase over the years until the 1990s, when they experienced a sharp increase. The remaining program—Unemployment Insurance—fluctuates, as would be expected, with the cycles of the economy. For example, the largest expenditures ever under UI were spent in 1982 (almost $21 billion), a year with a depressed economy and extremely high rates of unemployment (in the average week there were over 4 million unemployed workers receiving UI).

Social Security: The Social Insurance Programs

As discussed in Chapter 1, the act included programs that were based on social insurance concepts and programs that were based on social assistance concepts in that they were extensions of the existing Poor Law. The social insurance program of 1935 involved two complementary strategies and targeted two primary groups: (1)labor force participants and (2) those unable to participate in the labor force. Both programs incorporated the ideas of (1) universal coverage and (2) benefits as rights and not means-tested.

The first program—UI—offered a combination of employee benefits designed to protect the worker against disability, illness, and temporary unemployment. The second program—Old Age Insurance (OAI)—provided income support for those who were not connected to the work force because of retirement due to age. In time, the Social Security Act was amended to include additional groups not connected to the work force, e.g., widows raising dependent children (survivors insurance was added in 1939); and the disabled (disability insurance was added in 1956). Today, the social insurance program is known as OASDI (the Old Age, Survivors, Disability Insurance Program). While Medicare (the medical insurance program for those eligible under the retirement and disability criteria) was passed in 1965 as the Title 18 amendment to the Social Security Act) technically it is not an income maintenance program since funds are not transferred directly to the beneficiary.

The UI program is somewhat unique in that it is financed by employers through a special tax collected by the federal government (the Unemployment Insurance Trust Fund), which then passes these funds on to the states to administer. While some of Roosevelt's advisors argued that this program should be structured the same as the other insurance programs (i.e., administered by the federal government) to insure that all recipients would be treated the same way regardless of residence; in the face of some general resistance on the part of states to the growing role of the federal government, Roosevelt decided to include them more actively in the New Deal.

Unemployment benefits are provided as a right (there is no means test associated with either eligibility or amount of benefit) to workers who are unemployed through no fault of their own. Since the administration of the program has been given to the states, we find some differences in both the amount and duration of benefits. In general terms, we find that each state has enacted a minimum and maximum amount tied to the workers' previous earnings (i.e., the higher the wage, the higher the benefit); that the norm is 50% of earnings up to that maximum; and that benefits are available for up to 52 weeks during periods of extended unemployment. Previously, the upper limit had been 26 weeks, but lingering periods of high unemployment during the past 10 years have resulted in the increase. Approximately 97% of labor force participants worked in covered jobs.

The counterpart of the UI program is OASDI. While the former attempted to buffer the risks associated with temporary unemployment for those able to work, this program was to do the same for those who were not able to work because of age or disability or whose livelihood was threatened because of the death of the insured worker, e.g., children. This program is funded through a special payroll tax paid by both employer and employee. Self-employed workers are also required to participate in the program. These funds are deposited in special trust funds (the OASI Trust Fund and the DI Trust Fund). The monies in these funds are administered by a board of trustees and can only be used to pay benefits and operating expenses of the program. Unlike a number of other income maintenance programs, OASDI is totally operated with funds collected through the special tax and deposited in the trust funds. There are no subsidies from the general revenues of government (see Table 3.2).

In determining the amount each employer and employee in a given year will pay, two factors are considered. The first is the tax rate and the second is the amount of total wages that will be taxed. Changes are made periodically to ensure the solvency of the fund.

While there is considerable debate about the health of the Social Security system (specifically OASDI), much of this is clouded with misinformation. Numerous polls show that many, if not most, young workers believe that there will not be sufficient funds for them when they retire.

In the first three decades of the Social Security program, polls showed that most Americans thought highly of the program, but had little under-

Table 3.2. Social Security Trust Fund ($ Millions)

Year	Receipts	Expenditures	Balance at end of year[a]
1940	592	28	1,745
1950	2,367	784	12,893
1960	11,382	11,189	20,324
1970	32,220	29,848	32,454
1975	59,605	60,395	36,987
1980	105,841	107,678	22,823
1985	184,239	171,150	35,842
1990	286,653	227,519	214,197
1995	342,801	297,760	458,502

Source: Social Security Bulletin, Statistical Abstract of the United States. 1996. Washington, DC: USGPO.
[a] In 1982 the trust fund balance was at an all time low of $12,535,000.

standing about it—including the insurance issue. By the mid 1970s, however, this began to shift markedly and by 1978, over 60% had lost their confidence in the program (Sherman 1989).

In part this can be attributed to the belief that if OASDI is an "insurance" program, all contributors' payments should be set aside for their retirement, much like private annuity programs are operated. To put it another way, the insurance company is required to have sufficient funds on hand to pay off all of its contractual obligations in the event that it either goes out of business or if all of its policyholders decide at the same time to cash in their policies. OASDI is not an insurance program by this definition. It is, however, an insurance program in the sense that the program (1) is designed to continue indefinitely, (2) will accept new members, and (3) anticipates that revenues will be sufficient over a long range period to meet expenditures since (4) the program is compulsory (Schottland 1963). Rather than seeing the contribution as "paying" for the benefits, it is more accurate to think of these contributions as "qualifying" the individual for the benefits.

The data in Table 3.2 show that from its beginning and through 1975, annual receipts exceeded annual expenditures and that the trust fund's annual balance was continuously growing. By 1980, however, annual receipts had fallen below expenditures and the trust balances had decreased sharply.

This phenomenon can be attributed directly to the introduction in 1975 of the automatic cost of living adjustment (COLA) which is triggered to changes in the Consumer Price Index (CPI). Given the high rates of inflation, Congress passed a series of amendments in 1972 that not only introduced the automatic COLA but, in order to catch up with previous periods of high inflation, also increased the benefits by 22% that year and

11% for the years 1973–1974. While the policy change has had a positive impact on the quality of life of millions of people, while it has kept millions of recipients above the poverty line, it had the negative effect of almost wiping out the surplus in the Trust Fund.

Inflation, as measured by increases in the CPI, was relatively nonexistent for most of the years between 1940 and 1965 (see Table 3.3). With the exception of the postwar years (1945–1950), the average annual rate of inflation was less than 1%. During the late 1960s inflation began to creep up, but it was only during the 1970s and early 1980s that the country experienced a major problem.

Two bipartisan committees were established in the late 1970s (1977) and the early 1980s (1983) to deal with this problem. Their attention turned to possible changes in the current financing mechanisms. One option, that of channeling general revenue funds to "bail out" the OASDI trust funds, was rejected, first, on the grounds that the strength of the program—the notion of "right to benefits"—would have been compromised. Second, the committee believed that to do so would open the door to making basic changes in the program, such as moving from universal coverage (an entitlement program) to selective provision (means testing). The committees reaffirmed the value of the institutional approach and rejected the residual approach. Instead, their focus was on strengthening the program within its fundamental philosophy.

The changes the two committees recommended for both the tax rate and the tax base are significant (see Table 3.4). From 1937 through 1972 (35 years) the taxable base (the amount of wages that were taxed) remained under $10,000 and from 1972 through 1976 the tax base only increased

Table 3.3. Average Annual Increases in the CPI

Years	Increase (%)
1940–1945	0.80
1945–1950	1.22
1950–1955	0.56
1955–1960	0.48
1960–1965	0.38
1965–1970	1.46
1970–1975	3.03
1975–1980	5.76
1980–1985	4.80
1985–1990	3.60
1990–1995	3.50

Source: Social Security Bulletin, Statistical Abstract of the United States. 1996. Washington, DC: USGPO.

Table 3.4. OASDI Tax Rates and Taxable Base[a]

Year	Tax Rate[b] (%)	Taxable Base ($)	Maximum Annual Tax ($)
1937–1949	1.00	3,000	30
1950	1.50	3,000	45
1955	2.00	4,200	84
1960	3.00	4,800	144
1970	4.80	7,800	405
1975	5.85	14,100	825
1980	6.13	25,900	1,589
1981	6.65	29,700	1,975
1984	6.70	37,000	2,479
1985	7.05	39,600	2,792
1988	7.51	47,000	3,530
1989	7.51	48,000	3,605
1990	7.65	51,300	3,924
1995	7.65	61,200	4,681

[a] The table has been divided into a number of parts. The first (1937–1975) shows a pattern of steady but slow growth in both the tax rate and the taxable base. The second covers the early 1980s, when the 1977 amendments became operational. The third period reflects the dramatic corrections made in the system to deal with both short- and long-range problems.
[b] Rate for both employer and employee. The tax rate for the self-employed was somewhere between the combined employer-employee rate.

marginally. Following the recommendations of the 1977 committee, the taxable base jumped to $25,900 in 1980 and to just under $30,000 in 1981. Still, these were only stopgap measures attempting to deal with the current crisis. The balance in the trust fund, in spite of these measures, reached a historical low of $12 billion in 1982. The second set of more radical recommendations was implemented in 1984. Not only did the taxable base jump sharply, but for the first time in the history of the program, higher income beneficiaries were required to pay taxes on up to 50% of the benefit.

To put this into perspective, if a worker began paying into the Social Security system in 1937 and worked for 13 years, and if his or her income was the maximum to be taxed, he or she would have contributed approximately $435 during that whole period. If that same worker continued to work for another 10 years, he or she would have contributed an additional $855 for a 23-year grand total of $1,290. A worker beginning in 1980, however, earning the maximum to be taxed would have contributed more than the older worker in that single year—$1,589.

By the end of 1995, over 43 million persons—69% of whom are over the age of 62—were receiving benefits under the largest of the income maintenance programs, OASDI. As Table 3.5 shows, the proportion of retirees to those receiving benefits under the other two components—the

Table 3.5.   OASDI Beneficiaries (Thousands)

Year	Retirees	Disabled	Survivors	Total
1940	148		74	222
1950	2,326		1,152	3,487
1960	10,599	687	3,558	14,844
1970	17,096	2,665	6,468	26,299
1975	20,364	4,352	7,368	32,084
1980	23,336	4,682	7,601	35,619
1985	25,991	3,907	7,160	37,508
1990	28,400	4,300	7,200	39,800
1995	30,100	5,900	7,400	43,400

Source: Social Security Bulletin, Statistical Abstract of the United States. 1996. Washington, DC: USGPO.

disabled and survivors—has fluctuated over the past 60 or so years: the retirement program has always accounted for at least two of every three recipients. The data in Table 3.5 also show that the number of recipients in the other two programs had plateaued in the decade of the 1980s but that the number of disabled recipients increased markedly in the 1990s. What is remarkable is the fact that over 16% of all Americans are receiving benefits under this program. Of these, 54% are women, 37% are men, and 95% are children.

While average monthly benefits grew over the years, the growth following the introduction of the COLA trigger in 1974 was extraordinary (see Table 3.6).

Table 3.6.   OASDI Average Monthly Benefit ($)

Category	1940	1950	1960	1970	1980	1990	1995
Retiree
Worker	22.60	53.86	74.04	118.10	341.41	588.30	704.80
Spouse	12.13	23.60	38.72	61.19	171.95	439.00	491.00
Survivor
Widow	10.28	36.54	57.68	101.71	308.12	557.90	681.60
Child	12.22	28.43	51.37	82.23	239.52	462.00	502.90
Disabled
Worker			89.31	139.21	370.74	570.40	667.60
Spouse			34.41	42.55	110.48	380.00	492.30

Source: Social Security Bulletin, Statistical Abstract of the United States. 1996. Washington, DC: USGPO.

Average annual increases for the old-age program (OA) was 4% in the decade of the 1950s and 6% in the decade of the 1960s. Corresponding annual rates of increase for the survivors program and for those covered under disability were comparable, ranging from 5 to 8%. Given the high inflation of the 1970s *and* the automatic increases in the benefit level, we experienced double-digit increases: i.e., an average annual increase of 19% in the retirement program, 20% in the survivors program, and 18% in the disability program. Over the past 15 years (1980–1995) we have seen smaller but still considerable growth in all programs.

If we now combine the data in Tables 3.4–3.6 into Table 3.7, we see a pattern of moderate growth in the 1960s with the increase in expenditures a function of both an increase in the number of recipients and the average monthly benefit; sharp increases in expenditures in the 1970s caused by increases in the amount of benefits provided; relatively slow growth in the 1980s; and even slower growth in the 1990s. The so-called crisis in the OASDI program appears to be partially resolved and the program will continue to be solvent through the first 20 years of the next century or at least until the next period of sustained inflation. Moreover, while the Hart (1979) and Harris and Associates (1981) polls mentioned above showed a society pessimistic about the strength and value of such a system, Yankelovich, Skelley, and White (1985) found these trends being reversed and that 90% of Americans supported the Cost of Living Adjustment (COLA); that 67% agreed that social security taxes should be raised if needed; and that by a two-to-one margin, military expenditures should be cut back before social security expenditures.

Table 3.7. Average Annual Increase—Consumer Price Index (by Decade)

Decade	Category	Percentage Increase
1960–1970	Recipients	7
	Expenditures	13
	Monthly benefit	6
1970–1980	Recipients	4
	Expenditures	28
	Monthly benefit	19
1980–1990	Recipients	1
	Expenditures	11
	Monthly benefit	8
1990–1995	Recipients	1
	Expenditures	4
	Monthly benefit	6

Source: Social Security Bulletin, Statistical Abstract of the United States. 1996. Washington, DC: USGPO.

Recent Proposals for Reform

Rather than waiting for the next crisis and expecting Congress to step in and implement another adjustment to the system to add another decade or so of solvency, a number of groups are suggesting we at least explore some more permanent though radical solutions. Technical adjustments no longer seem sufficient. If less radical changes are implemented, it is argued that the system will collapse. As it is now, the only way to increase funds is to increase either the tax rate or the taxable base, or change eligibility criteria such as age or means-test benefits. And yet the tax rate is 6.2% for the employer and employee and the taxable base is over $62,000. To raise the tax rate would create a number of potential problems to both the employer (it might serve as a disincentive to hiring new workers) and employee (this creates a burden on the lower income worker). To raise the taxable base raises another type of problem. It has been estimated that if the income limit on the payroll tax were lifted so that all income were subject to the Social Security payroll tax (FICA), two-thirds of the projected actuarial deficit would be eliminated (*Economist*, June 14, 1997). This apparently is not a feasible alternative, since making Social Security more progressive would mean losing the support of the wealthy. And finally, traditionalists believe that to means-test Social Security benefits would move us away from an important principle: universal provision of benefits under an institutional model as discussed in Chapter 2.

To put the current system's deficiencies into a framework that most people can understand, conservative think tanks such as the Cato Institute and the Heritage Foundation have begun to prepare data showing what an employee might have expected to receive if he or she had had the option to invest an equal amount into the stock market rather than into a system that invests in more fiscally conservative treasury bonds. For example, assuming a 7% annual return, a worker born in 1948 who earns $30,000 annually can expect at age 65 to receive $1,083 a month in social security benefits but would receive $6,812 each month if their contributions had been privately invested.

Given these types of projections, it is no wonder that for the first time the Social Security Advisory Council has discussed the possibility of either the individual or the federal government investing a portion of FICA in stocks. Alternatives range from government itself investing 40% of Social Security income, to requiring individuals to invest a portion of their contributions in the stock market.

Hoskins (1996) reviewed a number of emerging efforts to privatize Social Security and arguments used to defend this evolution. He concluded that (1) private sector approaches may not result in lower public spending; (2) such approaches may provide protection to the fortunate few but not necessarily to the population at large; (3) the combined risks of inflation and commercial bankruptcy are historically frequent. In support of this last point, during the recession of 1982–1984, the government of Chile had to take over a number of private pension fund management companies that failed (after Chile privatized its Social Security system in 1981).

While Hoskins makes a number of recommendations, his overall warning needs to be emphasized:

> Even more than the issue of international competitiveness, the public/private debate on income security and health protection tends to be more emotional than intellectual. The discussions quickly tend to degenerate into either/or, black/white and diametrically opposed approaches, when in fact the experience of most countries demonstrates that there is virtually an unlimited mix and range of public and private approaches to risk protection. The combined configuration of public and private programs for social protection that works well in one country could well prove to be a public policy disaster in another. Private sector approaches are thus not automatically the cheaper or more effective solutions when applied to social security protection. (1996:74)

These concerns will be addressed at greater length in later chapters.

Social Security: The Social Assistance Programs

The Roosevelt administration concluded that even with the passage of the two insurance programs that were the centerpiece of the Social Security Act (OASDI and UI), a significant number of Americans would not be covered for quite a few years. Immediate steps had to be taken. For example, in 1933 approximately 15 million Americans were unemployed and 19 million (almost 16% of the population) were receiving some form of state-administered public assistance. The OASDI and UI were not designed to help all of these people.

While the social insurance program was seen as a long-range solution to a structural problem, the administration proposed a number of short-range income maintenance programs to complement the various employment-related strategies. Between the two efforts of (1) stimulating the employment sector and (2) transferring income to those unable to work, the administration assumed that the immediate crisis would be met. Unlike the insurance programs, however, it was thought that these efforts would be temporary and would provide support to a smaller and smaller residual of the population.

The evolving Social Security legislation was thus expanded to include a special program for those who were clearly in need and unable to help themselves. Need was to be defined as poverty, and eligibility was to be determined through a means test. As so often happens, those responsible for "creating" the program looked for comparable examples. As mentioned earlier, over half of the states had already implemented public assistance programs for the elderly and the blind and virtually all states had programs for children whose wage-earning parent had died. Furthermore, the federal government had already taken steps to support these states when they were in fiscal crisis by providing them loans. The Emergency Relief and Construction Act of 1932 provided $300 million for this purpose and the Federal Emergency Relief Act of 1933 made an additional $2.5 billion available. It was unnecessary to invent a new system—the infrastructure for the program was already in place.

The social assistance programs targeted these three groups: Old Age Assistance (OAA) to provide financial assistance to elderly persons who were poor; Aid to the Blind for those who were blind and poor; and Aid to Families with Dependent Children (AFDC) for children who lived in a family whose breadwinner had died. The important distinction between the insurance and the assistance programs is that the former is an entitlement program whose eligibility criterion is a demonstration of membership in a covered category (i.e., insurance coverage, age, level of disability), while the latter involves two sets of criteria for eligibility: membership in a category (e.g., age) *plus* documented poverty. These three programs were expanded in 1956 with the inclusion of the permanently and totally handicapped who were poor, thus mirroring the expansion of the social insurance program, providing coverage to handicapped and disabled workers (APTD).

These programs are referred to as "categorical programs" in the sense that they provide support only to those individuals who are poor *and* fall into one of the four designated categories: aged, blind, disabled, or dependent children. Unlike the social insurance programs, they were

- funded through general revenues and not a special tax;
- partially financed by the federal government and partially by state and local governments;
- administered by the states, which set eligibility criteria and benefit levels within a set of federal parameters; and
- means-tested and not needs-tested.

While the federal share tended to be more uniform in the earlier decades of the programs, in 1958 the sharing formula shifted in favor of those states with fewer resources, higher rates of poverty, and lower annual per capita income. While the formulas were (and still are in the case of AFDC) somewhat complicated, this share over time has averaged around 50% of total costs of the transfers (the federal share of some of the administrative costs have been higher).

In 1994, over 21 million individuals were receiving financial assistance under one of these programs. Approximately 7% are elderly, 23% disabled, 1% blind, and almost 70% dependent children and their parents (see Table 3.8). From 1980–1990, the total increase of all recipients was 21%. The number of disabled persons increased by 45%, the number of blind by 8%, the number of dependent children and their parents by 13%. The number of elderly recipients, on the other hand, increased by approximately 7%. During the 1990s, the number of disabled recipients continued to grow at a much faster rate than the others.

Three of the programs were consolidated and federalized in 1974 leaving AFDC as the sole state-administered program. The "new" program— Supplemental Security Income (SSI)—established a single set of eligibility criteria and standardized the amount of the benefits (see Table 3.9).

To understand the significance of this shift in program financing (the new program was financed totally by the federal government from general revenues) and administration, we need only look at the level of benefits provided by the programs before the transfer. The figures in Table 3.9 represent average monthly benefits paid to individuals under each of the four programs.

Under the earlier federal-state program, we find that the amount of a recipient's benefit was related to the specific category he or she qualified for, regardless of his or her resources. Each recipient had to pass the same

Table 3.8. Social Assistance Income Recipients (Thousands)[a]

Year	OAA	APTD	AB	AFDC	Total
1940	2,070		73	1,222	3,365
1945	2,056		71	945	3,072
1950	2,786	69	97	2,233	5,185
1955	2,538	241	104	2,192	5,075
1960	2,305	369	107	3,073	5,854
1965	2,087	557	85	4,396	7,125
1970	2,082	935	81	9,659	12,757
1975	2,307	1,933	74	11,346	15,660
1980	1,808	2,256	78	10,744	14,916
1985	1,504	2,551	82	10,855	14,992
1990	1,545	3,279	84	12,159	18,079
1994	1,466	4,745	85	13,974	21,222

Source: Social Security Bulletin, Statistical Abstract of the United States. 1996. Washington, DC: USGPO.

[a]These statistics are for the end of December each year.

Table 3.9. Social Assistance Programs—Average Monthly Benefits ($)

Year	OAA (Aged)	APTD (Disabled)	AB (Blind)	AFDC
1940	20.25		25.35	9.85
1945	30.90		33.50	15.15
1950	43.05	44.10	46.00	20.85
1955	50.05	48.75	55.55	23.50
1960	58.90	56.15	67.45	28.35
1965	63.10	66.50	81.35	32.85
1970	77.65	97.65	104.35	49.65
1973	80.00	106.10	112.85	53.95

Source: Social Security Bulletin, Statistical Abstract of the United States. 1974. Washington, DC: USGPO.

means test so we know that they all are equally poor. Historically, how ever, recipients who were blind received the highest benefit, and for the past 25 years, the disabled received the next highest level of benefits. Children received the lowest.

To put this into perspective, the benefit an elderly person received under the OAA program represented about 75% of that received by a disabled person under the APTD program, about 70% of that received by a blind person under the AB program, and 150% of that received by a child under the AFDC program. In part these differences were justified with the rationale that each group had more or less financial need depending on its status, i.e., blind poor persons needed more because they were blind; children needed less because they were children. In part, however, these differences can also be explained by the fact that when increases in benefits were made, some groups were more acceptable than others—or in the language of the Elizabethan Poor Law, some were "more worthy" than others.

The 1974 federalization of the social assistance programs for the old, the disabled, and the blind also had a major impact on the economic wellbeing of many of the recipients in that a national standard of benefit was developed. The data in Table 3.10 shows dramatically the range of benefits in each program in the year preceding this action. Under each program, the three states with the highest benefit levels are identified and then the three states with the lowest levels.

Although the average monthly benefit payment to an elderly recipient was $80 in 1973, benefits ranged from a high of $119 in Alaska to a low of $40 in New Hampshire. Similarly, benefits for the disabled ranged from $57 in Louisiana to $168 in Alaska; for the blind the range was a low of $66 in Mississippi to a high of $174 in Alaska; for a child the low was $14 in Mississippi, and the high was $86 in Hawaii. These differences were

Table 3.10. Social Assistance Monthly Benefits—Ranges among States in 1973

	OAA	APTD	AB	AFDC
High	AK ($119)	AK ($168)	AK ($174)	HI ($86)
	MA ($113)	MA ($159)	CA ($175)	MN ($83)
	HI ($112)	CA ($148)	MA ($155)	NY ($81)
Low	NH ($40)	LA ($57)	MS ($66)	MS ($14)
	MS ($54)	IN ($60)	NH ($74)	AL ($22)
	TX ($54)	MS ($65)	NM ($74)	LA ($25)

Source: Social Security Bulletin, Statistical Abstract of the United States. 1974. Washington, DC: USGPO.

defended with the argument that benefits should reflect regional differences in cost of living.

While costs of living do differ by region (especially in Alaska and Hawaii), it is difficult to argue that costs of living are 282% higher for someone living in Massachusetts compared to an elderly person living across the border in New Hampshire or 200% higher for that same person compared to someone living in Texas or Mississippi. We find the same wide range in the other three categories. A disabled person in Massachusetts received over 250% more than a disabled person living in Louisiana, Indiana, or Mississippi; a blind resident in Massachusetts received a benefit over 200% higher than his or her counterpart living in Mississippi, New Hampshire, or New Mexico. And finally, a child receiving AFDC benefits in Minnesota received a grant 600% higher than a poor child in Mississippi, a grant 377% higher than a child living in Alabama, and 332% more than a child in Louisiana. These differences, in some instances staggering in their magnitude, cannot be explained totally as responses to differences in cost of living. They were the direct result of allowing each state to determine the level of the benefit. Some states were more generous; others were more miserly. Some states were more progressive; others were still ruled by strongly held Poor Law beliefs. This is clear when we examine southern states and analyze the differences of benefits within a state between the categories. Earlier we pointed out that nationally an elderly person's benefit under the OAA program was 150% higher than a child's benefit under the AFDC program. In Mississippi, the difference was 386%! To a large extent this can be explained on racial grounds. While AFDC recipients included both white and minority children, the popular belief (and myth) held that the majority of AFDC recipients were African-American.

The passage of the SSI program solved the problem for the elderly, the disabled, and the blind. The problem remained, unfortunately, for dependent children (see Table 3.11). The same 1974 amendments that provided

Table 3.11. Aid to Families with Dependent Children

Year	Number of Families (000s)	Number of Children (000s)	Total Expended ($ millions)	Average Monthly Grant Constant 1995$
1955	612	1,673	617.8	404
1960	787	2,314	1,000.8	438
1965	1,039	3,256	1,660.2	497
1970	2,208	6,214	4,853.0	582
1975	3,498	8,095	9,211.0	578
1980	3,712	7,419	12,475.2	518
1985	3,263	7,334	15,001.2	498
1990	4,218	8,208	19,078.0	469
1994	4,981	9,469	22,867.0	394

Source: *Social Security Bulletin, Statistical Abstract of the United States.* 1996. Washington, DC: USGPO.

for automatic cost of living adjustments for OASDI recipients operate for SSI recipients. AFDC benefits, on the other hand, are not automatically increased to keep abreast of inflation. Increases have to be passed by legislatures in each state and most do so only sporadically. For example, the average monthly AFDC benefit for a family of three in 1994 was $394, but the same states we analyzed in Table 3.10 still showed wide variations. Furthermore, this amount was $184 less than a family of three received in 1975, controlling for inflation.

A final income maintenance program under the heading of social assistance is the *Food Stamp Program*, established in 1964 by the Food Stamp Act. Persons whose income and assets fall below nationally derived standards may receive coupons redeemable for food at most retail food stores. The amount each individual or family receives is determined by household size and income. Approximately 10% of Americans have received food stamps, and 67% of these recipients had incomes below the poverty line. Total costs of the program have risen from $35 million in 1965 to $4.7 billion in 1975, $12 billion in 1985, and $25 billion in 1994 (Social Security Bulletin 1996).

Welfare Reform

In 1967 Congress amended the Social Security Act to allow AFDC recipients to retain some of the money they earned in outside employment. Previously, for every dollar the recipient earned, the benefit was reduced by a like amount. Arguing that the policy was a work disincentive and one that discouraged the work ethic, recipients were allowed to keep the first $30 they earned and one-third of the remainder. Additionally, the Work Incentive Program was implemented, requiring AFDC mothers with children over a certain age to enroll in job training activities. Moreover, child care would be made available as an added incentive.

In 1981, however, this was seriously modified. The Omnibus Reconciliation Act (OBRA) lowered the amount of money that could be disregarded and limited the $30 plus one-third to four months. While the rhetoric remained the same—the work ethic was to be instilled in welfare dependents—the actions suggested that it was only that—rhetoric.

Female-headed families for the past 35 years found themselves in a catch-22 position. Many wanted to work (Handler 1972) but found that the jobs available to them were in the secondary labor force. Pay was minimal, the likelihood of mobility and career advancement was nonexistent, and—most important—the jobs did not provide benefits. Stigmatized by society because they were dependent and on welfare, they found that they could not take these jobs without seriously jeopardizing their children's well-being. Being on welfare meant being eligible for Medicaid, food stamps, housing benefits, and child care. Working in a job that paid minimum wages meant a family living with an income below the poverty level. Not only would the family be living in poverty, now they would not have health insurance and other basic benefits.

The welfare reform efforts of 1988 (the Family Support Act) rectified some of the more glaring anomalies. First, all states were required to implement the AFDC-UP program passed by Congress in 1967 but only on a permissive basis. The intent of this program was to support families before their problems became so severe that the father left. Second, job training would be available and required for parents with children over the age of three and required for one of the parents (in two-parent families) even when the children were under that age. Third, recipients were able to retain a number of their AFDC-related benefits, including Medicaid, for one year after they began working. Finally, a nationwide mandatory child support enforcement program was initiated.

The work incentive aspects of the 1988 policy did not, however, produce the hoped-for results of a shrinking AFDC caseload. In two years the number of recipients increased by 1.26 million (11%) and by 1994 recipients numbered almost 14 million, an increase of 28% since the reform efforts of 1988 (see Table 3.8).

A number of states requested waivers from the federal government to experiment with ways to achieve these objectives of reduced expenditures and increased self-sufficiency. The waivers were granted and various measures implemented that set out to reward families that moved toward independence (i.e., employment) and penalize families that did not. What was common to all was the idea of a limited period of time a family would be eligible for assistance.

These "experiments" led to the passage of the Personal Responsibility and Work Opportunity Reconciliation Act of 1996. The general purpose of this legislation was to "end welfare as we know it"—to overcome the numerous problems in the system that seemed to create dependency rather than support families so that they might become self-sufficient. The specific purpose was to provide assistance to needy families with children and to reduce dependency by promoting job preparation, work, and marriage.

This was to be achieved through the block grant mechanism (as discussed in Chapter 1) referred to as Temporary Assistance for Needy Families (TANF). This new program ended the federal entitlement program (AFDC) and gave the states complete flexibility to determine eligibility levels and set benefit levels. The historical partnerships forged in 1935 no longer operated and the role of the federal government was limited to that of providing a fixed amount of money to the states. In fact, the act severs the automatic categorical eligibility of AFDC recipients. States will be allowed to establish different income eligibility criteria for AFDC and Medicaid.

To some extent, a number of controls, both positive and negative, were built into the 1996 legislation. It tightened the work requirements and informed states that by the year 2002, 50% of all single parents must be participating in work-oriented activities of at least 30 hours per week, and by 1999, 90% of parents in two-parent families must be participating in similar work activities. Parents who do not meet these requirements will have their assistance reduced unless they are a single parent with a child under the age of six and the reason the parent is unable to work is due to a lack of child care. Finally, as an incentive, Medicaid and child care benefits will continue for 12 months once a recipient begins work.

The legislation also has a number of penalties or prohibitions also designed to further the objective of reducing dependency. (1) For the first time, public assistance would have a cap on the amount of time someone might receive benefits. States could not use the TANF program to provide financial support beyond 60 months over a lifetime. Provisions were made to allow states to exempt up to 20% of recipients if they could demonstrate hardship. (2) Teen parents—to receive benefits—must live at home or in an approved adult-supervised setting and, once the child is 12 weeks of age or older, must participate in educational or training activities. (3) Parents who refuse to cooperate in establishing paternity will have their grant reduced by 25%. (4) Benefits, including food stamps, will be denied to a person convicted of felony drug possession, use, or distribution. (5) Benefits (i.e., SSI, food stamps) will be denied to legal noncitizens until they become citizens; there is to be a 5-year ban on all programs for newly arrived legal immigrants, and illegal immigrants are to be barred from all federal benefits.

These reforms are radical and dramatically change the face of the welfare system we have had in place since 1935. The question we are left with is, To what extent will these reforms achieve the objective of creating real opportunities for previously dependent people to become and stay independent? This concern will be addressed in some detail in later chapters, especially those dealing with employment and poverty.

INCOME MAINTENANCE PROGRAMS: A CRITIQUE

Earlier in this chapter, three major rationales used to justify income maintenance programs were identified. This last section of this chapter will assess the current system against these rationales to determine the extent to which they have been successful and, based on recent developments in both the social insurance and social assistance programs, question whether additional rationales need to be discussed if we are to understand these developments as we move into the twenty-first century.

1. To Buffer the Risks Associated with Temporary or Permanent Unemployment. Within this broad rationale we suggested that three somewhat differing purposes are proposed, each of which needs to be addressed in turn: (1) to replace wages, (2) to prevent poverty, and (3) to meet basic needs. As we stated earlier, if the purpose of income maintenance programs was to replace wages, then the amount given to a recipient should vary according to his or her earnings history. If the programs are to prevent poverty, the amount of income to be transferred should be the difference between actual income and the agreed-upon poverty level. Finally, if the programs are structured to provide a minimum subsistence level, the task is to document what amount is required to meet basic needs. All of these would, moreover, have to have an anti-inflationary mechanism in place that would increase the amount of the transfer as the cost of living increased.

If we annualize the average monthly (or—in the case of UI—the weekly benefit), the average recipient in 1994 would have received the amounts shown in Table 3.12. Since the 1994 median family and per capita income were, respectively, $32,264 and $20,174, it is clear that none of these programs replace income if income is defined as prevailing wages.

A wage replacement program would also be more closely tied to individual earnings. In theory, a recipient's benefits under the OASDI and UI programs would vary according to previous wages. Higher earners, for

Table 3.12. Average Annual Benefit by Program (1994)

Program	Recipient	Benefit ($)
UI	Unemployed Worker	9,464
OASDI	Individual Retiree	8,364
	Retiree and Spouse	14,208
	Survivor and 2 children	16,380
	Disabled Individual	7,932
	Disabled/Spouse and 1 Child	14,460
SSI	All Categories	4,212
	Elderly	2,916
	Blind	3,168
	Disabled	4,608
AFDC	Parent and 2 Children	4,536
Median Family Income		32,264
Median Per Capita Income		20,174

Source: Social Security Bulletin, Statistical Abstract of the United States. 1996. Washington, DC: USGPO.

example, pay more into OASDI and receive higher benefits. However, there is a minimum and a maximum amount regardless of previous earnings.

Were the programs ever intended to replace wages? No, despite the belief many have that they were to do so. The architects of the 1935 Social Security Act, in looking to the insurance program implemented by Bismarck, incorporated most of the German system, including the philosophy that pensions should reflect income inequalities. This approach—the insurance approach—assumes that the more you have the more you should get, unlike the assistance approach, which assumes that the more you have, the less you receive.

However, the original recommendations found in the Social Security Act also included the provision for a voluntary government plan for old-age annuities to be sold competitively by the government (Derthick 1979). Apparently, the administration did *not* envision the new program to be a wage replacement program—otherwise there would be no need for such an annuity program. Rather it was to protect the employee by providing a floor or safety net. While there was early sentiment among some in Congress and in the administration for a universal, flat-rate benefit; most believed that such an approach would be unacceptable to most people since it seemed to resemble the existing public assistance system—the dole. Political acceptability meant promoting the program as an insurance program. The trick was to make a program whose purpose was really to meet basic needs look like a wage replacement program.

During the period when the Social Security system was being debated in this country, the British system was evolving. Beveridge, faced with the same issue (i.e., to what extent should benefits reflect prior earnings), came down on the side of flat contributions and flat benefits for all. Moreover, he believed that the benefits should be fixed at the *subsistence* level or—in his words—a "national minimum" (Beveridge, p. 143).

While Beveridge argued that social insurance was a collectivist solution to the problem of meeting basic need, he argued as strongly that to do more than meet that basic need was to interfere with the natural workings of the market. To provide for total need would interfere with individual responsibility and would act as a disincentive to competition— the life blood of capitalism. Instead, he created a system that provided for the basic needs of everyone but allowed "individuals to create individual differences" through voluntary savings and retirement plans (Marshall 1972).

In answer to our original question, then, it would be reasonable to conclude that the primary purpose of our income maintenance programs is not to replace earnings but to provide funds sufficient to meet basic needs. Although we do not have a flat benefit like the British system, the reality is that our system, even with its different benefit levels, is in reality similar in intent despite some rhetoric to the opposite.

To what extent does this system prevent poverty—the remaining stated purpose under this rationale? This is a more difficult question to answer, since many recipients also receive in-kind benefits that, if cashed out, might offer a more complete and realistic picture. These include food stamps, various housing subsidies, and medical care. For this analysis, we will focus only on the income maintenance programs.

The data in Table 3.13 provide a mixed response. The benefits an unemployed worker receives are above the poverty level if and only if the worker is single. It is important to note, however, that while the intent of the program is to protect workers who find themselves temporarily out of work, the average benefit has not kept up with inflation and, depending on the size of the worker's family, may provide an income that is below the poverty line. For example, the average benefit in 1988 was $182 per week. This works out to $4.55 an hour or $9,464 a year.

The OASDI programs do offer benefits that, on the average, are above the poverty level. However, when we speak of average, we are not talking about a floor below which no one falls. Sixty-two percent of OASDI beneficiaries aged 65 or over receive one-half of their total income from Social Security, 24% rely on Social Security for at least 90% of their income, and 14% obtain all of their income from Social Security.

Moreover, if the COLA provision had not passed in 1974, many more would be living below poverty. This was dramatically pointed out by

Table 3.13. Benefit as a Percentage of Poverty Level[a] (1994)

Program	Recipient	Percentage of Poverty Level
UI	Unemployed Worker	128
OASDI	Individual Retiree	114
	Retiree and Spouse	144
	Survivor and 2 Children	133
	Disabled Individual	108
	Disabled/Spouse and 1 Child	117
SSI	Elderly	40
	Blind	43
	Disabled	63
AFDC	Parent and 2 Children	37

Source: Social Security Bulletin, Statistical Abstract of the United States. 1996. Washington, DC: USGPO.
[a] The poverty level in 1994 was $7,360 for an individual, $9,840 for a two-person family and $12,300 for a three-person family.

James Roosevelt, a Social Security commissioner. Commenting on the proposed COLA cut a few years ago he stated:

> The 1985 COLA cut would have driven 500,000 elderly below the poverty line. Some will tell you that only 12.5% of the elderly are below the poverty line—they (most of the elderly) can afford it. But another 30% are just dollars and cents above the line and vulnerable. (1988:6)

It is precisely because of the COLA amendments that the program on the whole is a relatively successful poverty prevention program. We use the word *relative* only because not all recipients will have benefits that bring them above the poverty level. As Roosevelt stated, 12.5% of the elderly are still poor. However, we need only go back to the early 1960s when 50% of the elderly were poor (Orshansky 1966).

The social assistance programs offer a different picture. No program— neither SSI nor AFDC—provides benefits above the poverty line. Many of the SSI recipients are also receiving OASDI benefits and some of these may actually be raised above poverty. Still others, as discussed above, are eligible for a variety of in-kind programs that, if cashed out, might put them above the poverty level.

We conclude, then, that the income maintenance programs

- do not replace earnings,
- do provide for basic needs,
- do prevent poverty for some beneficiaries and not others.

2. To Stabilize the Labor Force and Prevent the Possibility of Civil Unrest. In Chapter 1, we pointed out that during the depression the Roosevelt administration, confronted with the possibility of civil unrest, enacted a package of radical (radical in that they redefined the role and functions of the federal government) employment and income-related policies. This strategy, however, was not invented in the twentieth century. Throughout history, governments have used similar tactics to maintain social control. Perhaps the most famous example is the successful efforts of Bismarck in the 1880s. As Briggs (1967), in commenting on Bismarck's introduction of compulsory insurance against sickness, accidents and old age points out:

> Many of Bismarck's critics accused him, not without justification, of seeking through his legislation (because of state contributions) to make German workers dependent on the state. . . . [T]he workers would put up with much because they had pensions to look forward to. . . . [He tried] to make German Social Democracy less attractive to workingmen. (p. 36)

Schottland (1963) reached this same conclusion:

> Bismarck saw in social insurance an opportunity to halt the rising tide of socialism by yielding to the workers' demands for income protection and at the same time, to strengthen the central German government. (p. 15)

The issue of social control also needs to be examined more closely at the program level. While the unemployment insurance program is a non–means-tested program and provides benefits as a matter of "right," it incorporates a number of social control features. The program offers benefits to workers who find themselves unemployed through "no fault of their own." In practice this means that a worker (1) did not quit his or her job, (2) was not fired for cause, (3) had a recent history of attachment to the work force, and (4) and was seeking work as evidenced by registering for work at a state employment office. Each of these requirements bonded the worker to the workplace—and the bond was as strong as those forged by the nineteenth-century architects of the Poor Law in that it reinforced the work ethic from both a psychological and legal set of conditions.

The social insurance benefits provided under OASDI also strengthened this bond in that benefits were only provided to individuals and families who had a previous attachment to the work force. Moreover, the level of the benefit was tied to previous earnings. This proved to be an incentive to the earner to work hard (assuming that hard work and productivity were related to higher wages).

Once assistance is given (i.e., the beneficiary is retired or unable to work because of a disability) whether it is through the OASDI or SSI programs, the social control element seems to become less important. As

Handler points out, the "aged are becoming less associated with the labor market. . . . [T]hus the giving of aid to this group does not conflict with the moral issue of work" (Handler 1972:14). The primary social control measure introduced under the Victorian Poor Law—the principle of less eligibility—was modified in this century and would apply only those who could be expected to work, whether these expectations were realistic or not.

Handler has written extensively on this issue and his titles are worth noting. In *The Coercive Social Worker* (1973) he suggests that social service professionals having disengaged from the War on Poverty, have returned to their "traditional mission of reforming the poor." In *Reforming the Poor* (1972) he carefully documents the numerous social control measures built into the AFDC program from the earlier "man-in-the-house" rules and the "suitable house" requirements to the more recent "work tests."

Piven and Cloward (1971), in their classic *Regulating the Poor*, offer data covering the period 1940–1970 to support their thesis that

[a]s for relief programs themselves, the historical pattern is clearly not one of progressive liberalization; it is rather a record of periodically expanding and contracting relief rolls as the system performs its two main functions: maintaining civil order and enforcing work. (p. xv)

Tom Joe (Joe and Rogers 1985) has offered a similar conclusion in his analysis of AFDC programs in the 1980s. Blending an analysis of legislation, secondary data, and interviews with a number of women in Georgia, he and his colleague Rogers show the direct relationship between the AFDC program and employment in the secondary labor market.

Do our income maintenance programs perform a social control function whose purpose is to stabilize the labor force and prevent the possibility of civil unrest? There is sufficient evidence on the whole (i.e., no one study is conclusive) to suggest they not only do, but that these functions are viewed by many as rational if economic goals are to be met.

Table 3.14. Distribution of Money Income among Families—Percentage by Selected Quintiles

Quintiles	Average (1947–1984)	1991
Lowest 20%	5	4.5
Middle 20%	12	16.6
Highest 20%	42	44.2

Sources: Adapted from Plotnick (1987, 1995).

3. To Promote a More Egalitarian Society through the Redistribution of Wealth. The third and final general purpose of income maintenance programs is that of moving our society toward one that is more egalitarian or, perhaps more accurately, to deal with some of the more glaring aspects of an unequal society. This argument becomes more tenuous than the above. While it is possible to analyze the extent to which we are or are not becoming more egalitarian, money income is only one aspect of wealth and income maintenance is only one form of money income. Still, public income maintenance programs accounted for a significant percentage of the gross domestic product (see Table 1.2).

Kuznets (1953), in an earlier study of the distribution of money income in the United States, shows that in 1913, the top 1% of American families received 16% of pretax national income. By 1920 this had dropped to 14%; by 1939 to 13%. This would suggest that some leveling had occurred.

However, if we look at the period 1947–1984 and analyze the distribution of money income by quintiles, a less optimistic picture emerges (see Table 3.14). While a totally level society is an impossibility, a more equal society would be one in which each quintile received an amount close to 20%. However, over this 37-year period, families in the top fifth received approximately 42% of all money income while families in the lowest quintile received about 5%. Plotnik reports that this skewing has continued into the early 1990s.

The most recent statistics suggest even more income inequality, with the highest income quintile receiving 49.1% in 1994 (Weinberg 1997).

We can thus conclude that our income maintenance programs have not created a more equal society if income alone is the criterion. We are left then with the question posed earlier in the chapter: Is Marshall's formulation about equality of status more realistic, or is perhaps the position of Keynes, Galbraith, and Beveridge—that equality of opportunity in a capitalist society is an appropriate goal, while the redistribution of income and wealth is inappropriate in that it will unduly interfere with the economic system? Or finally, are Titmuss, Tawney, and Crosland correct in suggesting that some combination of equality of opportunity and outcome will be required if our society is to remain one that fosters a sense of community and shared responsibility?

Finally, we need to begin a dialogue to determine what the purpose of income maintenance programs including the social insurance and social assistance programs in the next century should be. Have we lost sight of the vision of the 1930s, a vision concerned with establishing a program based on *trust*—one that would guarantee a security net or floor for all? Or is that vision no longer viable and does a new system and approach need to be developed for the future?

CHAPTER

4

Housing Policy

While the federal government has had a long-standing commitment to meet the housing needs of this country, a commitment that began to take shape in the depression of the thirties, housing policy remains an extremely ambiguous term. As an area of national concern it

> encompasses government expenditures, loans and loan guarantees for investment in structures; zoning regulations and building and housing codes; legal provisions concerning property rights and tax treatment of residential property or of income from it. (Aaron 1972:4)

Responsibility for the formulation and implementation of policy at the national level is presently diffused among several federal departments: Housing and Urban Development, Agriculture, Health and Human Services, Defense, Treasury, the Veterans Administration, the Bureau of Indian Affairs, and finally, several congressional committees. This diffusion has produced a great deal of confusion and has resulted in the absence of a clearly stated position beyond the rhetoric of the general goal found in the 1949 act:

> The general welfare and security of the nation and the health and living standards of its people require housing production and related community development sufficient to remedy the serious housing shortage, the elimination of substandard and other inadequate housing through the clearance of blighted areas and the realization as soon as feasible of the goal of a decent home and a suitable living environment for every American family, thus contributing to the redevelopment of communities and to the advancement of the growth, wealth and security of the nation. (Section 2)

We include a chapter on housing policy because of these stated goals. By including the goals of a "suitable living environment" and the "redevelopment of communities," Congress has identified housing as a social policy concern. Furthermore, housing was defined as a basic societal good—one that was essential for the "general welfare and security of the nation and the health and living standards of its people."

Over 60 years ago, the Congress of the United States passed a series of bills that committed this country to a course of action to solve a massive housing problem. This commitment, involving billions of dollars, was reaffirmed by Congress over the next four decades.

This historic commitment was grounded in five basic principles:

- The goal of housing policy is home ownership.
- The federal government has a major responsibility for the nation's housing problem.
- Federal government manipulation of credit is the preferred solution.
- Public housing is for the purpose of clearing slums.
- Slum clearance (and therefore public housing) is a cooperative effort between federal and local governments.

As clear and simple as these principles may appear, housing policy has always been torn between the goals of assuring an "adequate quantity" of housing and "decent quality" of housing for all Americans. However, because of our tendency to equate these two goals and the reluctance to recognize the implications of our stated commitment to decent housing as expressed in the Housing Act of 1949 (and reaffirmed by the Housing Acts of 1954, 1959, 1961, 1965, 1968, and 1974), we have succeeded in achieving neither goal to the satisfaction of anyone.

For decades, policymakers have expressed a belief and reliance on market mechanisms as the most viable strategy to distribute housing resources. Given this, they have approached both goals, i.e., the quantity and quality of housing, as an economic problem. The social dimensions of housing (housing as more than shelter) have been ignored or deemphasized.

THE CURRENT SITUATION:
DETERIORATION ON ALL FRONTS

Sixty years later, we enter the twenty-first century with the housing problem still with us—and, in the opinion of a growing number of analysts, with a problem that is worsening. Schwartz and his colleagues identified and discussed a series of trends in the housing market that have developed over the last ten years (Schwartz, Ferlauto, and Hoffman 1988). According to them:

   1. *We are experiencing a decline in home ownership.*   Contrary to popular belief, home ownership became the norm only after World War II. In fact, the percentage of home owners never reached 50% until then, and had been declining over most of the first half of this century: By 1980 almost two of every three families were home owners, and although the percentage dropped slightly in 1987, it reached almost 66% in 1996 (see Table 4.1).

This growth since the 1950s was not evenly distributed over the population. Young families—those headed by adults in the 25–34 age group—had a home ownership rate of 39%; Hispanic and African-American families had an ownership rate of 43 and 44%, respectively. Part of the reason for this is the skyrocketing costs of buying and maintaining a house:

- In 1975, the average family needed an income of $15,775 to buy an average-priced new home; by 1996, that family needed an income of income of $37,657.

Another part of the reason for this decline is the increase in the interest rates since the early 1970s—rates that rose four to five times faster than real household income. It is only recently that interest rates have declined. As some economists point out:

- A 1% increase in conventional interest rates will keep at least 10% of potential buyers out of the housing market.
- A 1% increase in Veterans Administration rates will keep over 1.5 million families out of the market.

Table 4.1. Home Ownership Rates 1890–1996

Year	Percentage of All Housing
1890	47.8
1900	46.1
1910	45.8
1920	45.6
1940	44.1
1980	65.0
1987	63.8
1996	65.6

Sources: For 1890–1920 see E. Wood (1939:37–38); for 1940–1987 see Schwartz et al. (1988:7); for 1996 see http:www.hud.gov / homstat.html.

A final reason is linked to lending institutions requiring larger down payments than previously; instead of 10%, they now require 20% or more. On the median-priced house in 1996, this would translate into $20,000 to $25,000 plus closing costs.

2. *The affordability, and availability of the nation's rental housing has decreased to the point where 30 million tenants live in substandard housing.* While there are no hard rules, common wisdom suggests that the average family should pay between 30 and 35% of their income for housing. And yet:

- Over 5 million poor families pay more than half their income for rent.
- Families with incomes of less than $10,000 income pay more than 60% of their income for rent.
- More than one-third of single-parent families pay over 75% of their income for rent.
- The number and percentage of female-headed families have increased from 3.5 million in 1950 (9% of total families) to over 9 million in 1980 (15% of total families), and reached 11 million in 1997 (16% of total families).

To compound these problems:

- Since the midseventies, the housing market has lost over 1,000,000 low-income units *each year* due to abandonment, arson, demolition, condominium conversion, and gentrification.
- In 1996, over 900,000 federally assisted housing units began to be lost to low-income families; by the year 2000, almost the entire stock of such housing (2 million units) will revert to market rates. Under previous federal legislation, developers receiving low-cost loans and subsidies were required to accept low-income families for 20 years. This requirement is now expiring.

3. *We are experiencing a decline in the quality of existing housing.* Over time, the federal–private market partnership has achieved some successes in expanding housing opportunities and in improving housing conditions, but we are still experiencing decline in the quality of existing housing stock. For example:

- More than 5.3 million households lived in seriously substandard housing and/or pay more than half their income for rent.
- However, 24.2 million American families lived in inadequate or overcrowded houses in 1985 compared to 19.1 million in 1975. Fur-

thermore, since 1975, conditions have deteriorated in seven of the nine modern indicators of housing maintenance and upkeep (National Association of Home Builders 1985).

4. *There has been a dramatic increase in the number of homeless families.* In 1983, the first year that statistics on homelessness were reported on a large-scale basis, various estimates of the homeless suggested that anywhere from 300,000 families (Department of Housing and Urban Development) to 3,000,000 families (Department of Health and Human Services) were homeless. The National Alliance to End Homelessness (Homeless in America 1997) has recently estimated that on any given night, 750,000 persons will be without shelter and that 1.3 to 2 million Americans will be homeless sometime during the year. Since then, it is clear that the numbers have grown, especially in the category of families with young children. It is estimated that 35% of all homeless persons fall into this category compared to 21% in 1985. A related phenomenon is the doubling up of families in the 1980s, i.e., a family unable to find/afford housing moves in with a family with housing. This is especially the case in single-parent, female-headed households. In 1987, there were 10 million such families.

How did we get to this point and where do we seem to be going? We begin this search with a discussion of the major theories and assumptions underlying government intervention in this area and then explore how these theories have shaped our policy initiatives. Following this, individual housing policies are analyzed on two different but complementary levels.

First, each program is discussed from a historical perspective. This is important since all the basic issues in housing policy have been continuously fought over for at least 60 years. Policies that have been proposed in the 1980s and the 1990s are not new ways of dealing with the "problem" and debates around these proposals are not dealing with "new" issues. The fundamental concern is, and has been, the appropriateness of increasing the supply of housing through the private market and the role of government in this process. The historical review attempts to analyze the extent to which this strategy has been successful. Second, each major program is analyzed in terms of its own goals and objectives. How was the problem defined? What specific strategy was introduced? How successful was it?

Following this, housing policy as a whole is analyzed, i.e., we look across programs. To do this, we reintroduce the notion that housing policy is a social policy and, as such, requires a broader set of criteria to judge its effectiveness.

THEORIES OF HOUSING MARKET FAILURE

In general, housing policy in the United States reflects a number of opposing views of what the housing problem is and what public policy should be. Although different strategies emerge from these competing groups in terms of program strategies, all accept the fundamental premise that the private housing market, in theory, is the best allocator of housing resources. Furthermore, while all accept that past and current housing markets have experienced some failures—that the private market is imperfect—they assume that marginal modifications to the market system will make the distribution of housing more efficient and equitable.

The major problems faced by the private market are its historic inability to provide decent quality low-cost housing due to certain inefficiencies and externalities that cause housing resources to be less than optimally distributed. These include (1) externalities, (2) lack of knowledge, and (3) racial discrimination.

1.   There are few incentives for owners in deteriorated neighborhoods to improve their properties because they are likely to receive little or no return on their investment. The upgraded property would continue to be surrounded by deterioration. In fact, the market often rewards those owners who do not invest in upgrading. An unrehabilitated building may increase in value at no cost to the owner simply because it is located next to a rehabilitated building. Although all owners would benefit if each upgraded his or her property, this collective good is not achieved because the private market, by definition, cannot dictate individual behavior.

2.   A second aspect of the market failure theory questions whether all households have equal capacity to obtain the housing and neighborhood they both want and can afford. A fundamental premise of free market economic theory is that knowledgeable, rational consumers weigh their individual perceptions of the costs and benefits of various combinations of goods and services and then make a selection that maximizes their individual benefit. However, in a survey of rent-controlled apartments in New York City, Schussheim found that tenants in high-income units were more likely to be aware of their rights under the city's rent control ordinance. None of these high-income renters paid more than the legally permitted rent. In contrast, low-income Hispanic and African-American tenants in Harlem frequently paid rents substantially exceeding rent control limits (Schussheim 1974).

3.   A third dimension of market failure is racial discrimination. From a purely economic point of view, discrimination is objectionable because it causes resources to be distributed inefficiently. In other words, some households presently living in substandard housing would be able to

afford decent housing if the private market did not arbitrarily inhibit how they spend their resources. And yet when entire classes of households are denied the right to choose where they want to live, their economic and social rights have been arbitrarily proscribed. Title VIII of the Civil Rights Act of 1968 prohibits discrimination in the sale or rental of housing on the basis of religion, race, or ethnic origin. However, discrimination continues to limit the housing choices of minorities.

In summary, market failure theory attributes the causes of inadequate housing consumption to certain inefficiencies that cause housing resources to be less than optimally allocated. Given market failure, government intervention is justified to eliminate these inefficiencies. However, as discussed in Chapter 1, some forms of government intervention are preferred over others and, in general, the less intrusive, the more acceptable.

Two overall strategies have been, to greater or lesser degrees, introduced by government over the past six decades: (1) efforts to increase the quantity and quality of housing stock and (2) efforts to increase the financial ability of some economically disadvantaged individuals and families who cannot afford adequate housing. The former is called a *supply-side* strategy; the latter a *demand-side* strategy. While both general strategies are theoretically acceptable, historically the emphasis has been on attempts to stimulate an increase on the production side.

Examples of supply-side interventions would include:

- tax incentives to developers,
- credit incentives to developers,
- mortgage insurance to lenders,
- public housing production.

Examples of demand-side interventions would include

- tax incentives to home owners,
- subsidization of owners and renters.

While there may be disagreement among policymakers and analysts about which of the above is more effective and therefore more preferable, there is almost unanimous agreement that government production of housing (public housing) is the least desirable and the most intrusive.

As Friedman argued:

> Public housing . . . can be justified, if at all, only on grounds of paternalism; that the families being helped "need" housing more than they "need" other things but would themselves either not agree or would spend their available resources unwisely. (1962:178)

Those who argue a demand-side strategy do not see the solution in the production of public housing units nor in the provision of incentives to builders, lenders, and developers. Rather, the solution lies with increasing the incomes of low-income householders who will improve their own housing conditions. Proponents of the demand-side position argue that supply-side strategies substantially benefit the builders and the developers, while demand-side strategies primarily benefit the targeted population. Underlying this position is the notion of *elasticity*. This term, used by economists, is the percentage change in demand that would result from a change in price of one percentage point. In their study of the relationship between income and housing demand, DeLeeuw and Ekanem (1970) concluded that the income elasticity of demand for rental property is approximately 1.0, i.e., for every given percentage change in income, they predict an equal change in the quantity of housing units.

Those who argue for more nonintrusive supply-side strategies point out that even if developers and builders limit their effort to providing more costly housing (and therefore more profitable) housing submarkets; all income classes will benefit through a process known as *filtering*. This argument is as follows. As one family sells its house to purchase one more costly, the original house is now available to a family with less income and so on down the line until the unit is eventually available to the poor. Aaron (1972) suggests that this notion of a filtering chain is a fundamental assumption underlying our housing policy, especially our housing-related tax policies. As early as 1935, during the initial debates on whether the federal government should build public housing, the President of the National Association of Real Estate Boards argued that

[h]ousing should remain a matter of private enterprise and private ownership. It is contrary to the genius of the American people and the ideals they have established that government become landlord to its citizens. . . . There is sound logic in the continuation of the practice under which those who have initiative and the will to save acquire better living facilities and *yield their former quarters at modest rents to the group below.* (cited in Keith 1973: 33; emphasis added)

While the idea of filtering is attractive, there is little evidence that the poor have benefited to the extent hypothesized. Stegman (1970) questions the effectiveness of the filtering strategy when he points out that for housing units to pass through the market, all units would have to sell for less than market value, i.e., individual owners would have to absorb losses.

Both supply-side and demand-side theorists agree that increasing housing consumption of low-income households has positive benefits for the poor as well as for society as a whole. However, the public policies derived from these theories tend to reflect a calculus weighted toward measuring only a few dimensions of housing deprivation. Until fairly recently, federal policy has followed the recommendations of those who argue supply-side strategies. Until the 1980s these strategies had some success in increasing the number of housing units produced each year. Combined with sporadic demand-side strategies, large numbers of low-income families, handicapped persons, and the elderly have been able to find adequate and reasonably priced housing. This progress, never adequate and now stalled, needs new stimuli.

To create an agenda for the future, we need to analyze these policies in some detail. The next section discusses, within a historical framework, major federal initiatives in the housing field. Moreover, it will analyze these programs against the backdrop of competing and often contradictory statements of purpose and strategy.

TRIGGERS TO GOVERNMENTAL ACTION

While initial governmental action in the housing market can be traced to the depression of the 1930s with its high unemployment, escalating number of mortgage defaults, and the general malaise in the world economy, an equally significant trigger was the growing awareness of documented scandals associated with urban tenement living.

Reformers such as Edith Wood observed in 1919:

Roughly stated, one-third of the people of the United States are living under sub-normal housing conditions . . . and about a tenth are living under conditions which are an acute menace to health, morals, and family life; conditions which tend to produce degenerative changes in those subject to them. (1919:31–32)

Others, such as Veiller, not only agreed with Wood's findings but were quick to offer cause-effect conclusions—though at times it was unclear whether the cause of these "degenerative changes" was the housing conditions (i.e., the tenements) or the tenants:

Democracy was not predicated upon a nation of tenement dwellers, nor can it survive as such. . . . This (lodger evils and overcrowding) prevails chiefly among the foreign elements of the population, more especially among the Italians and Poles, and in some cities, the Hungarians and other Slavic races. It also prevails among the Jews in the larger cities. It is fraught with great danger to the social fabric of the country. It means the breaking down of domestic standards. It frequently leads to the breaking up of homes and families, to the downfall and subsequent degraded career of young women, to grave immoralities—in a word to the profanation of the home. (1910:37)

In 1910, 3 million people in New York city lived in tenement houses. Of these, one million had no bathing facilities in their homes: 250,000 used outside privies and one family in two shared bathrooms. In city after city, surveys conducted by social reformers highlighted immorality, crime, saloons, overcrowding, inadequate water supplies and waste disposal systems, dark rooms, filth, high rates of disease, and infant mortality (Fish 1978).

At various times from 1890 to 1930, numerous coalitions fought for housing reform—reforms that either attempted to draft and pass federal legislation bringing existing housing stock up to acceptable standards (the so called *restrictive approach*) or legislation guaranteeing that a certain percentage of new units be set aside at or below actual market value (the so-called *constructive approach*).

Initially, Veiller (1914) and other reformers refused to support the latter, arguing that people living in tenement houses would have to learn how to live in these new homes, which otherwise would quickly be destroyed by tenants who did not know any better. However, they were forced to abandon the restrictive approach when such legislation was thought to be probably unconstitutional.

The second (and later) trigger was the large and growing number of mortgage defaults experienced in the early years of the depression. By the end of 1932, the monthly rate of foreclosures was approximately 26,000, or an average of 1,000 per day (Fish 1978).

At that time, lending institutions were unwilling to offer long-term mortgages (the norm was for three- to five-year loans) and were extremely conservative about the amount they would loan (a lender, on the average, risked about 40% of the value of a piece of real estate). Borrowers without sizable amounts of cash were forced to find second mortgages.

The home buyer usually paid the interest on the loan on an annual basis and the principal at the end of the loan period. Those who could not pay the principal would then refinance their loans. This system resulted in most borrowers refinancing their loans many times before retiring them. During the depression, many people lost their confidence in banks and began to withdraw their savings. The banks, in turn, having invested this money in home mortgages, found it necessary to call in their loans. When borrowers could not pay, the banks foreclosed and sold the property to recoup some of their money.

These distinct but equally pressing problems came to a head in the Roosevelt administration. As mentioned in Chapter 1, the historic role of the federal government was, by choice, minimal. In terms of housing policy it was virtually nonexistent with the exception of three housing laws passed in 1918 to provide housing for laborers in war related industries. These programs were short-lived and ceased after the armistice.

Two major strategies evolved during Roosevelt's first two terms—strategies that paralleled the two problems just discussed. The first involved a series of policies that attempted to strengthen the stability of lending institutions and thus prevent or slow down the number of foreclosures through various "insurance" programs. The second, and at that time the more controversial, was the direct involvement of the federal government in battling the problems of slums and tenement housing through the production of public housing. These two approaches have been, and continue to be, major thrusts of housing policy. While a variety of programs has been evolving over the past 50 years, they fall under one of the above two categories.

These two basic strategies can best be understood as strategies dealing with two distinct problems. The first (mortgage insurance and later the use of tax incentives) is concerned with the housing needs of "most" Americans—from the working class to the upper class; while the second (direct intervention in the market) is concerned with the poor and low-income families who cannot find adequate housing without substantial assistance. While the dichotomy cannot be equated exactly to the distinction made in Chapter 2 (i.e., institutional versus residual) there are enough similarities to at least suggest that the former are more institutional in approach and the latter more residual. When benefits and services are institutional they tend to be viewed by recipients as *rights*, they carry no stigma, and their purposes are rarely questioned. When benefits and/or services are residual, however, they are not seen as rights, they are stigmatized, and expenditures are scrutinized continuously. Given this, housing policies will be discussed not in chronological order but as two distinct sets of policies—those that have been formulated for the problems of low-income and poor families and those for "the rest."

HOUSING POLICIES FOR LOW-INCOME AND POOR FAMILIES

Early Efforts: Public Housing

Public housing is considered today, by both conservatives and progressives, to have been a major social failure. The term "public housing" conjures up the depressed and deteriorated areas of the South Bronx,

Cabrini East in Chicago, and Pruitt-Igoe in St. Louis. This general perception of the failure of public housing is, however, one-sided and a relatively new attitude. Public housing had been strongly supported by most liberals from the early years of this century up through the 1950s and was proposed during this earlier period as a solution to the problems of the slums and tenement housing.

The public housing movement began in earnest in 1931, when social workers from the settlement houses, urban reformers, city and regional planners, and others established the National Public Housing Conference [later organizations influenced by this group included the National Association of Housing Officials (1933) and the Labor Housing Conference (1934)]. Moreover, they were able to forge a coalition between these groups and the trade unions, the National Urban League, the National PTA, and the NAACP—a coalition that eventually succeeded in pressuring Congress to pass the Housing Act of 1937 (P.L. 75-412).

The seeds of the 1937 act are found in the National Industrial Recovery Act (NIRA) of 1933, which authorized funds for the Public Works Administration (PWA) for slum clearance and for building 21,769 rental housing units for low-income families in 37 cities (Myerson and Banfield 1955). Almost immediately, like so much of the New Deal legislation, the program was attacked on constitutional grounds.

In 1935, the federal court first ruled [*U.S. v. Certain Lands in Louisville*, 9 F. Supp. 137 (1935)] that the federal government did *not* have the right to take property under the principle of eminent domain—the taking of property by a government from a citizen for a public use—and later ruled [*Township of Franklin v. Tugwell*, 66 D.C. App. 42, 85 F. (2nd) 208 (1936)] that the federal government was not empowered to purchase land and build housing. A final test case carefully crafted by the federal government was successful and later became the legal basis for the 1937 Housing Act. The Court ruled [*New York Housing City Housing Authority v. Muller*, 279, N.T.S. 299 (1935)]. that the federal government could *finance the building* of housing and the states could use the power of eminent domain and could *own* housing.

Based on this finding, social reformers and housing advocates drafted legislation for large-scale public housing projects. The legislation, sponsored by Senator Wagner of New York, was defeated in 1935 and 1936 through the efforts of a coalition made up of the National Association of Real Estate Boards (NAREB); the United States Chamber of Commerce and the Mortgage Bankers Association, who argued it was an attack on the free enterprise system; and the National Retail Lumber Dealers Association (NRLDA), who opposed the legislation because it excluded the use of wood in the newly built housing (Johnson 1952).

Wagner, aware of the pitfalls facing any bill proposing a national public housing program, went to great lengths to neutralize the opposition of the housing industry by assuring them that the program would only cover the poor—those who could not possibly be served by the private sector. He stated:

> The object of public housing, in a nutshell, is not to invade the field of home building for the middle class or the well to do which has been the only profitable area for private enterprise in the past. Nor is it even to exclude private enterprise from major participation in a low cost housing program. It is merely to supplement what private industry will do, by subsidies which will make up the difference between what the poor can afford to pay and what is necessary to assure decent living conditions. (cited in Keith 1973:32–33)

Roosevelt, ever the pragmatist, and concerned with another downswing in the economy, demanded solutions that dealt simultaneously with the housing problem and unemployment. At this time, one in three of the unemployed were in the building trades and housing represented the largest part of this. While there were no data at that time, later analyses have confirmed Roosevelt's position. It is now estimated that each $1 billion of expenditures on multifamily construction will create over 25,000 jobs; each $1 billion on single-family units will create 22,000 jobs. Moreover, the multiplier effect for each $1 billion will be responsible for an additional 276,000 jobs (Ball 1981).

Wagner, now with the active participation of the White House, reintroduced his legislation, which was signed into law on September 1, 1937. The stated purpose of the Housing Act of 1939 (P. L. 75-412) was

> to provide financial assistance to the States and political sub-divisions thereof for the elimination of unsafe and unsanitary housing conditions, for the development of clean, safe, and sanitary dwellings for families of low income, and for the reduction of unemployment and the stimulation of business activity. (Section 2)

Under the legislation, municipal governments established local housing authorities (LHAs), which in turn were responsible for obtaining a federal subsidy for the construction of housing units. These subsidies included up to 90% of development costs. The projects were developed, owned, and managed by these LHAs. Commissioners determined need, set rent scales, and established income limits and eligibility.

The federal government, in turn, marketed short-term notes to finance the construction of the units. Upon completion of this phase, it marketed the long-term bonds (up to 60 years) issued by the Local Housing Authority. The federal government also entered into an annual contract with the

LHA, agreeing to make yearly contributions to pay off the debt service on these bonds. The 1937 act proposed an annual target of 135,000 units for a six-year period—a total of 810,000 units. Finally, the legislation required that for each new unit built, one slum dwelling had to be eliminated.

The Housing Act of 1937 is an important piece of social legislation for a number of reasons. First, it reinforced the emerging pattern of the new "federalism." As with a number of programs under the Social Security Act of 1935, responsibilities were to be shared among federal, state, and local units of government. Moreover, while the program was a national effort, critical powers were delegated to local government, e.g., coverage, eligibility, and standards. Second, the legislation reaffirmed the principle of federal intervention when an imperfect market exists: in this case the market failed the poor and those with low incomes. Intervention was direct (unlike later housing policies) in that government produced and managed the units. Third, housing was defined as a basic need—one for which society, through the public sector, has responsibility.

Such was the intent. What was accomplished, given Wood's estimate of 11 million substandard housing units in the United States? From 1937 to 1942, 170,000 units of public housing in 260 communities were built. However, even this production figure, as small as it was, is misleading. Eighty-five percent of the units were built on slum sites that had been cleared for the new units and only 18,000 units were built on vacant sites (Myerson and Banfield 1955). Very little "new" housing was added to the nation's housing stock. From 1949 to 1966, over 400,000 houses occupied by low- and moderate-income families were torn down under the slum clearance component of the public housing program.

In an eight-year period, 1940 to 1948, 255,300 public housing units were built (see Table 4.2). This represented less that one half of one percent of all housing units built during this period. The average annual production was a little over 28,000 units but this figure is somewhat misleading in that in some years the production was very high and in others almost nonexistent.

Congress reaffirmed the 1937 National Housing Act in 1949 against considerable pressure from lobbying groups representing private housing interests. The act authorized $1.5 billion for slum clearance and urban renewal and authorized 810,000 additional units of public housing to be built by 1955. Six years later, only 263,800 units had been built—one-third of the targeted goal.

In 1954, the commitment to public housing was again reaffirmed and Congress authorized 140,000 new units be built over the next four years; 179,000 were actually built. It is interesting that it was only during a Republican administration (Eisenhower) that public housing targets were actually achieved—albeit modest targets compared to previous adminis-

Table 4.2. Public Housing as a Percentage of All
Housing Starts (1,000s) 1940–1959

		Public	
Year	Total	Public (no.)	Public (%)
1940	602.6	73.0	12.1
1941	706.1	86.6	12.3
1942	356.0	54.8	15.4
1943	191.0	7.3	3.8
1944	141.8	3.1	2.2
1945	326.0	1.0	0.3
1946	1,023.0	8.0	0.8
1947	1,268.0	3.4	0.2
1948	1,362.0	18.1	1.3
1949	1,466.0	36.3	2.4
1950	1,908.1	43.8	2.2
1951	1,419.8	71.2	4.8
1952	1,445.4	58.5	3.9
1953	1,402.1	35.5	2.5
1954	1,531.8	18.7	1.2
1955	1,626.6	19.4	1.2
1956	1,324.9	24.2	1.8
1957	1,174.8	49.1	4.0
1958	1,315.2	67.8	4.9
1959	1,494.6	36.7	2.4
Total	22,084.8	716.3	1.0

Sources: Adapted from Tables cited in Fish (1979:245, 300).

trations. At the end of the 1950s, public housing had ceased to be a
desirable housing policy. Granted, later legislation did deal with public
housing but not on the previous scale. The Housing Acts of 1961, 1965,
1968, and 1974 attempted to solve some of the existing problems, such as
size, density, and location (e.g., scattered housing strategies and eventually ownership) but with little success. This does not mean that the production of public housing stopped. It did, however, slow down. Whereas
716,300 units of public housing were built in the 20-year period 1940–1959
(still far short of the six-year target established in the 1937 legislation), the
total stock in 1977 had grown only to 1,200,000 (an increase of 484,000
over a 17-year period), and to 1,300,000 in 1985. What had happened?

It was clearly not our success in dealing with the "tenement problem."
As late as 1944, approximately 2 million people in New York City still
lived in tenements condemned by the 1915 Tenement Housing Act
(Strauss 1944).

It was also equally clear that it was not a lack of demand for such housing. In 1987, we had approximately 1.3 million public housing units and over 800,000 families on waiting lists (in some cities the wait was 15 to 20 years) for public housing. It could hardly be argued that the federal government was unfairly intervening in the private market. Not only has the private market not been able to keep up with demand, the total federal involvement from 1940 to 1959 represented only 3.2 per cent of all housing starts (see Table 4.2).

The situation was, in all likelihood, in part associated with the characteristics of the tenants of public housing. Through the 1940s and into the 1950s

> they were poor, but most of them were employed and accustomed to urban living. . . . In those days Local Authorities carefully screened out, or imposed quotas on applicant families receiving relief, those who had unpleasant social histories or living habits, or those who were not normal. The ideal was to rehouse a cross-section of the low-income families of the community, in terms of income, of family-size and of source income. (Silverman 1971:6)

This had changed by the 1960s: (1) in part because of a conscious reversal of discriminatory practices that had excluded many minorities from participating in the general economic growth that would allow them to be able to purchase adequate housing on the market; (2) in part because of civil rights advances that prohibited discriminatory practices in housing (e.g., quotas for different subgroups to mirror the larger community), and (3) in part because of other programs that opened up the suburbs to young white families. Whatever the full list of reasons, Rainwater's description of the 33 eleven-story buildings Pruit-Igoe Project presents a picture quite different from the earlier period:

> Open(ing) in 1954, [it] has 2,762 apartments of which only 2,000 are currently occupied, and has as tenants a very high proportion (over 50 percent) of female headed households of one kind or another on public assistance. Though originally integrated, the project is now all Negro. The project community is plagued by petty crimes, vandalism, much destruction of the physical plant, and a very bad reputation in both the Negro and white communities. (Subcommittee on Executive Reorganization 1966:2837)

This project, then comprising 43 buildings, was dynamited in the early 1970s.

By emphasizing those in the greatest need, public housing has created ghettoes of the poor: ghettoes that other city residents did not wish to live near and in which most of the poor would rather not live. Public housing has a threefold stigma: one has to be poor to be eligible (average family income is 28% of the average family income in the United States); 87% of public housing residents are either minority or elderly; and finally the physical environment carries a spatial stigma.

In addition, as implemented the policy emphasized shelter and ignored the multiple dimensions of housing. This narrow definition has produced a continually troubled program. By providing only shelter, the community aspects were nonexistent. These failures, so painfully brought to the surface by Pruitt- Igoe, are repeated again and again in large projects in metropolitan areas. Pruitt-Igoe, named for two World War II heroes, one African-American and one white, was designed by an internationally famous architect and incorporated a large park with the latest playground equipment and extensive landscaping. As the original costs began to escalate, all of the elements, including the landscaping and playgrounds, which are important for the creation of human environments and a sense of community, were dropped. Given these failures, numerous alternatives to public housing have been and continue to be proposed.

In 1984, for example, the Department of Housing and Urban Development (HUD) under the rubric of "privatization" initiated the Public Housing Home Ownership Demonstration Program (with its legislative basis in the 1974 amendments to the 1937 Housing Act). Following the lead of British Prime Minister Margaret Thatcher, whose government sold 80,000 units of public housing, the administration began selling 1,600 units of public housing in 18 cities. By the end of the Bush administration only a few thousand units had been sold, in part "because subsidized housing is restricted to the very poor who cannot pay for routine operating expenses much less the costs of major repairs required in older and run-down buildings" (Dreier and Atlas 1995).

Low-Income Housing: Alternatives to Public Housing

By the 1960s, both the Congress and the administration concluded that the 1949 housing goal of a "decent home and a suitable environment for every American family" had not been realized, especially for lower income families. A series of major initiatives were introduced to deal with these shortages. While they differed in terms of specific programs, they all emphasized private sector solutions. Some attempted to increase the financial position of those who were excluded from the private market (e.g., rent supplements); others attempted to stimulate housing developers to produce new units (e.g., interest subsidies and direct low-cost loans).

It is clear that these efforts reflected a belief

- that public housing was not the hoped-for solution to meet the housing needs of the nation,

- that public housing would continue to be a necessary but undesirable program—one for a small residual of the population,
- that new strategies needed to rely on the private sector.

It also became clear that housing policy initiatives emerging in the 1960s and continuing through the 1970s and 1980s were not the result of systematic and comprehensive planning. Rather, these developments can be characterized as piecemeal engineering efforts with the engineers working in isolation from each other. Some used a supply-side blueprint while others looked for a solution in demand-side strategies.

Interest Subsidies

By the mid-1960s this criticism of federal housing policy had grown to the point that members of both sides of Congress as well as advocacy groups were demanding more "radical" approaches to the housing problem. Most of the proponents for change proposed that the federal government play a much more limited role and that greater reliance be placed on the private sector. The solution, they argued, was not public housing with its resulting dependency, but private housing and self-help. The strategy of preference: the stimulation of new low-income housing production by offering developers interest subsidies, i.e., below-market interest loans.

The 1959 Housing Act (P.L. 86-372) had authorized a similar program on a small scale. Under Section 202, Congress authorized the making of such loans to nonprofit corporations to build housing for the elderly or handicapped. These loans were long term (often 50 years). The program was small—for the first 10 years the average number of units built on an annual basis was less than 5,000.

The Kennedy administration modified the program in the Housing Act of 1961. The interest subsidy program was expanded to include low-income families and families displaced by urban renewal projects, but as with the Section 202 program, the appropriations were small. It took President Johnson and the Great Society to bring the interest subsidy program to center stage with the passage of the Housing Act of 1968 (P.L. 90-448), which pulled together all existing interest subsidy programs into two programs: Section 235 (assistance to low-income families to buy homes) and Section 236 (subsidies to developers to build rental units for low-income families).

In its discussion of the bill, Congress found

> that the goal of "a decent home and a suitable living environment for every American family" (as expressed in the Housing Act of 1949) . . . had not been fully realized for many of the Nation's lower income families; that this

is a matter of grave national concern; that there exists in the public and private sectors of the economy the resources and capabilities necessary to the full realization of this goal. (Fish 1978:354)

Congress directed the president to set forth a

plan for the elimination of all substandard housing and the realization of that goal within ten years by constructing or rehabilitating 26 million housing units, 6 million of these for low and moderate income families. (ibid.)

The Section 235 program provided subsidies to low-income families to the point that they paid as little as 4% interest on their mortgages, were required to make very small down payments (3%), and would pay no more than 20% of their adjusted income for their mortgage payment. Families could then purchase new or rehabilitated units. Through 1977, almost 500,000 units were insured under this program, with a value of about $8.6 billion.

Under the Section 236 program, HUD provided the developer a subsidy that reduced his or her actual loan interest to 1%. The developer, in turn, agreed to accept eligible families (their income could not exceed 135% of the income ceiling for public housing residents) and charge them 20% of their income for rent. Unlike in public housing, renters would not be forced to leave the unit if their income exceeded this ceiling.

By using existing mechanisms of home financing and attracting more private capital, HUD believed that the supply of housing for low- and moderate-income families would increase substantially. Moreover, the subsidies would make fewer demands on the federal budget, would minimize resentment on the part of the lower middle class by allowing them to benefit from the program, and would attract private developers into the low- and moderate-income housing market.

In absolute terms, the increase of available housing units was substantial. In the first nine years of the program, 939,000 units were produced compared to the 1.2 million units produced in the first 40 years of the public housing program. This figure is, however, somewhat misleading. Various analysts suggested that

for every 100,000 units subsidized during the 1960s and early 1970s, perhaps as few as 14,000 represented net additions to the housing stock. The reason for this is that many builders dropped plans to construct nonsubsidized units when more profitable opportunities to build subsidized units became available. (Rice 1978:355–56)

The program, in hindsight, was a failure. Homes were poorly rehabilitated, FHA inspectors received kickbacks to look the other way, and inexperienced families were bilked into buying homes that would not last the life of the mortgage. While the cost to the family was designed to be 20% of their income, the program did not include in that amount the cost of utilities, heating, and repair bills, which often ran as high as 55% of income for low-income families (Stegman 1970). When repair costs exceeded the ability of families to pay for them, many simply walked away from the homes. Tens of thousands of units were abandoned nationwide, making the federal government the largest slum owner in history (Department of Housing and Urban Development 1974).

The Section 236 program experienced a default rate in excess of 7%—much greater than any other housing program except the Section 235 program. Thousands of the recipients of Section 235 subsidies for ownership defaulted. In Detroit alone, HUD foreclosed on 5,000 units. By 1974 HUD estimated that the defaults for both programs were costing the federal government $2 billion annually.

The scandal became so great that the interest subsidy programs were suspended and production strategies were shifted to rental subsidies in the 1974 housing bill.

Rent Supplements

The alternative to subsidizing the developers (a supply-side intervention) was the subsidization of those seeking housing (a demand-side strategy). While the former assumed that developers would produce more and higher quality units if they were provided incentives in the form of below-market interest rates, the latter held that if the economic power of poor and low-income families was increased, developers would respond by either building more or rehabilitating existing housing units.

While the major rental assistance initiative is found in the 1974 Housing Act (P.L. 93-383), its beginning, on a much smaller scale, goes back to the Johnson administration and the Housing Act of 1965. Under this program, eligible families would pay 25% of their income toward the fair market rent established by the Federal Housing Authority (FHA). The federal government would pay the difference.

The administration sought $110 million to subsidize 375,000 housing units over a four-year period (1966–1969). The proposal met with tremendous opposition during the congressional hearings. Numerous members of Congress argued that the federal government was overstepping its bounds by attempting to force economic, ethnic, and racial integration. Lobbying groups such as the National Association of Homebuilders and Redevelopment Officials (NAHRO), the Chamber of Commerce, and the National Lumber and Building Material Dealers Association argued that all federal efforts should subsidize production costs and not subsidize rent. Although the bill did pass, Congress approved only $36 million, and of the targeted 375,000 units, only 4% or 16,567 units were subsidized under this program.

This rent supplement program, better known as the housing allowance program, differed from the earlier effort in that eligible families obtained certificates from local housing authorities, and with these certificates found their own housing in the market. It was assumed that if owners received the fair market rent for their units (the family still paid only 25% of income with the remainder paid under the program), they would have an incentive to upgrade the quality of the units and then maintain them if they were to remain competitive. This increase in demand would produce an increase in the supply of standard housing for low- and moderate-income families.

Eligible families (their income could not exceed 80% of the area's median income) were seen as having much more opportunity than in earlier housing programs, because they were free to choose the housing that, in their opinion, best met their needs or preferences—in economic terms they were able to maximize their choice of location and neighborhood. The only restrictions were that the housing authority had to certify that the housing met existing codes and standards and that the owner had to sign a contract obligating him or her to maintain the property and observe the legal rights of the tenant. By the end of 1977, three years after the program began, almost 1 million units had been reserved under the Section 8 program and almost 300,000 were occupied—a significant improvement over the 16,567 units produced in the earlier rent subsidy program.

A more recent variation of this demand-side intervention emerged in 1983, when Congress authorized HUD to provide housing vouchers to a number of families on an experimental basis. As with Section 8 certificates, the vouchers subsidized tenants in units that met housing codes and standards. It differed from the Section 8 program in a number of ways. The administration admitted that this strategy would not stimulate the production of additional housing units; families were allowed to pay more than 25% of their income for more expensive units; the owner agreed to a 5-year commitment rather than the earlier 15-year commitment.

The theoretical benefits of a housing allowance / rental subsidy program is that, in allowing a family to choose the housing that maximizes their choice, the spatial stigma found in the earlier public housing efforts and the first subsidy program would be avoided. Neighbors would not know that the family was receiving the supplement. This assumes, of course, that the issue of discrimination has and is being successfully dealt with—an issue that was first addressed by President Kennedy in his

executive order "Equal opportunity in Housing," which "prevented discrimination in the sale, lease, or occupancy of residential property owned
or operated by the Federal Government" (Subcommittee on Housing and
Community Development 1975:314) and which was not only reaffirmed
but broadened in the Civil Rights Act of 1964.

The disadvantage of relying on the private market is that if the supply
of housing is low, choice is restricted through a voucher program. In
1986–1987, for example, 62% of the families holding housing vouchers in
New York City and Boston—low-vacancy areas—could not find housing.
Furthermore, over 50% of all participating families were paying more
than 30% of their income for rent (Schwartz et al. 1988).

HOUSING POLICY FOR MIDDLE- AND
UPPER-INCOME FAMILIES

The picture that emerges when we trace through our efforts to improve
the housing conditions for the poor and low-income families is one of
ambivalence. Government has produced and managed housing units, it
has also attempted to stimulate the production of housing in the private
sector, and finally it has increased the buying power of low-income families. Under the first and third efforts, the targets of the policy were people
who needed housing, while the second emphasized the developer. At
times the policies seemed to be concerned with social objectives; at other
times, economic needs including employment. Furthermore, at various
periods the federal government dealt with supply-side and demand-side
strategies simultaneously. These efforts have to be seen as a lack of consensus among policymakers as to the nature of the problem, its causes,
and solutions. This ambivalence has been notably absent in policies targeting middle- and upper-income families. Since the 1930s housing policy
has been quite consistent for these families. The following sections analyze these policies.

Mortgage Insurance Programs

Since the late 1920s, a major housing goal of the federal government,
stated and restated on numerous occasions over the next 70 years, was
home ownership. This promotion of home ownership was actively supported by different groups and for different reasons.

The early social reformers mentioned in an earlier section of this chapter saw home ownership as the solution to most of the country's moral and social problems:

[W]here a man has a home of his own, he has every incentive to be economical and thrifty, to take his part in the duties of citizenship, to be a real sharer in government. (Veiller 1910:6)

[Home ownership] goes to the very roots of the well being of the family, and the family is the social unit of the nation. It is more than comfort that is involved. It has important aspects of health and morals and education and the provision of a fair chance for growing childhood. Nothing contributes more to happiness or sound social stability than the surroundings of their own homes. (Gries and Ford 1932:xv)

Others suggested that a major strategy to deal with the economic problems of the depression including the growing problem of unemployment was the stimulation of increased home ownership. Still others argued that home ownership was American and more in ideological harmony with our beliefs about capitalism and free enterprise. It was a combination of these beliefs that led to a series of government efforts to support families who were or would become home owners.

As discussed in an earlier section, by 1933, home mortgages were being foreclosed at a rate of over 1,000 per day. Congress in 1932, with the active support of President Hoover, passed P. L. 72-304 (the Federal Home Loan Bank Act), which established a new agency empowered to buy mortgages from lending institutions so that they in turn could make new loans. Eventually, a system of district home loan banks were organized and a nationwide pool of mortgages established. This legislation also established the federal government's right to regulate the savings and loan associations. However, by 1933, 49% of the $20 billion home mortgage program was in default and in serious financial trouble (Fish 1978).

The Roosevelt administration took a number of new approaches to the same problem. The first was the Home Owner's Loan Corporation (HOLC), established in June 1933 to help families who were in danger of losing their homes through mortgage foreclosures. Through a combination of bonds and other guarantees, loans of up to 80% of appraised value with a life of 15 years were offered at 5% interest. Applications were accepted up to June 1935 and the last loan was closed one year later. Over a relatively brief period 1.9 million applications were received: slightly over 1 million were approved and $3 billion loaned. Although there were some defaults, by 1951 when the program ended, the corporation was liquidated at a profit.

In 1934, Congress expanded its efforts. Since the HOLC only assisted families who already owned their homes and were in default, legislation was needed to support those who wanted to buy their own homes. This legislation, the National Housing Act of 1934, had three main objectives: (1) assisting families to purchase homes, (2) encouraging investment in housing construction and (3) providing employment for the building trades. This act established the Federal Housing Administration (FHA), which was authorized to

- establish the Federal Deposit Insurance Corporation (FDIC) to insure banks,
- establish the Federal Savings and Loan Insurance Corporation (FSLIC) to insure other lending institutions,
- establish national mortgage associations to buy up mortgages.

Because they were insured, lenders were to offer mortgages on 80% of the appraised value; the interest would not exceed 5% and the loans would be for 20 years. Borrowers would be charged a percentage of the monthly payment (usually 0.5 to 1% of the face value of the mortgage) as an insurance premium.

This legislation literally revolutionized the housing industry. It enabled more people to buy homes; it lessened the need for second mortgages; it brought stability to both borrowers and lenders; and it stimulated more investments in the housing market by diminishing the lender's risk.

In 1944, Congress passed another mortgage insurance program—the Serviceman's Readjustment Act (more commonly known as the G.I. Bill of Rights)—which authorized the Veterans Administration to guarantee loans for purchasing, building, or improving private homes. About 40% of World War II veterans bought their homes under this program. This program, more than any other program, was the major stimulus for moving this country from a nation of renters to one of home owners by 1950. The peak year of the Veterans Administration's program was 1959, when 393,000 new homes (24% of all new homes) were financed through this program.

Secondary Mortgage Market Activities

Concurrent with the insurance program, the federal government introduced another, somewhat more intrusive program—intrusive in the sense that while the insurance program supported the workings of the market, this approach actually shaped the market. Earlier, the Federal Home Loan Bank Board was given the authority not only to regulate the savings and loan industry, but also to set interest and deposit rates and even make cash advances to a bank experiencing cash flow problems. These regulatory activities were considered to be needed because of the vulnerability of the industry to shifts in the money market and operated until the deregulation of the savings and loan associations by the Reagan administration in the early 1980s.

Faced with another economic downturn in 1937, Congress created the Federal National Mortgage Association (FNMA, known as Fannie Mae), which sought to encourage the flow of money from regions of the country where the demand for mortgage money was low to regions where it was greater. The FNMA purchased FHA mortgages from lenders and then sold them to interested investors. The agency, moreover, had the power to actively intervene in the market and affect monetary policy. It was able to increase the flow of money when credit was tight and offset restrictive monetary policies on the part of the Federal Reserve Bank. Within one year it had purchased 26,276 mortgages worth $100 million.

As Aaron (1972) notes, the federal government's creation of a secondary mortgage market and its regulation of the savings and loans banks greatly benefited the housing market. By expanding the flow of credit, it stabilized a turbulent market, lowered interest rates, and attracted capital into a market experiencing problems in attracting investors. As with the mortgage insurance programs discussed in the previous section, these programs principally benefited single-family homeowners, who had middle and upper incomes. In 1968, Congress created the Government Mortgage Insurance Association (GNMA, called Ginnie Mae), which expanded opportunities for families with incomes below the median by allowing for the purchase of multifamily units.

Tax Policies

Of all policies affecting the housing market, tax policies have had the greatest impact. These policies offer the home owner the following benefits:

- interest deduction on home mortgages,
- property tax deductions,
- capital tax deferment if the seller buys a more expensive home.

Furthermore, in order to attract more private investment into the rental housing market, the Tax Reform Act of 1969 allowed owners to depreciate their residential buildings at an accelerated rate. These massive tax shelters offered over the first years of the project stimulated many investors to enter the market. Furthermore, investors who substantially rehabilitated their properties were given even more tax benefits if they kept the property for more than ten years. The rationale for these tax benefits was that incentives were needed since the risk was high and investors were shying away from this market.

The 1986 Tax Reform Act, however, has made investments in rental units less attractive by lengthening depreciation schedules and taxing capital gains at higher rates. These changes resulted in a 28% increase in rents over the following few years and a production decline of up to 300,000 units each year (Schwartz et al. 1988).

The total amount of tax revenue forgone is staggering. In 1987 (Harney 1989), for example, the federal government's loss of potential tax revenue reached $55 billion—three and a half times HUD's entire budget for that year ($15.2 billion). By 1996, forgone tax revenue grew to $64 billion, while HUD's budget grew to a little over $19 billion. Whereas HUD's programs benefit low-income and poor families, these tax policies provide benefits to those who are financially better off. Almost 44% of the mortgage subsidy goes to the 5.2% of those taxpayers whose incomes are above $100,000. One-half of all homeowners do not claim the deduction and only 20% of the 28 million households with incomes between $30,000 and $50,000 receive any subsidy.

HOUSING POLICY: A GENERAL CRITIQUE

Basic Assumptions

A number of assumptions clearly emerge from this analysis of past and present housing policies:

Home ownership is a desirable national objective.   Throughout this century, the argument has been made that ownership develops a sense of pride and commitment on the part of the owner. Indeed, Congress in 1968 affirmed the belief that ownership would solve a number of social problems (a large number of cities were experiencing riots and other forms of racial disturbance) and would create "a new dignity, a new attitude toward their jobs and a sense of participation in their communities" (Housing Act of 1968).

Market mechanisms, for the most part, are adequate to determine the quantity and quality of the nation's housing stock.   The beliefs that a balance between the supply and demand for housing and that profit and self-interest are legitimate values are *the* fundamental driving forces in the housing market.

While market mechanisms are adequate, the market is not perfect. Occasionally there will be distortions in the supply-demand equilibrium. At times the demand for housing will outstrip the available supply; at times certain groups (e.g., low-income, minorities) will experience barriers in their search for housing.

Availability of adequate housing for all is a legitimate goal for the state. Adequate has come to be defined as decent, safe, and sanitary. While the goal implies that housing is a right of citizenship, the goal seems to have been justified more from an externality rationale, i.e., poor housing and a poor physical environment are believed to be associated with disease and social pathology and thus detrimental to the stability of the community.

Government can and should intervene in the housing market. This intervention however, should be as indirect as possible and specific strategies should not distort natural market mechanisms. Policies should favor fiscal and monetary strategies to counteract supply-demand fluctuations. The actual production of housing by government is the least favorable since it is the most intrusive form of intervention.

Assistance to moderate and low-income families should be indirect thus minimizing the role of government. This assistance should be limited to those bypassed by the private market and should require that families contribute a percentage of their income to the purchase or renting of the housing unit.

Housing: Economic or Social Policy?

Taken literally, the goal of a "decent home and suitable living environment for every American family" is clearly a social goal. In fact, it is a radical statement of societal responsibility. The irony of U.S. housing policy is that both the 1949 and 1968 Housing Acts

> contain a national commitment which not only could never be afforded, but are likely not supported by a sufficiently large constituency to be carried out even if more funds were to become available. . . . Yet . . . there seems to be little overt interest among low income housing advocates and our political leaders in modifying the nation's goal of putting every ill-housed family into a new quality house in a good neighborhood in spite of the fact that fewer and fewer superior quality units can be built each year per million dollars of public assistance. (Stegman 1970:330–31)

To better understand the dissonance between rhetoric and actual practice we need to ask, Who benefits from our housing policies? The answer—middle- and upper-income families. "Subsidized" housing programs attempt to direct some resources to poor Americans, but in terms of level of benefits and numbers of units produced, they do not counter-balance the overall thrust of national policy. Indeed, this overall thrust is so strong that even "subsidized" housing programs reveal the pressure to aid middle-class families at the expense of low-income and poor families.

Was our housing policy ever intended to produce enough units to meet the needs of the poor and the low income? To answer this question we need to reexamine the initial statement of housing goals:

> the realization as soon as feasible of the goal of a decent home and suitable living environment for every American family, thus contributing to the redevelopment of communities and to the advancement of the growth, wealth and security of the nation. (Housing Act of 1949, Section 2)

Which of these goals are more important: the social goal of decent housing, the economic goal of growth and wealth, or the societal goal of security and stability? As Rein (1970) points out, multiple goals cannot be maximized at the same time, they are often contradictory, and choices have to be made.

As we have argued, the housing problem has been defined as an economic problem and as such we have emphasized economic solutions. While there might be some sentiment that decent, safe, and sanitary housing is a basic need of all citizens and society, which government has an obligation to meet, especially for those who are unable to obtain housing in the market, government also sees that it has an obligation to the well-being of society as a whole. Thus decent housing is not defined as a right to which all members of society are entitled but a necessary component of general well-being and stability for a prosperous nation. Is this so different from Bismarck's development of a social security system in the latter part of the nineteenth century—a system whose purpose was to maintain social order among the working classes who were threatening civil unrest?

From this perspective, housing assistance for the poor and lower-income families is justified as long it does not threaten other more important social values—the social well-being of the nonpoor. Housing policy was never meant to produce sufficient housing of acceptable standards for all people. It has been grounded in a filtering strategy with some intervention at certain points along the filtering chain. The interventions were to increase low- and moderate-income housing opportunities by closing obvious gaps in the filtering process. Although there may be some elements of conscience-soothing in a nation proud of its high standard of living, these elements have always been subordinate to the larger goal of increasing economic prosperity.

How else can we explain the decades of the 1980s and 1990s? The Reagan administration, with its concern for reducing taxes and thus revenues, its concern for increasing military expenditures, and its stated promise to balance the budget, looked to other areas of the budget to locate possible cuts. Housing expenditures were slashed. The total budget authority of HUD was reduced from $35.7 billion in 1980 to $15.2 in 1987: from 7% of the federal budget to 1%. This trend continued through the Bush and Clinton administrations. In 1996, the total budget for HUD was slightly more than $19 billion (less than 53% of the 1980 budget) and represented about 1.5% of the federal budget.

Public housing construction and improvement and rental assistance for the elderly, handicapped, and low income were cut by 70% in the 1980s. Rent burdens (the percentage of income renters were to pay) was raised from 25 to 30% and new eligibility criteria resulted in only the poorest being eligible.

The Clinton administration has continued this general policy. Proposals have been made to replace 100,000 units of public housing with Section 8 vouchers/certificates, to implement a moratorium on any future building of public housing, and to change existing policies so that families with higher incomes and steady employment would be attracted to the remaining public housing projects. Eventually, these units will be sold and the federal government's role in the housing sector will be limited to the Section 8 program.

These program cuts (with the exception of the voucher programs) have virtually ended all federal efforts to assist low-income and poor families, the elderly and handicapped, and Native Americans. Less than one-third of poor renters receive a federal housing subsidy and of the 13.8 million low-income renter households eligible for assistance, almost 10 million (72%) receive no help. Of those who do receive assistance, 26% are covered by Section 8, 33% live in public housing, and 40% live in private subsidized developments (Dreier and Atlas 1997).

However, this strategy raises a number of concerns. In 1998, 4.4 million Section 8 contracts (90% of whom are elderly, disabled, or families with children) will expire and Congress has been reluctant to extend funding. This is, however, the tip of the iceberg. Within a decade all of the current Section 8 contracts will have expired and, if continued, will be converted to one-year terms, thus introducing an element of uncertainty into the lives of low-income and poor families.

These policies need to be questioned given the evidence (1) that such a strategy (i.e., vouchers) will not significantly increase the quantity and quality of our deteriorating housing stock; (2) that a significant number of units that the elderly and handicapped have come to rely on are now being "privatized" (i.e., converted to condominiums or rented at fair market value) thus creating more homeless; (3) that there is more stress on families who will have to provide housing to their elderly parents; and (4) that there has been a serious decline in the quality of life of millions of people.

5

Health and Medical Care

While we have been concerned about the rising costs of medical care for the past 30 years, the level of this concern has escalated over the past 15 years. Government at all levels, insurance companies, businesses, and providers have searched for and experimented with numerous strategies that, while they differ in philosophy and assumptions, have one common objective: to curb what has been referred to as uncontrollable expenditures through some combination of cost containment mechanisms. These mechanisms have included such different approaches as

- health planning to create a health care "system" that would discourage unnecessary duplication and encourage the sharing of scarce resources,
- self-policing by physicians through professional standards review organizations,
- placing limits on the amount of reimbursement a provider can receive for treating a patient, e.g., Diagnostic Related Groupings (DRGs),
- restructuring the way medical care is delivered, e.g., managed care in its many forms.

In developing these mechanisms, new partnerships have formed between those who pay for the services and those who provide the services. New partnerships have also been developed between the public and private sector and roles that were once clearly drawn have become blurred.

This chapter will explore these efforts in some detail, not only in terms of their success in dealing with the problems of costs, but also with a view to analyzing their impact on other areas with special emphasis on the ultimate target of these policies: the consumer. To do this, the analysis traces the evolution of the medical care system over the last century, the policies enacted by government, and finally discusses the assumptions and theoretical underpinnings of these developments.

THE PROBLEM OF RISING COSTS

As of 1995, total national health expenditures (public and private) reached $950 billion. This amount represents almost 14% of the gross domestic product (GDP). Furthermore, the Health Care Financing Administration (HCFA) projects that this could reach 18% in the year 2000 and possibly 32% by 2030 (an estimated $16 trillion). This translates to per capita expenditures of $48,000 in 2030 compared to $6,000 in 2000 and $3,500 in 1995 (HCFA 1995; Levit et al. 1996).

To fully appreciate these numbers, we need to locate them in a historical context (see Table 5.1). From 1946 to 1960, medical prices in general and hospital prices in particular grew at a rate slower than or similar to the growth rate experienced by the consumer price index (CPI). Growth in this area was comparable to the inflationary growth in most areas of consumption. With the passage of Medicare and Medicaid in 1965, prices in these two areas began to grow at a faster rate and by 1970, we begin to see a significant rise far in excess of general inflation.

In 1930, national health expenditures represented only 3.6% of the GDP. By 1950 they grew to a high of 4.7%—a relatively small increase over a two-decade period. However, in each ten-year period since 1960, national health expenditures as a percentage of the GDP have grown by 2–3% (see Table 5.2). Furthermore, the share of these expenditures taken on by government in general and the federal government in particular has grown significantly.

To put these statistics into perspective, this country's health care system is the most expensive in the world (see Table 5.3). For example, total personal health care expenditures per person in 1990 averaged $836 in the United Kingdom, $1,035 in Japan, $1,232 in West Germany, and $1,683 in Canada. In the United States these costs averaged $2,359.

What tends to frustrate many is that despite our wealth, education, technology, medical schools, hospitals, research facilities, and the stagger-

Table 5.1. Consumer Price Index For all Items and Medical Care Items (1957–1959 = 100)

Year	CPI—All Items	CPI—Medical Care	Hospital charges
1946	68.0	60.7	37.0
1960	103.1	108.1	112.7
1965	109.9	122.3	153.3
1970	127.7	155.0	256.0

Source: USDHEW, "Medical Care Prices Fact Sheet." *Research and Statistics Note,* USGPO, Washington, D.C. Note Number 2, February 23, 1970.

Table 5.2. Health Care Expenditure Data

	1960	1970	1980	1990	1994
NHE[a] ($ BIllion)	26.9	73.2	247.2	697.5	949.4
% GDP[b]	5.1	7.1	8.9	12.1	13.7
Per capita $[c]	141	341	1,052	2,688	3,510
% Public $[d]	24.8	37.8	42.4	40.8	44.3
% Federal of public[e]	44	64	69	69	72

Source: Levit et al. (1995).
[a]NHE: National Health Expenditures from all sources including out-of-pocket.
[b]% GDP: percentage of the gross domestic product spent on health care.
[c]Per capita $: per capita expenditures spent on health care; total amount spent divided by total population.
[d]% Public $: of all expenditures (NHE) percentage paid by government of all levels.
[e]% Federal of public: that share of all public expenditures paid by the federal government.

ing amount we are spending on health care, international health indices give the United States not only poor ratings but ratings that are getting worse relative to other countries. At least 16 European countries in 1967 had a higher life expectancy for males and 11 had a higher expectancy for females. Whereas in 1950, the infant mortality rate (IMR) of this country

Table 5.3. International Comparisons (1993)[a]

Country	Rank on IMR Lowest-Highest	Per Capita Income 1 = Highest	% GDP spent on Medical Care 1 = highest
Switzerland	1 (3.4/1,000)	1	5
Japan	2 (4.2)	2	19
Finland	3 (4.4)	11	18
Norway	4 (5.0)	5	14
Denmark	5 (5.6)	4	10
Germany	6 (5.8)	6	12.5
Netherlands	7 (5.9)	13	12.5
Ireland	8 (6.0)	17	5.5
Austria	9.5 (6.1)	7	9
Australia	9.5 (6.1)	16	5.5
Canada	11 (6.2)	14	15.5
United Kingdom	12 (6.3)	15	7.5
Italy	13 (6.7)	12	3
New Zealand	14 (7.2)	19	4
France	15 (7.3)	9	12.5
Belgium	16.5 (7.6)	10	7.5
Sweden	16.5 (7.6)	3	17
United States	18 (8.2)	8	1

Sources: Department of Economic and Social Information and Policy Analysis, *Statistical Yearbook,* 40th ed., Statistical Division, United Nations, New York, 1995. United Nations, *1994 Demographic Yearbook,* UNO, New York, 1996.
[a]The figure in parentheses is the actual IMR for that country.

was the sixth lowest in the world, by 1962 the United States had dropped to 11th place and by 1967 to 18th place (United Nations 1968).

In 1993, our ranking was unchanged and 17 countries had lower infant mortality rates. Moreover, of the 18 countries listed in Table 5.3, only one country had a lower life expectancy for men and none had lower expectancies for women. This occurred despite the fact that the United States spent more of its GDP on health care than any of these countries and that average per capita costs were lower in 10 of these countries.

Given these results, many question whether any future increase in health care expenditures, let alone the projected $16 trillion in the year 2030, would improve our position relative to these other countries. If the results were more favorable, we could conceivably argue that the costs were acceptable. Such an argument, however, cannot be sustained with three decades of less than optimal outcomes.

It can be argued that while many factors influence mortality and morbidity levels, a major reason other countries have not only lower rates, but also less variation in their rates for different socioeconomic groups and provide medical care services more economically, is that their medical care systems are organized more efficiently and effectively. In general, the chief problems seem to be

- an increasing fragmentation in the delivery of services, artificial separation between preventive and curative services, and depersonalization of the patient through categorical disease emphasis and medical specialization;
- an increasing lack of comprehensiveness and continuity of care resulting from this fragmentation and depersonalization;
- underserved areas, e.g., rural areas, reservations, and inner cities due to a maldistribution of health services and health providers;
- the absence of a defined locus of responsibility that would assume responsibility for effecting solutions and accountability for the results.

HISTORICAL ANTECEDENTS OF THE CRISIS

Prior to the arrival of newer diagnostic tools, highly sophisticated technology, specialization within the medical profession, and various third-party payers (e.g., insurance companies and government), the medical care system was rather simple. Most patients were seen in their own home and only those with highly communicable diseases, mental illness, or in need of extensive surgery were sent to the hospital and frequently these were not expected to return. Patients preferred to be treated at home, where they received care seldom improved upon in institutions graphically described as "public dumping grounds for the aged, the poor, the insane, feebleminded, epileptics, blind and deaf mutes, sufferers from chronic disease" (Stewart 1925:3)

The practice of medicine, as practiced by the solo professional of the premodern era, the general practitioner, was minimal and best depicted by the famous painting of Sir Luke Fildes—"The Doctor." This painting, dating from the nineteenth century, shows a doctor sitting, head in hand, beside a young girl. The father is standing helplessly beside her and the mother is sitting off to the side with her head down on a table. The scene is one of frustration and futility and demonstrates how little the physician has to offer.

At the turn of the century, the overall mortality rate in the United states was 17.8 per 1,000 and the average life expectancy was 47 years. The leading causes of death were communicable diseases—pneumonia, influenza, tuberculosis, and gastritis—accounting for one-third of all deaths. In 1915, the maternal mortality rate was 61 per 10,000 live births and 1 in 10 babies did not survive the first year of life (Anderson and Lerner 1959).

The American Medical Association (AMA), established in the middle of the nineteenth century, began to organize the rapidly proliferating facets of medical care. During the early 1900s the medical care system was not only simple, with limited specializations in the professions and institutions, but also had relatively few standards or controls. Medical schools consisted of little more than lecture halls and apprenticeships. Accreditation was unheard of. Not all hospitals, of course, fit this characterization. Proprietary hospitals, usually founded by physicians, were exceptions as well as the leading public institutions along the eastern seaboard. However, access to these facilities was limited by economic and geographic constraints for most people.

In 1910, Abraham Flexner, concerned with the disparity between American and European standards in medical practice, documented the need to establish controls in medical education and was instrumental in the closing of many marginal medical schools. Over the next few decades the profession, through the AMA, initiated changes in both medical education and hospital practices. Environmental control activities all but eliminated gastritis, yellow fever, and typhoid, and reduced the incidence of tuberculosis. Similar advances in the laboratory sharply affected the incidence of diphtheria.

These advances, however, brought with them a host of new problems. As mortality was reduced with the control of communicable diseases and the overall reduction in infant and maternal mortality, longevity increased. The decline of the death rate was accompanied with increased survival of those with illnesses and disabilities. In other words, as mortality rates were reduced, morbidity rates increased: this is, as Somers and Somers (1965) remarked, the paradox of medical progress. Each increase in scientific knowledge and technical skill was accompanied with a sharp rise in demand for medical care. This increase also, by necessity, transformed medical care from an individual practitioner's enterprise into a highly organized institutional effort.

In the 1920s and 1930s more and more physicians accepted the fact that efficient and effective services required a hospital-based practice around which highly institutionalized activities were centered and hospitals emerged as the primary locus of medical care. The growth of a highly complex professional organization built around sophisticated knowledge and technology was far removed from the era when individual physicians armed with a black bag represented medical practice. The construction of new hospitals as centers of this technology increased sharply and had a secondary effect of concentrating the energies of medical science more and more on the treatment of acute short-term illnesses.

THE BEGINNINGS OF THIRD-PARTY PAYMENT AND ITS IMPACT ON COSTS

This new practice of medicine required the use of large amounts of capital not only in the form of hospitals and operating rooms but also for services such as nursing, laboratories, x-rays, and various therapies. These additions to the "black bag" were costly, and when the depression occurred, hospitals found themselves in serious financial difficulty. Individuals lacked the means to pay for hospital care and there was no precedent for the federal government to play a role in the financing of individual health care. Up to this time, local government and charitable organizations provided minimal health services to the poor. There were, however, no effective mechanisms to deal with the great numbers of the newly unemployed.

Voluntary health insurance was a response to the growing crisis. The movement was given significant impetus when, at the height of the depression, a group of schoolteachers in Dallas, Texas, contracted with Baylor University Hospital for the provision of health benefits in exchange for a fixed fee (Goldman 1948). This successful demonstration and a variety of similar programs, later incorporated under the name Blue Cross, drew considerable interest from hospitals, which in general were in serious financial difficulty. In response to the fiscal crisis, other health insurance plans, both nonprofit and commercial, were developed. These early insurance movements had a tremendous and perhaps unanticipated impact on the organization of medical care services, first because of assumptions they made about where services should be delivered, and second because of how they defined their role in the health care system.

Whatever the intention, the health insurance industry exacerbated the trend toward centralizing medical services in the hospital by limiting reimbursement to those services delivered in those settings. Not only was this accepted as the most economical arrangement, but it also encouraged the practice of medicine under the most ideal conditions for health care professionals. It centralized the physician's place of work, provided the opportunity for peer review and consultation, and provided the practitioner with an expensive technology that could not be duplicated in a private practice setting (Somers and Somers 1965). While the hospital-based practice offered an ideal setting for practitioners, it was not necessarily ideal in terms of the needs of patients nor of keeping overall medical costs manageable. Less costly settings might have served just as well for many medical needs.

The second effect of health insurance is related to the way the industry defined its role in the provision of medical care services. In the face of political pressure from organized medicine and its concern for physician independence in determining what medical care would be provided, insurance carriers argued that they were only fiscal agents and "maintained that the carrier had no legitimate reason to interfere in the practice of medical care directly. These matters, they insist, should be left strictly to the vendor and consumer of care" (ibid.:226). This explicit and public disclaimer of any responsibility for supervising medical care was accompanied, however, with implicit controls. The insurance industry covered only a limited range of medical services, offering protection from certain kinds of medical costs and requiring that services be delivered in hospital settings. These implicit controls were likely motivated by the insurance carriers' need to define health services in a tangible way and to establish fiscal formats that were in keeping with a business orientation. However, intended or not, the industry was unable or unwilling to stimulate different patterns of utilization and delivery of services given its focus on hospital-based care.

The voluntary (i.e., the not-for-profit) health insurance industry experienced tremendous growth from 1935 to 1950. By 1939, over 5 million people were covered by some form of health insurance, of which 4.5 million were in various Blue Cross programs while commercial (i.e., for-profit) carriers accounted for the remainder. Over the next 10 years, the numbers of insured grew to almost 70 million. While both the voluntary and commercial companies experienced growth, the latter's share of the market was almost half in 1950. A residual of about 5% held membership in group insurance plans, most notably the Kaiser-Permanente and the Health Insurance Program of New York. These latter were early prototypes of what has become widely know as health maintenance organizations. This increase was stimulated to a large extent by the wage stabilization programs of World War II, which froze wages but permitted increased employee compensation in the form of fringe benefits. The court held that health and welfare benefits were open to negotiation, and as a result, health insurance coverage drew a great deal of attention at the collective bargaining table.

This increase in health insurance coverage was accompanied by a similar increase in the number of acute care hospitals, the number of hospital beds, and utilization. Over a 20-year period, 1928–1948, admissions rose by 87%, hospital days increased by 63%, and length of stay decreased by 39%. Medical technology, armed with more effective tools for assessment and treatment of acute illnesses, and encouraged by tremendous success, began to focus more sharply on these activities.

But not all patients were in need of acute care. Many of the specific medical needs of the aged population were not effectively met by the general hospital and few alternatives within the system were supported by the medical profession. Those with chronic illnesses who went to hospitals used resources that were more sophisticated and expensive than they required and, to some extent, used resources that were then unavailable to patients with acute medical needs. But many aged persons and others with chronic care needs went to hospitals, partially because of the absence of acceptable alternatives and partially in response to the stimulus of insurance programs, which provided coverage only for hospital-based care. The end result was a heavy but inefficient use of hospital facilities. This increase in hospital utilization and the impact of the health insurance industry on this utilization was directly related to the issue of rising costs and was not effectively addressed for over 30 years.

THE EVOLVING ROLE OF GOVERNMENT

The role of government, including federal, state, and local, has changed considerably over the past century. Basically, these roles can be characterized by five patterns:

- direct provision of medical care services,
- the purchase of services from private vendors,

- the purchase of health insurance,
- requiring employees to purchase health insurance and employers to share in these costs, and
- the setting of standards (Somers and Somers 1965).

During the nineteenth century, government assumed two major responsibilities: (1) the public health or sanitation function with a focus on the health of the community and (2) the care of specific groups within the population. This latter involvement included the development of a network of federal hospitals for military and merchant seamen, the provision of medical care in local Poor Law institutions and the development of reservation-based medical care services for Native Americans. (Rationales for this involvement have been discussed in Chapter 1.)

The public sector saw its role as primarily supportive to the private sector and dealt only with those groups that were unable to obtain medical care on their own. The inclusion of additional groups was incremental and, even as these groups became larger, the nature of the involvement was, with few exceptions, one that tended to favor the purchase and not the direct provision of services.

The passage of the Social Security Act did have a significant though indirect impact on the medical care system. For the first time in this country's history, an economic floor was established and large numbers of people (especially the aged) could expect financial assistance on a continuing basis. Many no longer were forced to suffer deprivation in their own homes or go to county infirmaries or homes for the aged. Given the means to make a choice, the elderly turned to nursing homes and boarding homes. In fact, by law, the grants were not available to retired persons residing in county homes or almshouses.

Just as the emergence of the health insurance industry strengthened the role of the physician as the primary provider in the medical care system and the hospital as the locus of medical practice, so also federal monies through the Social Security Act affected the medical care system by providing a potential source of funding for nursing and convalescent homes resulting in a rapid growth of these facilities. However, since the federal government saw these programs as cash assistance programs and not medical care programs, no restrictions were placed on the beneficiaries as to how these funds were to be spent and no measures were developed to protect the individual and establish minimal standards of care.

Beginning in 1950, the federal government modified its policy of providing only cash payments to recipients, and made funds available to those states willing to provide medical services to those who were receiving public assistance benefits, i.e., those who were categorically eligible [recipients of Old Age Assistance (OAA), Aid to Families with Dependent children (AFDC), and Aid to the Blind (AB)]. States, in turn, would match these federal funds, and establish and administer a vendor system to reimburse providers. This policy was developed because experience indicated that regular cash payments did not cover medical expenses for all recipients.

In 1950, government spending on medical care was a little over $100 million. By 1960 it reached almost $500 million, and by 1964, after the introduction of the Medical Assistance for the Aged program (MAA) and one year before the passage of the Medicare/Medicaid legislation, this financing of medical care reached a little over $1 billion. From 1950 to 1964, governmental expenditures increased 13-fold. Still, this involvement of the government through vendor payments, as large as it might appear, was still small compared to the amounts controlled by other third-party payers.

The passage in 1960 of Medical Assistance for the Aged (MAA), known more popularly as the Kerr-Mills Bill, substantially increased federal sharing in medical care vendor payments. Under this legislation (P.L. 86-778) the federal government would share in all state expenditures without any limit. In practice, the federal government's share ranged from a low of 50% in the wealthier states to a high of 80% in the poorer states. If a state chose to participate in the program, it was required to expand its medical care coverage to aged who were poor and unable to purchase needed medical care even if they were ineligible for OAA. Finally, to encourage states to emphasize preventive services and to support elderly persons who wanted to remain in their own homes, the legislation required a state to provide both institutional and noninstitutional services. Despite fierce opposition from the AMA, which charged that legislation such as this would open the door to socialized medicine, the Eisenhower administration was successful in effecting it passage.

Two far-reaching principles were established in this legislation. The first was that medical care policies were to be seen as extensions of income maintenance (retirement) policies, "protecting elderly persons against the cost of episodic illness on the rationale that such costs are unbudgetable and cannot reasonably be met by a regular monthly pension" (Ball 1971:21).

Second, the role of government would continue to be nonintrusive. The medical care market would not be interfered with other than government paying for the care provided to the elderly by the private sector. This principle would be strengthened by the decision that the program would pay "usual and customary fees" as determined, not by government, but by the provider.

The passage of the Kerr-Mills Bill was the first major initiative on the part of the federal government in paying for medical care services. In 1950, the total federal outlay for medical care under the OAA program was $36 million. Ten years later, these expenditures amounted to $280 million; an absolute increase of $244 million and an average annual increase of $24 million. One year after the passage of the MAA program, expenditures increased by 145% over the previous year or $408 million (see Table 5.4).

By 1965, federal outlays had reached $800 million: an absolute increase of $523 million since 1960 and an average annual increase of $100 million. While the program was clearly developed within the *residual model* of social welfare, i.e., the program was means-tested, selective in coverage (only the elderly who were poor were eligible), and initially viewed as serving only a relatively small number, it quickly became a major source of funding for a large number of recipients. The role of the federal government had increased considerably over a relatively short period of time; and however reluctant the federal government had been in the past to become involved in this particular market, there was no turning back.

MEDICARE AND MEDICAID

Arguably, the most significant piece of social legislation to be passed since the original Social Security Act of 1935 was P.L. 89-77. Operationally, medical care was recognized as a right and government assumed a direct responsibility in assuring that right. As with other programs, the role of government was to be unintrusive, i.e., government would finance medical care but would not interfere with the way that medical care services were organized and delivered: it would support the existing free market system. The two programs, one a health insurance program and the other a welfare program, though differing in administration and pur-

Table 5.4. Government Expenditures for Medical Care ($, millions)

Year	OAA	MAA	Total[a]
1950	35.9	—	100.7
1960	280.3	—	492.7
1964	420.9	381.7	1,147.6

[a]Includes AB, AFDC, and APTD.
Source: Department of Health, Education and Welfare, *Trends,* S-96, Part 1, Washington, D.C., USGPO, 1965.

pose, had one goal in common: to meet the medical needs of high-risk groups. Again, similar to the Medical Assistance for the Aged Program, government chose to work within the current delivery system. Both were primarily vendor programs and reinforced the assumption that the removal of a financial barrier would improve the health status of people.

The legislation, at least in part, received widespread congressional support because of the sudden jump in the cost of medical care. Throughout the decades of the forties and the fifties, prices for medical services and hospital care were actually lower than the prices for other goods and services. From 1960 to 1965, however, increases in medical and hospital prices began to outstrip increases in the CPI (as shown in Table 5.1). This proved disastrous to the elderly, most of whom were living on fixed incomes, which did not rise as prices rose (OASDI and OAA became inflation-proof only in 1974). Moreover, one year before the implementation of Medicare, only 47% of the aged had health insurance and even these numbers had been declining (HEW 1968).

In addition, one in two elderly nursing home patients were receiving some form of public assistance, usually Old Age Assistance (OAA) and Medical Assistance for the Aged (MAA) and 88% of all nursing home patients were elderly.

The 1965 amendments reflected the major principles introduced in the original act. Just as there were two major initiatives in the income maintenance programs, i.e., a social insurance program that provided benefits as entitlements (OASDI and UI) and a social assistance program that provided benefits to those who could demonstrate eligibility by passing a means test (OAA, AB, APTD, and AFDC), so also there were two similar emphases in this health care legislation.

As mentioned above, the federal government spent $800 million on medical care services in 1965. As significant as this amount was relative to previous expenditures, it paled in comparison to subsequent years. In the two years after the passage of Medicare, the federal government spent $3.4 billion on hospital and nursing home care alone. Twenty-five years after the passage of the legislation, these Medicare and Medicaid expenditures had reached the staggering total of $135 billion annually. Of this, the federal share was $110 billion and the remainder was the Medicaid share paid by states. By 1995, these expenditures reached $255 billion, of which $187 billion represented the federal share. Furthermore, the elderly have been and continue to be the major beneficiaries of these programs.

Medicare

Title 18 (Medicare) falls into the *social insurance* category since it provides a range of services to OASDI recipients (later certain groups of persons with disabilities regardless of age were added) as an entitlement. Like OASDI, eligibility is not a function of passing a means test, but is strictly a matter of having participated in the Social Security system while working. The program has two major components.

Part A (also referred to as "Hospital Insurance") is mandatory for all OASDI recipients and pays for hospital care and skilled nursing care and home health services. The program is financed almost entirely through the Social Security Tax and entitlement is earned while the individual is still working and not yet retired. Initially (1966) the specific percentage of FICA set aside for Medicare was 0.35% (of the total 3.85% tax). This percentage has risen over the years, and by 1998, of the 7.65% FICA tax, 1.45% is set aside for Medicare payments. Additionally, until recently, the maximum taxable income for Medicare and OASDI was the same. Now, however, all income is subject to the Medicare tax. Over 90% of all expenditures are paid from the trust fund and the rest from general revenues.

Part B (referred to as SMI—Supplemental Medical Insurance) pays for physician services, hospital outpatient services, home health care, and a variety of laboratory and other diagnostic services. All individuals receiving Part A are eligible for Part B, but unlike the former, participation is not mandatory. Furthermore, while the recipient of Part A has contributed to the program while working, Part B is financed, in part, from monthly premiums paid by the retiree (the premiums pay for approximately 25% of costs). The remainder comes from general revenues.

Over the years, the federal government, concerned with rising prices, has introduced a number of cost containment measures—measures that are intended to provide a disincentive to unnecessary utilization. The two most notable of these are (1) the deductible and (2) the coinsurance payment. Deductibles, also known as first dollars, require the individual to pay a certain amount before Medicare begins paying and coinsurance requires that the individual pay a percentage of all costs after that deductible has been paid.

Medicaid

Medicaid (Title 19) also established in 1965, is a residual program that falls in the *social assistance* category. The program was an extension of the earlier programs discussed above that were established to pay for the medical care needs of low-income elderly (MAA). The new program initially paid for medical care only for those needy persons who were eligible for one of the existing social assistance programs, i.e., OAA, AB, APTD, and AFDC—they were categorically eligible. Beginning in the late 1980s, the federal government required states also to provide coverage to children living in families with incomes below the federal poverty level.

These children were phased in by age group starting with the youngest. As of 1996, children 13 and under were covered and, unless there is a change in policy, all children under the age of 19 will be eligible as of the year 2002. As with the other social assistance programs operating at the time (OAA, AB, APTD, and AFDC), Medicaid utilized matching grants and strict means tests to determine eligibility.

States were allowed to set these criteria and choose the services to be covered under the program. The federal government established parameters and basic criteria, but gave the states considerable control. For whatever services the state chooses to provide, the federal government provides matching funds ranging from 50 to 83% of total costs. Specific matching formulas were consistent with those developed in the Kerr-Mills legislation of 1960. In 1995, the federal share of the $133 billion Medicaid budget was 64%. Allowable services include hospital care, nursing homes, physician services, outpatient services, diagnostic services, and prescription drugs.

States were also encouraged to provide coverage to individuals and families who qualified for the program since their income was low enough (income eligible) but were not categorically eligible for AFDC or SSI. These were referred to as medically indigent (MI) and medically needy (MN). The federal government, however, would not share in the costs of that care.

While Medicaid is a social assistance program for all age groups, the program has become a major source of support for the categorically eligible elderly and the disabled. For example, in 1995, while 36 million people received some type of Medicaid benefit,

> [c]hildren and adults in families with dependent children represented over 68% of all recipients and yet consumed only 26.2% of the expenditures. Nearly one-half of all Medicaid recipients were children (17.2 million), who consumed only 15% of all Medicaid benefits. . . . Conversely, the aged, blind and disabled represented just over a quarter of all recipients but consumed nearly three-quarters of the program benefits. (Levit et al. 1996:197)

Long-Term Care

Long-term care includes care received in nursing homes and from home health agencies. In 1995, $106.5 billion was spent in this area, with the public sector, primarily Medicaid and Medicare, accounting for 57% of these expenditures (Levit et al. 1996).

These expenditures, while representing only 12.2% of all personal health care expenditures compared to expenditures for hospital care (39.8%) and physician services (22.9%), have become a major concern.

This sector represents one of the fastest growing areas (in 1960, expenditures for long-term care were 3.8%) and will continue to grow given current demographic projections. While the overall rate of institutionalization among the elderly is between 5 and 6%, as many as 25% of the elderly will spend some time in a long-term care facility—usually a nursing home. Furthermore, 18% of those 85 years of age and older were institutionalized compared to 2% of the population between 65 and 74. In addition, the population aged 75 to 84 is also growing and is among the higher consumers of home health services.

Given demographic shifts toward a more elderly population (e.g., the frail elderly) it is conservatively estimated that institutionalization for men will increase by 53% and for women 67% by the year 2000 (Moon and Smeeding 1989). To compound this problem, nursing home costs have risen considerably. Average length of stay is 465 days and costs averaged $127 per day or more than $46,000 per year in 1995 (ibid.).

Medicaid is the major source of public funding for long-term care and an increasing proportion of Medicaid funds are spent on long-term care. In 1995, Medicaid spent a total of $36 billion on nursing home care. This single program paid over 46.5% of all nursing home costs while Medicare paid less than 10%. The rest were out-of-pocket expenditures (ibid.).

Catastrophic Illness

The latter part of the 1980s witnessed an unexpected turn in policies for the elderly. Both Congress and the administration agreed that one piece remained to be put in place if the country were to establish a comprehensive set of health care policies.

On July 1, 1988, President Reagan signed the 1988 Medicare Catastrophic Coverage Act into law. This new addition to the Social Security Act was designed to protect elderly and disabled OASDI beneficiaries who incur catastrophic medical expenses due to illness or injury. The legislation reflected three basic objectives. It would

- cap beneficiary out of pocket expenses,
- be self-financing,
- be affordable.

The basic purpose of the legislation was to assure every elderly person against financial ruin because of illness or disabling condition. The benefits therefore did not provide assistance for early costs associated with an illness but emphasized services *after* the original Medicare benefits were exhausted. The number of days of coverage for skilled nursing homes were increased and ceilings were lifted from hospice care and inpatient acute hospital care. Copayments were either removed (Part A for inpatient hospital care) or ceilings were established (Part B). Moreover, services not covered under the existing Medicare program were added, e.g., prescription drugs.

The new program was to have been funded through an across-the-board increase in the amount of premiums paid by each recipient. All would pay an additional $4 per month. A smaller group would pay still additional premiums based on their incomes and the amount of federal taxes they paid. Individual recipients would pay $22.50 for each $150 paid in taxes up to a maximum of $800 in a single year. One year after passage, the Catastrophic Illness legislation was repealed. The reasons for this and its impact will be discussed in the chapter on the elderly.

COST CONTAINMENT EFFORTS

Over a 35-year period (1960–1995), national health expenditures increased 35-fold. Moreover, public expenditures increased by 63-fold and of this, the federal spending 112-fold. These increases were considerably higher than growth in the GDP (12-fold) and population increases (43%). The federal government attempted to contain these cost increases by introducing a number of new policies and programs. Strategies to deal with this concern focus on modifying one of three factors that affect costs:

- reducing the number of consumers,
- cutting back on the volume of services provided,
- lowering the unit prices for medical care services, especially hospital costs and physician fees.

Over the past 25 years, government has developed policies to accomplish changes in one or more of these factors. The first effort focused on the third factor—the lowering of hospital costs. However, anticipating possible resistance on the part of two powerful groups representing organized medicine and hospitals, these groups were invited to participate in and assume major responsibility for achieving these goals.

Health Planning

One year after the passage of Medicare and Medicaid, Congress passed P.L. 89-749 as a first attempt to deal with rising costs. This legislation, the

Comprehensive Health Planning Act, defined the problem as one of un-necessary duplication, especially in the area of hospital beds and expensive technology. At the local level, hospitals operated as independent providers of care and demonstrated little interest in functioning as part of a larger hospital system.

As an individual hospital reached dangerously high rates of utilization, it attempted to increase its bed capacity by building new beds even if other hospitals in the community were experiencing underutilization. Moreover, all hospitals believed that to be competitive and attract patients, they had to offer the most comprehensive array of services and technology. For example, during this period, every hospital believed they needed a CAT scanner even though it might be used only intermittently. Although such equipment contributed to the rising costs of hospital care, not to have this technology might be perceived by the community as evidence of a hospital's lower capabilities.

The legislation established a number of planning bodies at the state and local level that were charged with assessing the health care needs of their community and future resource requirements if there were unmet needs. In part, this process entailed a communitywide inventory of additional resources. Together these products became the basis for that community's plan to be used as a mechanism to review requests by individual hospitals for permission to build additional beds. The health planning agency would then forward its recommendation to the state planning agency, which in turn would do its own analysis and send its recommendation with the local recommendation to Washington.

The legislation operated on the assumption that the problem was a fragmented service delivery system and that, once this became apparent, the major providers in that nonsystem would change their practices in the public interest. The planning process would efficiently and effectively identify objectives, define problems, and untangle cause-and-effect pathways to problem resolution. Planning would introduce rational perspectives and methodologies, and while decision-making was, of course, influenced and even shaped by political factors, rationality, dialogue, and persuasion were to replace ad hoc myopic problem-solving. Reason, not sanctions, was the tool of choice.

While there were examples where this approach did seem to curtail the addition of "unnecessary" hospital beds and the purchasing of extremely expensive equipment, in too many communities, rational decisions were circumvented by political end runs by hospital boards and physicians.

Congress attempted to strengthen the process by giving more power to the planning agencies. The National Health Planning and Resource Development Act of 1974 required that in order to obtain permission to expand, a hospital had to receive a Certificate of Need (CON) from the local health planning agency. This new power, however, was as susceptible to political influence as the earlier, more permissive legislation, and local planning agencies were often unable to resist the pressure to award the certificate.

Health planning was further weakened with the passage of the Omnibus Budget Reconciliation Act of 1981. Reaffirming a belief in the free market system and a less intrusive role for government, this act gave governors the option of eliminating their health planning agencies. Furthermore, it weakened existing regulatory powers and significantly reduced federal funding (McKinney 1995).

Diagnostic Related Groupings (DRGs)

Recognizing that these efforts had not achieved the goal of cost containment, Congress passed legislation in 1983 that escalated the role of the federal government from one of facilitator of and partner in a planning process to one of actually setting prices. The legislation introduced the idea of prospective payments and mandated that any hospital receiving federal dollars (i.e., Medicare) would be reimbursed only so much for providing care.

The use of DRGs—a classification system that clusters patients into 468 categories on the basis of patient illness, disease, and medical problems—provided the basis for determining these costs. Once these costs were determined, hospitals knew how much they would receive for someone with a particular DRG. If the treatment cost the hospital less (e.g., the hospital stay was shorter than the DRG allowed), the hospital "made money." If, on the other hand, the treatment costs exceeded that allowed under that particular DRG, the hospital would be financially responsible for these additional expenses. The federal government did not anticipate that there would be one set of prices for all hospitals and providers, but allowed for variation based on the type of hospital (e.g., regional hospitals, teaching hospitals, etc.) and their costs of providing care. This policy targeted the last two factors listed above, i.e., the volume of services and unit prices. While more successful than the earlier health planning efforts, by themselves DRGs did not have the hoped-for effect on rising medical care expenditures. One limitation is that they only apply to inpatient care. However, when they were coupled with more formal managed care efforts, more progress was achieved.

In 1999, Medicare spending for outpatient care will also be based on prospective payments as an attempt to meet mandated reductions in federal spending for these services. Moreover, it now appears that private payers will also introduce a prospective payment system (PPS) for inpatient hospital care.

Managed Care

During the 1940s, two independent prepayment plans, the Kaiser Foundation Health Plan and the Health Insurance Plan of Greater New York, came into being. These programs were radical departures from the traditional fee-for-service system, emphasizing the delivery of a comprehensive package of services including prevention measures for a negotiated annual fee. All needed medical care services would be provided for the participant for that fee, which could only be changed at the end of a particular year. However, while these plans demonstrated that such an approach could significantly lower hospital admission rates (Densen, Balamuth, and Shapiro 1958) and surgical rates (Anderson and Sheakley 1959), the expansion of this first "managed care" model lagged considerably. As recently as 1986, 90% of employees covered by employment-related health insurance plans were in traditional fee-for-service plans. However, by 1993, this percentage had dropped to 50% (Levit et al. 1966). This transfer, to a large degree, was the direct result of rising insurance premiums in these conventional plans and the belief on the part of employers that managed care would make this dimension of work-related costs more reasonable.

By 1995, almost one-half of the U.S. population were covered by a Health Maintenance Organization (HMO) or a somewhat less restrictive form of managed care—a Preferred Provider Organization (PPO). These plans typically charge lower average premiums than conventional plans, involve lower out-of-pocket costs to the participant, and provide for the agreed-upon premium a comprehensive array of services including not only hospital-based care but community-based services, which can result in fewer or shorter hospitalizations thus reducing the overall costs of medical care for the individual, preventive, and health maintenance services. Experience to date would suggest that managed care has been the most successful approach to cost containment. There is evidence that growth in inpatient expenditures as well as overall Medicaid expenditures has slowed because of managed care.

Reforms to Control Medicaid Costs

Up to this point, the cost containment efforts we have discussed primarily focused on two of the three factors that influence the costs of medical care: the volume of services and the prices of those services. The third factor—reducing the number of recipients or consumers—was not feasible in the programs we covered. This was not, however, seen as a constraint under the Medicaid program. Beginning in the 1980s, changes in Medicaid policies targeted all three factors.

By the early 1980s, a growing number of states were experiencing fiscal problems with rising Medicaid costs. At the same time, the Reagan administration was attempting to redefine the federal role by shifting more and more responsibility back to the states. Medicaid became a major target.

The Omnibus Budget Reconciliation Act of 1981 reduced the amount of the federal share for Medicaid but also allowed the states to develop strategies to curtail the growth of the program. Bovbjerg and Holahan (1982) report that states, over the years, attempted to deal with all three of the factors. The outcome, however, was less than hoped for. In many states, AFDC caseloads were reduced by changing the eligibility criteria, thus shifting the total costs of care to state and local governments. Physician fees were cut to the point that physicians were unwilling to accept Medicaid patients, causing these patients to seek care at higher cost hospital emergency rooms and outpatient departments. The volume of services was cut back in areas such as medications and prenatal care to the point that some recipients eventually required more intensive care at much higher costs.

Bovbjerg and Holahan suggest that the program's cost problems were inherent in the program's structure. Because Medicaid is an entitlement program, costs cannot be directly controlled through rationing or a fixed budget. Because it is a vendor payment program, prices increase during periods of inflation. And because it is an income-tested program, the number of people eligible increases during periods of high unemployment. Bovbjerg and Holahan conclude that cost containment can only be achieved through policy and program changes that allow alternatives to the fee-for-service approach. These, however, were prohibited in the legislation.

Eventually, the federal government accepted these realities and not only allowed but encouraged states to enroll their Medicaid recipients in managed care systems. Two kinds of Medicaid managed care waivers were established. The first—"freedom of choice waivers"—permitted states to require Medicaid recipients to enroll in managed care plans. The second allowed states to test new approaches through demonstrations, or pilot or experimental programs. In 1991, 9.5% of all Medicaid recipients were covered under managed cared plans. By 1995 the percentage of recipients in managed care plans increased over threefold (32.1%) or 11.6 million individuals (HCFA 1996).

The recent welfare reform initiatives will potentially reduce the numbers of Medicaid recipients significantly. Given the radical changes introduced in 1996, including the limited amount of time a family or individual will have to receive financial assistance (60 months over a lifetime); tighter eligibility criteria affecting children receiving SSI benefits due to change in disability determination; the loss of benefits to persons convicted of felony drug possession, use, or distribution; and loss of eligibility because of noncitizenship status (see Chapter 3). These persons, numbering in the hundreds of thousands, had been eligible before welfare reform and now will not be covered.

The question that must eventually be addressed is, To what extent will these changes, if enacted, produce short-term savings and long-term problems? When Medicaid caseloads were cut during the 1980s, overall costs did not go down, but were merely shifted to other payers. People still needed medical care and they found that care in public hospitals and the emergency rooms of nonprofit hospitals.

Reforms to Control Medicare Costs

More than 80% of Americans believe that Medicare has "major problems" or is in a "state of crisis" (*USA Today* / CNN / Gallup, 9 September 1995). This widespread consensus is supported by the 1996 Medicare Trustee Report, which suggests that if no changes are made in the current system, the Medicare Hospital Insurance Fund will be depleted by the year 2001. The report recommends that a strategy be found that would simultaneously increase Medicare taxes and decrease expenditure growth. This would provide sufficient time, then, to generate solutions to the long-term imbalance between costs and income (Levit et al. 1996).

To achieve the former, Congress has debated the possibility of increasing monthly premiums (Part B—the Supplementary Medical Insurance program) as much as 100% by 2002 and requiring even higher premium costs for higher income individuals. Accompanying this would be a series of annual increases in deductibles for both Part A and Part B. This strategy is, of course, similar to that proposed for the Catastrophic Illness program passed in 1988 and repealed in 1989—a strategy that was fought against by the more affluent elderly.

To decrease the growth of Medicare expenditures, two major policy changes have been discussed. The first would raise the eligibility age from 65 to 67, thus reducing the number of beneficiaries at least for a time; the second would involve the introduction of a means test into the program, similar to that proposed in the effort to reform the Social Security retirement program (OASDI). Means testing might involve some exclusionary process, e.g., individuals with incomes over a certain limit would be responsible for obtaining their own insurance, or, in conjunction with increased deductibles and premiums, they would be required to pay a much higher share of the costs than those with more moderate or lower incomes.

While the above focuses on reducing the number of beneficiaries as a way to control expenditure growth, another set of discussions focuses on more structural changes. Although persons enrolled in employee-sponsored managed care plans have increased considerably over the past 10 years (over 50% in 1995); and while the percentage of Medicaid beneficiaries enrolled in similar programs has also increased (from 12% in 1992 to 32% in 1995); most Medicare beneficiaries are enrolled in conventional fee-for-service programs. However, the number of Medicare recipients in managed care programs is growing (in 1996 there were 4.5 million enrollees representing 12% of all beneficiaries, compared to 6% in 1992; HCFA 1996). To stimulate more retirees to shift to managed care programs, a number of incentives have been discussed, including coverage of prescription drugs and the waiver of copayments.

Fundamental to these reform efforts (as well as the reforms discussed dealing with the Social Security retirement program) is the implicit questioning of the long-standing value of maintaining a system based on the concept of universal coverage. There seems to be a growing consensus that this system needs to be replaced with one that is residual in approach and selective in the provision of services if costs are to be contained.

UNRESOLVED ISSUES

The Uninsured Population

As discussed earlier, in 1965, the year Medicare and Medicaid were enacted, approximately 85% of the population were covered by some form of private health insurance. Thirty years later, this percentage dropped to 70.3%. Additionally, 15% of the population were covered by Medicare and Medicaid. (Note: these are not unduplicated counts.) Three decades later, the same percentage of the population was without health insurance or government entitlement: 15% (U.S. Bureau of the Census 1996a).

Despite the existence of Medicare and Medicaid, one-third of the poor had no health insurance, with disproportionate numbers of minorities, those with little or no education, and those who worked part-time. These are, of course, the characteristics of those who are working in the secondary labor market. Only 40% of workers earning $5 an hour or less had employers that offered any health insurance benefits. Only 13% of employees earning $5 or less had coverage for both themselves and their families. The irony of this is that these workers, who are unlikely to receive health insurance through their employment, are contributing to the insurance coverage of the aged through the mandatory Social Security tax system.

Medicaid, established to provide health coverage for the poor, only covered 46% of the poor in 1995. Children are the most vulnerable of this group. Even with the modifications discussed above that provided coverage to children whose family income was too high to meet the means test of AFDC but whose income was below the poverty level, one-fifth of all poor children—nearly 2.7 million—were income eligible for Medicaid but were neither enrolled nor covered by any other form of health insurance (Summer, Parrott, and Mann 1997).

Rise of the For-Profit Hospitals

For-profit hospitals have existed since the 1950s. However, until recently, with the exception of a few periods of growth, usually followed by a period of retrenchment, the numbers remained low relative to the number of not-for-profit and public hospitals. In 1984, there were over 5,700 community hospitals. By 1993 the number had declined to 5,300 (American Hospital Association 1994). In part this is due to a number of aspects of managed care, especially the shifting of patient care to less costly settings and cutbacks in Medicare and Medicaid payments. Not only have hospitals closed down, large numbers have merged with other institutions including for-profit hospitals.

By 1996, 15% of all hospitals operated on a for-profit basis and 86% of all of these hospitals were either owned or managed by three companies. Throughout the country there is evidence that the for-profits are attempting to expand, not only in terms of hospital care but also nursing home care, home health services, and HMOs. In fact, whereas 18% of all HMOs were for-profit in 1980, 75% were for-profit in 1995.

A basic concern is that we have little data to understand the real impact this evolution will have. There are concerns that an industry that is driven by the profit motive will develop policies that will not be in the best interest of patients. Services might be withheld because they are too costly; low- or no-revenue departments might be abolished even though they provided needed health care services; the medical needs of the poor and near poor might be ignored, especially if they do not qualify for Medicaid.

SUMMARY

Over a 60-year period, we have seen the role of government, especially that of the federal government, change from one of noninvolvement in the health care field to one that can only be described as preeminent. Initially, with the passage of the Social Security Act, the federal government expressed the belief that if at-risk people were given financial assistance, they would be able to obtain needed medical services.

Even when the federal government became more directly involved in programs such as Medical Assistance for the Aged (1959) and Medicare/Medicaid (1965), it did so on the premise that it would not interfere with the way medical care was practiced. Professionals would be in control, the fee-for-service system would not be changed, and "usual and customary fees" would be honored. Its role was compatible with that of the commercial and not-for-profit insurance companies.

As expenditures grew, government in the 1970s and early 1980s did attempt to contain costs by introducing new policies, but even these implicitly expressed a belief in the free market approach to health care delivery. In part, providers were encouraged to police their own efforts (e.g., professional standards review organizations) and, in part, they were invited to join with consumers and community leaders to develop a more rational and cost-effective system (e.g., comprehensive health planning).

Most of these efforts were recognized as ineffective in the 1980s and a period of more direct involvement began. The federal government attempted to deal with cost containment first by establishing limits to the amount it would pay providers (DRGs) in the Medicare Program. Next, following the lead of payers in the private sector, it encouraged the states to initiate a managed care approach for Medicaid recipients. This was a radical departure and involved structural change in that two key elements of the free-market system were discarded, i.e., fee-for-service and freedom to choose a provider.

Finally, developments in the 1990s show a greater move toward privatization in the health care field, especially toward for-profit providers.

Still, on the whole, these changes have been incremental. While they might depart from historical relationships between government and the private sector, they still only represent incremental modifications of the traditional medical care system, i.e., to change one of the three factors discussed above: (1) the number of recipients, (2) the volume of services provided, or (3) the prices of those services. Furthermore, most of these policies appear to emphasize a concern for rising costs and do not as aggressively target the quality issue, deteriorating health indicators.

6

Families and the Care of the Dependent

In the best tradition of the modern welfare state, this country has repeatedly expressed its commitment to meeting the basic needs of its families. Yet this same tradition has produced a series of policies, programs, and services that are often contradictory and counterproductive when assessed as a whole. This does not mean that specific policies, taken individually, have not been of value; rather it means that intervention has often created new problems in other areas or operated at cross purposes to other policies. More often than not, the secondary effects were never intended or anticipated.

For example, Aid to Families with Dependent Children (AFDC) is a program intended to provide financial support to needy families, but as designed and modified, it actually penalized two-parent families and encouraged fathers to desert (Stack and Semmel 1974). Housing policies of the 1930s were successful in providing improved shelter to tens of thousands of families who were living in tenements and slums, but often also had negative effects on neighborhoods and informal support networks (Subcommittee on Executive Reorganization 1966). Finally, recent efforts to deinstitutionalize the mentally ill and the mentally retarded, defensible on both therapeutic and economic grounds, have created increased pressure on families since the discharges have not been accompanied by a comparable expansion of community-based resources (Moroney 1986a, 1986b).

The secondary effects of these and other social policies have, in turn, generated continuous and often bitter debates. The debates can be reduced to a number of fundamental questions:

- Should services be provided as a right or made available only when individuals and families demonstrate their inability, usually financial, to meet their basic needs?
- Should benefits be provided to the total population or restricted to specific target groups, usually defined as "at risk"?
- Should government develop mechanisms to continuously improve

and promote the quality of life, or should it restrict its activities to guarantee some agreed-upon minimum level of welfare—a floor below which no one should be allowed to fall?

- Should government seek to prevent or minimize stressful situations, both environmental and personal, or should it merely react to problems as they arise?

These questions, of course, are raised and discussed in general terms in Chapter 2 and in one form or another have recurred in later chapters. Despite this ambivalence and disagreement, however, there seems to be a general consensus that when policies are proposed, the family should be considered in all deliberations. Whether for political or moral reasons, legislators argue that the family should be protected and strengthened as a basic social institution. Even a cursory review of the past 60 years shows that social legislation has been promoted on the premise that it would benefit the family and thereby benefit the country. Opponents of such action counter with the argument that the same legislation would weaken the family.

This latter position has gained considerable currency over the past 15 years. Sir Keith Joseph, a leading theorist for the Conservative party under Prime Minister Margaret Thatcher and a former minister of the Department of Health and Social Services has argued:

> They (the family and civilized values) are the foundation on which the nation is built; they are being undermined. If we cannot restore them to health, our nation can be utterly ruined, whatever economic policies we might try to follow. . . . The socialist method would try to take away from the family and its members the responsibilities which give it cohesion. Parents are being divested of their duty to provide for their family economically, of their responsibility for education, health, upbringing, morality, advice and guidance, of saving for old age, for housing. When you take responsibility away from people, you make them irresponsible. (Joseph 1974:5)

In this country, similar charges, in strikingly similar language, have been leveled at the social policies formulated in the New Deal of the 1930s and expanded in the Great Society of the 1960s. We are told, echoing Sir Keith Joseph's position, that families should not be relieved of traditional caring tasks because when this happens families begin to feel that they are neither capable of nor expected to continue their traditional responsibilities. For example, under the "profamily" banner, the New Right has argued that

> families are strong when they have a function to perform, and when government takes over the functions of a family, then as sure as the night

follows the day, families are going to disintegrate and fall apart because they have no reason to exist. . . . [T]oday we have well intentioned causes saying that we'll provide your food and we'll take care of your health, and we'll provide you with everything you really need, and then you can be a strong family. It doesn't work that way. Families are strong when they have a job to do. (Marshner 1981:163)

For over five decades the federal government had assumed a proactive stance in minimizing risk and enhancing social functioning as exemplified by the Social Security Act (e.g., retirement benefits, benefits for the handicapped and unemployment insurance), various housing programs (e.g., public housing and numerous forms of subsidized housing), and education programs (e.g., the G.I. Bill of Rights and mainstreaming the handicapped student). Today this role and function are being redefined and the federal government has taken a more reactive stance, intervening only when it is absolutely necessary to do so. Many of the New Deal and Great Society programs have been cut back, dismantled, or turned back to the states through the block grants strategy, as discussed in Chapter 1.

Proponents of both positions argue that their formulation of the welfare state provides the most effective set of guidelines for strengthening the family. How is it that one group can argue that proactive social welfare measures are the solution while another can argue that the real solution is the dismantlement of those very measures?

CHARACTERISTICS OF THE AMERICAN FAMILY

How do we deal with these anomalies? What "families" do we have in mind when we formulate policies? If policies are always proposed "with the family" in mind and if policies are proposed to "strengthen" families, how realistic is our view or understanding of the American family? How capable is the family in terms of our expectations for it to care for its own?

It is impossible to offer many generalizations or universal statements that some authority will not challenge. While one expert argues that the family as a social institution is not only dissolving but has actually become an anachronism (Zimmerman 1974), another applauds its state of health (Levy 1966), and a third maintains that though there have been some changes in family structure, the family is evolving toward a more viable form (Folsom 1943). Each position is accompanied with an impressive array of data. Each conclusion is credible if the reader is willing to accept each authority's implicit definition of what a family is and what it should be.

The single proposition that might be allowed to stand unscathed is that all societies have been characterized by some form of family structure and this unit usually carried out certain key functions. While the form of the structure, the specific ways by which the family fulfilled these functions, and the extent to which they were shared with other institutions has changed over time, there has always been, in recorded history, some basic social unit that could be called a family.

Whether family life was natural or created in the sense of a social contract is largely a matter of speculation. Regardless of how it came into being, as an institution it was more capable of fulfilling the survival needs—including both physical and social needs—of its individual members than they were on their own. Specific family functions are usually described as procreation, protection, social control, socialization, nurturance, and physical and emotional care. While major historical social scientists such as Durkheim, Weber, Tonnies, Simel, and Parsons have debated whether families have retained these functions or transferred them to other institutions, whether the nuclear or extended family is the dominant form of family structure, whether one form is superior, in theory, to the other given the demands of modern society, the more important issue is to arrive at a realistic and reasonable picture of the family and its ability to support (whatever that support is) individual members.

From whatever perspective we approach the situation of the modern family, the community and with it the traditional family are perceived to have gradually deteriorated. But is this the case? Are we, in fact, being nostalgic about the "world we have lost" (Laslett 1965), rather than being objective?

Families today do differ significantly from those of the nineteenth century and a number of those differences potentially affect a family's capability and willingness to provide social care for its dependent members. Families have become smaller. More of their members have become older and dependent as the age composition of the population has shifted upward. Women have entered the work force in significant numbers and their earnings account for an important part of the average family's total income. The number of single-parent families has increased sharply. It is clear that the family is undergoing profound and rapid change.

Perhaps the most notable of these changes is the size of the family (see Table 6.1). Almost 70 years ago, one in three families had five or more persons compared to one in seven in 1992. We also see a significant shift in the percentage of two-person families: 42% in 1992 compared to 26% in 1930. Finally, the size of the average family dropped by 20%, or almost one person.

Even though women have been marrying earlier in each successive generation since the turn of the century and theoretically were more likely

Table 6.1. Family Size 1930–1992

# Persons	1930	1940	1950	1960	1970	1980	1990	1992
2	26.1	29.3	32.8	32.3	34.5	40.0	40.8	42.0
3	22.5	24.2	25.2	21.7	20.6	24.0	23.9	23.2
4	18.8	19.3	19.8	20.5	18.8	21.0	21.1	21.1
5	12.8	11.7	11.1	12.9	12.3	9.0	9.1	9.0
6	8.1	6.8	5.6	6.5	6.7	4.0	3.2	2.9
7 or more	11.7	8.7	5.5	6.1	6.0	2.0	1.8	1.8
Mean	4.04	3.76	3.54	3.66	3.30	3.25	3.17	3.17

Source: U.S. Bureau of the Census, "Household and Family Characteristics." *Current Population Reports*, Series P-20, No. 292, Washington, DC: USGPO, 1976, p. 3; U.S. Bureau of the Census, *Statistical Abstracts of the United States*, Washington, DC: USGPO.

to have more children, the birth rate has actually dropped. Although the rate did swing upward between 1950 and 1960, it began to drop again in the 1970s.

The average number of children 75 years ago was 2.9 per family; today it is 2.2. These trends have had a significant impact on family structure and family life. For example, in the middle of the last century, the average mother was still bearing children well into her forties; by 1900, she had completed her childbearing functions at 33; and by 1990 this age had dropped to 29. Unlike her predecessor, the present-day mother is likely to have completed her child-rearing functions in her forties (although it should be noted that a small but significant number of mothers are postponing childbearing until their thirties and raising their children in their forties).

One argument for these changes is that as a society becomes more industrialized, it develops some form of social security or social insurance system. Before this, many parents, however erroneously, viewed their children as their old-age insurance, and the greater the number of children, the greater the insurance (Schottland 1963). With collective social insurance mechanisms available, the need for large families diminished. Related to this was the dramatic reduction in infant mortality rates (see Table 6.2). When the rates were extraordinarily high, the norm was to have a large number of pregnancies on the assumption that only a few children would survive. For example, it has been estimated that 100 years ago, one child in five died before reaching the age of one, and one in three died before reaching his or her fifth year. Another reason was the nonavailability and/or nonreliability of fertility control measures.

A final factor is related to changing expectations and roles of women over the past 60 years. In the past, women had fewer opportunities for careers outside the home. Furthermore, prior to World War II, mothers

Table 6.2. Birth, Infant Mortality, and Maternal Mortality Rates[a]

| | | Mortality Rates | |
Year	Birth Rates	Infant	Maternal
1920	27.7	85.8	79.9
1940	19.4	47.0	37.6
1960	23.7	26.0	3.7
1970	26.0	26.0	2.1
1980	16.0	12.6	0.1
1985	15.8	10.6	<0.1
1990	16.7	9.1	<0.1
1991	16.2	8.9	<0.1

[a] Birth rates are per thousand population; infant mortality rates are per thousand live births; maternal mortality rates are per 10 thousand live births.
Sources: U.S. Bureau of the Census, *Historical Statistics of the United States, Colonial Times to 1957,* Washington, DC: USGPO, 1960, pp. 23–25; U.S. Bureau of the Census, *Statistical Abstracts of the United States,* Washington, DC: USGPO, 1977, pp. 55, 70; 1989, pp. 61–62; National Center for Health Statistics, *Monthly Vital Statistics Report,* Vol. 41, No. 13, Washington, DC: USGPO, 1993, pp. 14–15.

were under heavy societal pressure not to work. Since then, not only has this sanction disappeared, but women have been encouraged for economic reasons to limit the size of their families. Large families are now viewed as a barrier to social mobility and to a higher standard of living. Mothers, then, having completed their childbearing function by 30, had the time and opportunity to begin or resume other careers, many with paid employment.

In 1900, 20% of women between the ages of 16 and 64 were employed. Over the next 40 years, this figure gradually rose to 26%. The figures for married women rose from slightly under 5 to 15% during this same period. Older women (45–64) were less likely to be in the labor force: 14% in 1900 and 20% in 1940.

These trends accelerated over the next 60 years, until almost 60% of all women are now employed (see Table 6.3). Even now, married women living with their husbands make up 61% of the labor force. While the total number of women in the labor force increased, by 1992 almost 68% of women with children under the age of six were working outside their homes and 54% with children under the age of one.

The reasons for these shifts are multiple and have been reported on extensively (Kanter 1978; Ridley 1968). While the specific reasons may differ by social class, they can be grouped under three major headings: (1) the need for income, either to supplement a husband's earnings or, in the

Table 6.3. Female Labor Force Participation Rates

Age	1950	1960	1970	1980	1990	1995
16–19	41.0	39.4	44.0	51.8	55.2	52.2
20–24	46.1	46.2	57.8	68.4	75.2	70.3
25–34	34.0	36.0	45.0	57.4	63.5	74.9
35–44	39.1	43.5	51.1	58.3	63.0	77.2
45–54	38.0	49.8	54.4	57.1	60.3	74.4
55–64	27.0	37.2	43.0	41.9	42.3	49.2
Total	33.9	37.8	43.4	48.4	51.4	58.9

Source: U.S. Bureau of the Census, *Current Population Reports: A Statistical Portrait of Women in the United States,* Special Studies Series P-23, No. 58, Washington, D.C.: USGPO, 1976; U.S. Department of Labor, Bureau of Labor Statistics, *Employment and Savings,* Washington, D.C.: USGPO, 1996; Hayghe (1994).

case of families where the woman is the main provider, to survive; (2) increased opportunities; and (3) the need for self-fulfillment. Not only have the stigma previously attached to working mothers and exclusionary labor practices diminished, but women are not tied down by large families and extended periods of child-rearing.

These changes have, however, created new and unanticipated pressures on today's families. Although child-rearing years have been reduced, families are faced with a growing demand from the other end of the dependency continuum: the elderly. Whereas in earlier decades of this century children were likely to be our largest group of dependents (e.g., in 1910 there were 12 children for every elderly person), today children are sharing demands on the family with their grandparents (e.g., in 1990 there were only 3 children for every elderly person).

These shifts in the dependency ratio are creating new pressures for families, especially mothers, since it is not simply a matter of transferring the care from children to elderly parents. For most families there is a significant hiatus in years. As discussed earlier, mothers were able to complete their childbearing years in their twenties and were in their early thirties when the children went to school. Fifteen to twenty years later, the new dependent group—their aged parents—needed care. Furthermore, the type of care required was not the same as required by their children.

Previously this had created fewer problems. There were fewer aged and when a family did have an aged member, some family members were available to provide care. Few mothers were employed and, more important, many families had unmarried daughters of other relatives living with them. Theoretically women in this group, especially those between the ages of 45 and 54, were the caregivers, as they were the generation immediately following the elderly group (see Table 6.4). This does not mean, of course, that the caregivers were only women in this age group.

Table 6.4. Caretaker Ratios, 1990–1994

Year	Women 45–54/ 1000 Elderly	Single Women 45–54/1000 Elderly
1900	966	76
1910	974	83
1920	983	94
1930	937	84
1940	837	72
1950	708	55
1960	625	44
1970	600	29
1980	561	25
1990	479	22
1994	456	20

This pool of potential caregivers has shrunk throughout this century. Over half the women in this age group are in the labor force. Moreover, 86% of married women between the ages of 45 and 64 are employed. These women, once a major source of caregiving, are either unavailable or working and caring. (We want to be clear on this point that we are not concluding, with regret, that this pattern of informal care is no longer available. Our point is more one of historical description. These women did provide substantial amounts of care because they were not employed).

Another characteristic of the modern family with implications for its capacity to provide care is the growing divorce rate. There is no question that divorce is becoming a common occurrence. In fact, it has been projected that between 40 and 50% of all marriages of women born between 1940 and 1944 will end in divorce. However, this trend needs to be tempered with the likelihood that 80% of divorced persons will remarry (Norton and Glick 1976).

This increase in the divorce rate can be attributed to changing attitudes and the liberalization of the divorce laws (Goode 1975). Whereas most Americans feel that divorce is preferable to an unhappy marriage and that divorce no longer carries the stigma it did in the past (Yankelovich, Skelley and White 1977), divorce still brings stress to those involved and impairs the family's ability to provide care (Heatherington, Cox, and Cox 1977; Schorr and Moen 1977).

Eighty-five per cent of all divorced women (including those with children under the age of six) are employed. Furthermore, even those who remarry will spend a considerable amount of time as the head of a single-parent family. Moreover, one in two children born in the 1970s will see his or her parents divorce or have one of his or her parents die. However, few children are in single-parent families for their entire childhood, the average period being about five or six years (Bane 1976).

While most children do live in a home with a mother and a father, the last two decades have seen a substantial increase in the number of children living in single-parent families, most of which are headed by women (see Table 6.5). The trend toward an increasing number of single-parent families is likely to continue throughout the remainder of this century. Not only has the proportion of children under six living with both parents declined during this period, but the number of children who lived only with their mothers increased from 5 million in 1960 to just over 15 million in 1993.

Not all children, however, have the same likelihood of growing up in a single-parent, female-headed family. For example, in 1993 the percentage of children living in a single-parent, female-headed family differed significantly by race and ethnicity: 21% of all white children, 32% of all Hispanic children, and 57% of African-American children were living in single-parent, female-headed households. Still, in absolute numbers, and contrary to popular belief, 72% of all children living in families headed by women are white.

Furthermore, 16% of all children live in single-parent, female-headed families in which the mother was "never married" and of these, half were born to young women who became mothers in their teens, two-thirds of whom did not finish high school. Moreover, although the average for single motherhood is one child, slightly more than 40% have had two or more children.

Although most women who are single parents work, one in three children living in a single-parent, female-headed family lives in poverty, a ratio that rises to 6 in 10 for all black children living in single-parent families. Although incomes in general have increased over the years, the income of a female-headed, single-income family continues to be just about two-thirds the income produced by male-headed, single-income families ($18,545 compared to $29,649 in 1994).

Table 6.5. Living Arrangements for Children under 18

	1960	1970	1990	1993
Total (000's)	62,124	67,090	61,537	65,502
2 Parents (%)	90.6	86.1	74.7	72.0
1 Parent (%)	9.4	13.9	26.3	23.7
with mother	87.0	86.0	92.0	87.0

Source: U.S. Bureau of the Census, "Marital Status and Living Arrangements, March, 1993," *Census Population Reports*, P20-478, Washington, DC: USGPO, 1994, Table 6.

The final trend affecting the family's capacity to provide social care is the change in the expectations that people have toward family life and marriage. These changes have produced significant tensions, especially in terms of role expectations and sex-differentiated tasks. Bott (1955) describes these tensions in terms of joint and segregated conjugal role relationships. In the former, tasks are shared; in the latter, they are differentiated along sex lines. More and more, both men and women are stating a preference for the joint conjugal role. A 1976 poll, for example found that while 90% of women preferred marriage *with* children, over half wanted both children *and* employment outside the home, a percentage that was even higher among women under thirty (61%) and women who were college graduates (65%). Approximately one-half of the men responded that they would support their wives if they wanted to work for wages (Roper and Associates 1976). A number of polls indicate that mothers and fathers, whatever their stated preference for a shared marriage, still have fairly traditional responsibilities toward child care and maintenance of the home. Yankelovich, Skelley and White (1979) reported that 78% of the respondents disagreed with the assertion, "It is the wife's responsibility to insure that the house is clean if she holds a job outside the house." And yet Yankelovich also found that women continued to have primary responsibilities in the areas of meal preparation (77%) and house cleaning (65%). When asked, "How much time does your husband spend in various household activities?" and "How much time do you think he should?" respondents' answers indicate that beyond the rhetoric of shared marriages lies the reality of sex-differentiated roles.

These findings appear to be consistent with more recent data from the 1987–1988 National Survey of Family and Households, which suggest that gender-differentiated family roles still exist, that men acknowledge that their wives do a disproportionate share of household tasks, and that wives view this as an injustice (Chadwick and Heaton 1992).

Young and Wilmott (1973) support these findings and speak of the "three job family"—a phenomenon also discussed by Poloma (1970):

[T]he assumption of a professional role by the wife does not mean a drastic change in family roles. . . . The wife was responsible for the traditional (homemaking) tasks. (p. 87)

Gordon (1973) adds:

[T]heir domestic responsibilities are not lightened to any degree . . . and thus are doubly burdened. They work full time and take care of their homes as well. (p. 93)

Summary

The trends described here are familiar facts of modern life. They are but a few of a large number of social and demographic realities reported regularly by the media. The tendency has been to treat these trends as individual statistical phenomenon and to pay little attention to their broader or combined implications. In examining these trends it is important that we avoid the romantic view that families were once better off than they are today. It is not appropriate now—if indeed it ever was—to look back nostalgically and devise policies whose primary purpose is to re-create things as we imagine, usually erroneously, they once were. Families are not worse off than they were in the past. They have undergone changes, to be sure, and these changes have taxed the coping capabilities of many families. But families have always been under pressures of some sort or another.

Despite the increasingly complex demands placed on parents, and the continuing pattern of stress and limited family support, parents are expected to carry out their tasks as if they were automatically capable and autonomous. There is mounting evidence, however, that this expectation is unrealistic. As a result, families—not just low-income families—need resources and supports to permit adequate family functioning in general.

Families are smaller than they were. When we factor in changing fertility patterns and significant increases of working women (especially mothers), it would seem that families are deterred from carrying out caring functions for their dependent members, that—on a number of levels— families are not in a position to be caregivers, and they should not be expected to be.

Still, the trends discussed above cannot be equated with problems. A dual-career family, a single-parent family, and a childless family cannot be defined as problem families. Some might be at risk in that they experience stress other family types do not. A working mother heading a family may have problems in interacting with external social service agencies and the educational system because their hours of operation conflict with her work schedule, but is she the "cause" of the problem? Similarly, families providing care to handicapped members may have problems, but more often than not, it is because the social welfare system does not support them.

Finally, the issue of defining the family or families for social policy purposes needs to be addressed. What is clear is that there is no one dominant type. There are nuclear isolated families—units with no or few contacts with other family units, extended families—units that are residentially near other kin, and modified extended families—units that are spatially dispersed, but are characterized by considerable interaction and exchange. There are families in which both spouses work, families in which only the husband works and the mother stays home to care for the children, single-parent families where the parent works and others where he or she stays home, families with and without children.

As valid as these family types are in a descriptive sense, it is simplistic and somewhat counterproductive for policy purposes to divide America's 67 million families into these categories. To do so assumes that families are static, since most data are a cross-sectional snapshot of families. A more realistic approach is to recognize and analyze the fluidity, change, and transitions as individuals live in a variety of family types over time. There are periods in the life cycle when an individual family may be one in which the father works and the mother stays home with the children. This stage is relatively short-lived when the total family life course is analyzed. There are periods, also, when women (and men) find themselves raising children without a spouse present, but again, for many this is a transition period. None of these types or stages, however, should be viewed as the dominant or "ideal" family type. No one family type is superior to another.

Effective policies and services should be sensitive to the needs and stresses of certain types of families and recognize that some families are at greater risk (in the statistical sense) than others and therefore need greater amounts of supportive services. However, to conclude that because a group of families has a greater need for services that type is "deviant" or "inferior" is spurious. The evidence, instead, suggests that all families are experiencing stress and would benefit if supportive services were made available. The evidence is equally clear that some families are experiencing greater levels of stress and need additional services. Given this, what has been our response?

THE IDEOLOGY OF OUR WELFARE STATE

Our approach to families since the depression of the 1930s can best be understood as falling under two contrasting paradigms. The first might be labeled the "old" paradigm, a paradigm that emerged during the 1930s and held center stage until the 1970s. Briefly stated, it encompasses four major principles. As a society we believed:

1. *That a number of group-identified needs warranted public action.* This is a variation of the public goods argument and the public interest rationale and would include programs ranging from public education to social insurance to national health insurance.

2. *That family life is enhanced if family caregivers are provided some relief from onerous caregiving tasks.* Examples of these policies would include homemaker/home care services for the frail elderly and respite care for parents with mentally retarded children.

3. *That social welfare organizations, both public as well as private, are efficient and responsive in meeting human needs.* Aspects of this principle include notions of imperfect market mechanisms, economies of scale, and a combination of centralized and decentralized service delivery systems.

4. *That professionals are central to the provision of effective services.* Examples of these policies are regulations that deal with staffing requirements in day care, nursing home care, and child welfare.

Under the old paradigm then, we believed that families recognized their natural obligation to care for one another. We believed, however, that families were at risk and under stress due to the rapid changes in the twentieth century. Continuing shifts in our economic system created risks and produced consequences that negatively affected the quality of family life. This, in turn, required society, through the state, to create a safety net.

Under the "new" paradigm that emerged in the 1980s, as a society we now believe:

1. *That government efforts to improve the quality of life of individuals and families are not only undesirable but are likely to be harmful.* This is a variation of the argument that governmental intervention invariably weakens families by creating dependency.

2. *That families should not be relieved of traditional caring tasks as they were under the old paradigm.* This is another variation of the dependency argument. Intervention becomes interference and will be interpreted by families as a lack of trust in their caregiving capability.

3. *That decision-making and organizational responses should be decentralized.* This assumes that the further away decision-making is from those in need, the less sensitive and responsible the effort.

4. *That professionals are self-serving and intentionally create dependency.*

Under the new paradigm, we now believe that too much has already been done, that families are spoiled, and that they need to reassume more of their traditional caregiving tasks—even if they do not want to do so.

Under the old paradigm, government assumed a proactive stance, which tended to generate policies that were universal in coverage. Under the new paradigm (actually this paradigm has its roots in nineteenth-century Poor Law tradition and utilitarianism) government assumes a reactive stance, i.e., it only intervenes when there is clearly defined pathology.

This approach, the "new paradigm," is consistent with the *residual approach* to social welfare—a concept that has been discussed in a number of chapters in this book. Fundamental to this approach is the belief that most people, most of the time, will be able to take care of their own needs. Given this, the front line of our social welfare system should be existing informal support networks, e.g., the family, the neighborhood, the churches. Only a small number will need help from the more formal and impersonal institutions beyond this immediate system. We also believe that, to some degree, when people seek help they do so because of personal or family deficits.

These perspectives are tied to deeply held notions about the family and community. The "traditional" family was seen as the basic unit of community life. As Demos suggests:

> Families were the building blocks from which all larger units of social organizations could be fashioned. A family was itself a little society. . . . The family performed a multitude of functions, both for the individual and for the aggregate to which it belonged. Thus, most of what children received by way of formal education was centered around the home hearth; likewise their training in particular vocations, in religious worship, and in what we would call good citizenship. Illness was also a matter of home care. (Demos 1983:164)

Communities then were settings in which families interacted with other families for mutual support. All of us can relate to the classic example of a barn raising—where the total community came together to build a home or barn for a new family or for an established family after theirs had burned down. Families willingly gave of their time and resources to help others with the understanding that if they ever needed help, other families would help them.

This idea of the family, real or not, is the type of family much of our policy is built around. Given this, we assume that state intervention should be considered carefully before actions are taken. Consistent with our belief that government intervention in the economy should be minimal and only after there are clear imperfections in specific markets, so also we believe that the state should not interfere with family life. Intervention should be limited to those instances where family functioning has been clearly impaired.

There is a widely held belief that family life is and should be a private matter. The family, moreover, is viewed as a sanctuary from the harsh economic world and therefore the state should not interfere. Furthermore, the family is perceived as a fragile institution, one that is "besieged," and must be protected (Lasch 1977).

This approach supports the notion of intervention in family life only when necessary. It is not that we are not interested in all families (at least so goes the argument); nor does it mean that we do not recognize that all families could use supportive services. The concern is a fundamental one: that intervention might result in families giving up their responsibilities—responsibilities they would prefer to keep. Instead of helping families remain strong caregiving units, the "support" might result in weakening the family. Intervention becomes interference. Therefore, it is argued, the more appropriate role for the state is to become involved only when there is clear evidence of family breakdown. By waiting until the family declares that it can no longer care for a handicapped member, for example, the state is assured that its involvement is necessary. There is, in conclusion, such a fine line between intervention and interference that caution is the preferred course.

This line of argument is usually supported with the assertion that families have deteriorated—an assertion based on any number of social indicators, e.g., rates of out-of-wedlock pregnancy, divorce, family violence, delinquency, adolescent pregnancies, and chronic economic dependency. The resultant list of weak family types, then, includes single-parent and "broken" families, families in which parents abuse themselves or their children, families whose adolescents behave in sexually or violently disruptive ways, and families on public welfare. The argument inevitably leads to proposals to rehabilitate these families by making them more like strong families—families that care for their own members with little outside help.

Given this emphasis, policies affecting families and children tend to be restricted to a smaller subset of families and children. These are the families that have demonstrated their inability to function and since there is sufficient evidence that pathology already exists, there is little danger that the intervention will cause harm, create dependency, or weaken the family unit. The harm has already been done; the family members have lost their ability to be independent; there is little strength to be found in the family.

In terms of expenditures, the major program targeting the family, prior to welfare reform, was the Aid to Families with Dependent Children (AFDC) program. The stated purpose of the program was to maintain children in their own home by providing income when the wage earner dies, is incapacitated, or is absent from the home. This program has, since the 1970s, provided income support to between 3 and 4 million families, and between 7 and 8 million children.

Title XX, enacted in 1974 (replaced in 1981 with the Social Services Block Grant), is another major "family" program. In some respects, Title XX evolved from the 1967 amendments to the Social Security Act, which attempted to expand social services to families at risk of becoming income dependent (AFDC)—a preventive function. As discussed earlier, Title XX mandated that at least 50% of social service expenditures go to AFDC and SSI recipients or those who were income-eligible for these programs. This gave some discretion to the states to provide services to "nonpoor" families (those whose income was 115% of the median family income). The reality, however, was that with the exception of child and adult protection services, over 90% went to income recipients or income-eligibles—the poor and very poor.

Day care for children was the largest program funded under Title XX (22% of all expenditures) and about 800,000 children received this service. Head Start is another source of funding for day care. This program, within the Office of Human Development, provides comprehensive health, educational, social, and nutritional services to approximately 350,000 children from low-income families.

Child welfare, another major source of support for families, has two major goals: (1) to strengthen the family through the provision of preventive services (e.g., counseling, parent training, and chore services), (2) to develop appropriate alternatives when necessary (e.g., foster care, and adoption). However, the primary efforts as measured in funds and services are spent in achieving the second goal.

The above approach is supported by the efforts of most policy analysts, who typically limit their concerns to specific and exceptional classes of families, e.g., poor families, minority group families, single-parent families, families with handicapped children, or otherwise "unlucky" families. Data are marshalled to show that these families experience special stresses, are uniquely "at risk," and have special needs. It is then argued, and often vigorously advocated, that such families be given special consideration in allocating scarce resources. This exceptionalist approach is not without value and, in fact, has a number of advantages. First, by focusing on discrete special groups, analysis can be narrowed and concrete recommendations made. Second, inequities can be pinpointed, including gaps and shortages in needed resources and services. And, finally, how can one argue against this approach in light of the following statistics:

- In 1994, more than 6 million children under the age of six lived in families with incomes below the poverty level—a poverty rate of 26%.
- In 1994, 20% of all children under the age of 18 lived in families with incomes below the poverty level.
- In 1994, over 9.5 million children lived in families supported by AFDC.
- In 1994, 650,000 children lived in foster homes.

- In 1990, 65,000 children lived in institutions.
- Between 1.5 and 2 million children are abused each year.
- Between 60,000 and 100,000 of these children are sexually abused each year.
- Between 10 and 20% of all families experience some form of spousal abuse.
- More than 1 in 10 teenagers become pregnant each year; over 500,000 babies are born each year to teens; 96% keep their babies.

AMBIVALENCE IN PRACTICE

While the above argument appears to be logical, rational, and even compelling—an argument that dominates the current debate—many of our policies are not as logical or rational. A few examples will make this clear.

Policy Position 1A: Children Should be Raised by Their Mothers and Not by Strangers

The family (so it is believed) throughout history has always been the major force that has provided societal stability and continuity between the past and the present by carrying out its responsibility to transmit acceptable values to its children. It is now being argued that the family has defaulted in this responsibility over the past 20 to 30 years. For the well-being of this and future generations, the family needs to reassume its responsibilities. However, families cannot achieve this if they continue to place their children in day care programs. The rationale: existing research clearly demonstrates that day care is harmful to the growth and development of children. Therefore, mothers should stay home and raise their children.

Policy Position 1B: A Variation of the Above

AFDC mothers should not be allowed to stay home, even if they have very young children, but should be required to work. Not only is this in the public interest (it would slow down the rising cost of welfare) but it is also in the mother's best interest in that she will learn to become independent. Furthermore, research strongly supports the conclusion that children benefit when placed in day care. *Therefore, AFDC mothers should leave the home and enter the labor force even if they have very young children.*

Policy Position 2A: Families Should Not Be Paid to Carry Out Natural Caregiving Functions

The very idea that society should provide financial support to families caring for handicapped members (beyond tax credits, deductions, or exemptions) is abhorrent. It is inconceivable, if not unnatural, it is argued, to pay families to provide such care. They are expected to do so. Families should want to care, whether from a sense of duty or love. The basis for this position emerges from a historical belief in what constitutes acceptable moral practices. *The payment of money to carry out "natural" family functions is viewed as unacceptable in that the moral reasons for caring—duty, love, responsibility to care for one's own—are replaced by nonaltruistic motives and the total fabric of society is threatened.*

Policy Position 2B: A Variation of the Above

Money can be given, however, to people who are willing to "serve as families." Foster parents can be paid to care for children without natural parents or whose parents are incapable of providing a caring environment. Others are paid to care for handicapped persons and the elderly residing in institutions. These people, in effect, are paid to function as substitute families—for providing for the physical and, in some instances, the social needs of the residents. Policies have been initiated to provide financial incentives to prospective adopting parents especially when the children are hard to place, e.g., older children, handicapped children, and minority children. Another example was the effort of DHHS in the mid-seventies to both prevent institutionalization of physically and mentally handicapped adults and ensure a reasonable quality of life while they lived in the community. The department, in its efforts to enable SSI recipients to "live within a family setting," increased their monthly grants by an average of 43% if they lived in a foster care type home and not by themselves. However, the same legislation reduced the monthly grant by one-third if the individual were living with his or her family. On the one hand the policy paid more money to stimulate the development of surrogate families, on the assumption that families provide better environments than institutions. On the other hand, this same policy reduced the benefit when the recipient lived with and received care from a relative. How else can you justify the higher monthly payments to foster parents and the much lower AFDC payments to natural parents? *Natural families are penalized when they care because they are "family," while unrelated persons are paid to function as families.*

We are forced to return to our earlier questions—but this time we expand them to include the notion of bilateral exchange:

- What is the most desirable, effective, and feasible division of responsibility between the family and extrafamilial institutions in meeting the needs of individuals, and in what ways can these institutions relate to each other so as to maximize benefits to families?

Earlier, we pointed out that our policies toward families are shaped by our implicit belief in a residual approach to social policy: wait until the problem occurs before doing anything. However, many today also blame the family for many of the social and economic problems facing society and argue that families have to reassume their responsibilities. To support this position of weakness and deterioration, a number of family indicators were listed. But most children do not spend their whole childhood in single-parent families. Over 47 million children live in two-parent families. Most parents do not abuse their children; nor do most spouses abuse each other. In fact, on the whole, one might argue that most families, despite the stress in their lives, are coping. The concern, however, for family well-being remains and needs to be addressed. We cannot expect that families will return to traditional ways. While a reactive approach may be less costly in the short run, it is likely to be more costly over the long run.

An Alternative Formulation

We need to reexamine some of these basic assumptions if we are to move ahead in the public debate about policies affecting families. Is it useful to continue assuming that it is the family's responsibility first, and that the state should become involved only when they cannot or will not provide the needed care? While we understand that the above has ideological value, is the introduction of a dichotomy (either the family *or* the *state*) of any practical value other than keeping expenditures down for the time being? Assuming that it does not, what competing principles or assumptions might we build our social policies on (Baldwin 1985)?

In searching for this reformulation, two major questions emerge:

1. Is social welfare (we use the term broadly to include health and social services as well as financial support) a matter of charity, of generosity, of humanity?

If the answer is yes, then the family would have no legal or moral right to what it receives. By definition, one individual cannot have a right to another's charity—it is a gift freely given. Furthermore, the type and amount of service given will vary depending on the benevolence of the giver and need not reflect the type and amount of service needed by the object of the charity.

If the answer is no:

2. Is social welfare, then, a matter of strict obligation on those who have resources?

If the answer is yes, then the recipient has a moral claim on those who are better off in society, a claim that includes rights and entitlements and will involve, in most instances, redistribution—the "taking" from those who have and the "giving" to those who do not. How do we, society, choose or decide between these two?

Are there rationales to help us choose? We introduce and discuss four major rationales that are currently used to justify intervention: (1) economic rationality, (2) compassion, (3) need, and (4) entitlement.

1. *Economic Rationality.* Many of this country's social policy, including policies affecting families, are justified under this rationale. We begin with the assumption that there are not enough resources, including money, to meet all the legitimate demands on those resources. Given this we are faced with making choices among competing demands, all of which we would probably like to fund. To complicate the situation, we are also faced with "opportunity costs," a term that simply means that if we allocate our resources to one program, we are not able to fund another program now, and perhaps in the near future. This type of thinking forces us not only to choose the objectives of one program, but also forces us to do so with a full understanding of the objectives we will not be able to achieve.

With this as a foundation, we argue that it is important that the decision to fund a particular program is the result of analysis that identifies the funding to be a "wise investment"—an investment that will provide us with an acceptable monetary return. How then, do we conclude that an investment is "wise" and that the return is acceptable? How do we conclude, furthermore, that the investment in program A is a wise investment compared to investing in program B?

This argument assumes, moreover, that investments are rational *only* when there is a return and that the most rational choice involves finding that investment with the greatest return. In theory, this position sounds not only reasonable but the flip side of the coin—that to invest in a program with a lesser return is "irrational"—is equally compelling.

This approach, sometimes referred to as the "human capital rationale," is often used as an argument to support families. We should allocate resources to children *because* they are our economic resources of the future. Our programs for the handicapped, another example, are justified on the grounds that rehabilitated persons will become independent and contribute to the general well-being of the economy by working and paying taxes instead of being dependent on welfare.

In practice, however, this approach has serious implications. First, analyses such as these require that a common denominator be used if proposed results (or benefits) from different programs are to be compared. The primary common denominator used is money (all benefits or objectives need to have a dollar value assigned) and even then, in a special way (earnings over a lifetime maintained or improved because of the program).

Furthermore, if we assume that resources are scarce and inadequate, we often find agencies and advocacy groups competing against each other—attempting to convince policymakers that their disabilities are better investments than others, e.g., the blind over the severely retarded); that some age groups are a better investment than others (e.g., adult workers over retired persons); that some families are better than others. Although each group is sincere and "rational" in what it does, the enemy becomes other groups, and survival is achieved only at the expense of others—in the planning literature this is referred to as a win-lose or "zero sum game" scenario.

Given this somewhat narrow definition of benefits, some groups in our society are "a priori" better investments than others. In a sexist society, for example, where women's salaries represent only 75% of comparable male salaries in 1995, our investment policies will always favor men over women. In a racist society where certain groups are relegated to the secondary labor market, it would be "irrational" to favor blacks, Native Americans, or Hispanics over whites. On a different level, it would also lead us to favor programs for people who are physically handicapped over programs for those who are chronically mentally ill and programs for those who are mildly mentally retarded over programs for those who are severely mentally retarded. While the surface argument is reasonable—we are not choosing between and among people, we only want to get the biggest economic return for our investment—the more subtle analysis that requires weighing the economic value of groups is disturbing, especially in a society with many inequalities.

2. Compassion. This rationale offers a different perspective. Unlike the above rationale, which supports investments only if they return more than they cost—they make economic sense—this rationale suggests that we provide services if and when the situation "touches" us.

The basis for this response, one that is ingrained in most of us, is found in Judeo-Christian teachings and, at least in part, explains our generosity to many fund-raising efforts in the voluntary sector. For example, telethons raise millions of dollars annually for children who are victims of muscular dystrophy, cancer, and other conditions. Other examples include recent efforts to raise funds for U.S. farmers who were losing their homes and livelihood, and efforts to collect food and medical supplies for starving people in third world countries.

If we were to use this rationale to justify supporting families caring for handicapped children, for example, we would, in essence, be arguing that (1) all children are vulnerable but these children are even more vulnerable; (2) while parenting in general is important, it is more difficult to raise a handicapped child; (3) disability is an unexpected crisis. The same line of argument might be made in those instances where adult children are experiencing family stress because they are providing care for a frail elderly parent.

Compassion is grounded, however, in other dynamics also. Three of these are pervasive in our culture. The first is simple. I feel "good" when I help someone else, a modern-day version of the "salvation through good works" argument. The second, and not necessarily exclusive of the first, is a variation of John Rawls's "veil of ignorance" thesis (Rawls 1971). He suggests that lacking full knowledge of future conditions (e.g., whether my future unborn child will be handicapped or not) a rational person will analyze alternative possibilities in terms of how they will negatively affect him or her and then choose the alternative that will harm him or her the least. The rational person will support the "best of the worst scenarios." While the overall strategy is clearly defensive, it is rational—though rational in a different way from the previous use of the concept, i.e., economically rational. An everyday version of this position would be, "There but for the grace of God go I," with its accompanying sense of relief (Moroney 1986a).

A third, and growing dynamic is the apparent transformation of what was initially "compassion" into frustration—frustration that the problem or condition is still with us after we have given support. A vivid example of this is the "Hands Across America" event held in the summer of 1987. With much publicity, and with the promise that "the poverty problem would be solved," millions of people formed a human chain across America to raise money. National and local media offered human interest stories, most of which showed people who were happy, who were excited, who seemed to care. They were doing something to solve a problem. A year later, when the problem of poverty was not only with us but growing, when there was evidence that more people than ever were homeless, many participants were at first confused, then frustrated, and finally an-

gry. This anger, unfortunately focused not on the causes of poverty—
such a focus would raise questions about many basic beliefs related to our
economic system; not at the organizers who represented many of our
community leaders and entertainers; but on the poor. Participants seemed
to be saying in so many words, "What right do they have to still be poor? I
stood in the hot sun for a whole day for them. How ungrateful!"

This rationale, then, can not only appeal to the more generous nature of
people, but has the potential for eventually turning us against the recipient. Compassion implies that the recipient has no rights or claims for
support. Rather, the recipient depends on the generosity and charity of
the giver—a giver who may require or even demand the recipient to act
or behave a certain way. This issue of reciprocity becomes critical (Pinker
1973; Moroney 1986a, 1986b).

3. *Need.* This rationale shifts our thinking from the provision of services to people because we "feel" for them to the position that suggests
persons with needs should be supported simply because they have needs.
This position begins with the argument that industrialization and modernization have brought with them a number of risks and consequences
that potentially affect *all* people and not just a small percentage of the
population. As a result of significant social changes, families are experiencing considerable stress.

It argues further that the free market system has not been able to
achieve a just allocation of goods and services, resulting in significant
hardships for a number of people. Social policies become essential, then,
if we are to correct social inequalities and provide a buffer to these societal stressors.

Richard Titmuss is the best known and one of the earliest proponents
of this position. As discussed in Chapter 2, within this framework, which
demonstrates strong linkages between common stressors, common risks,
and common needs, he argues the necessity of recognizing collective
responsibility on the basis of moral claims and the ethics of mutual aid
and cooperation (Titmuss 1968, 1971). Social policy, he suggests, is concerned with different types of moral transactions embodying notions of
exchange or reciprocal obligations necessary to bring about and maintain
community relations. Others such as Boulding (1967), Macbeath (1957),
and Tawney (1961) support this position.

To speak of moral claims and the ethics of mutual aid and cooperation
is to speak of community. Boulding, in fact, argues that the major purpose
of social policy is to build the identity of persons around some community because we need to be concerned with questions of identity and
alienation. While integrated people believe in common risk and common
need, the alienated attempt to destroy any sense of shared responsibility.

The glue of this moral sense of community is the notion of trust: I will give to others who have a need because I believe that, if and when I have a need, some one will give to me. Not only this, but I have responsibilities to people I do not even know (the "community of strangers") and they have responsibilities toward me. This is, of course, the rationale behind our intergenerational Social Security system. We are paying into the system to support currently retired persons, trusting that a generation to come will contribute when we are retired.

4. *Rights or Entitlements.* While for thousands of years many authors have offered insights into the issue of rights, I will briefly comment on the formulations of only two: John Rawls and Alastair MacIntyre. MacIntyre (1981) suggests that when we address the question of rights, we are confronted with the issue of claims that need to be validated. Those that can be validated, we accept as "rights"; those that cannot be validated, we reject. This validation process, in turn, usually involves some reference to law, custom, or logic. Under the first category, law, the process usually involves an interpretation of existing law (including the Constitution) to cover additional categories. Within this framework, for example, we might argue that P.L. 94-142 (Education for the Handicapped) was an *extension* of existing civil rights legislation, which in turn was validated in the Constitution. The second, custom, involves another type of argument— one that would eventually rest on the prevailing sense of what a moral community is or should be. Within this framework, we might argue that P.L. 94-142 was a *good* policy. Finally, an appeal to logic would involve not only the argument that such a policy was good, but would require our demonstrating how this is logically consistent with a whole value system (Dokecki et al. 1986). MacIntyre continues to argue that once a right has been validated, we assign it a moral status. Finally, he concludes that the entitlement that evolves from the right will have contractual dimensions and often will result in some compensation.

Rawls offers a different perspective—that of "justice as fairness"— though he does conclude with a formulation of rights based on contract theory. Today, many professionals in the human services are familiar with his principles (1971:302–3):

- Each person is to have an equal right to the most extensive total system of equal basic liberties compatible with a similar system of liberty for all.
- Social and economic inequalities are to be arranged so that they are both (a) to the greatest benefit of the least advantaged, (b) attached to offices and positions open to all under conditions of fair equality of opportunity.

- All social primary goods—liberty and opportunity, income and wealth, and the bases of self-respect—are to be distributed equally unless an unequal distribution of any or all of these goods is to the advantage of the least favored.

This formulation is appealing to the issue of family care: a case can be made that handicapped persons are at a disadvantage compared to non-handicapped persons; parents of retarded children compared to parents with nonhandicapped children; adult children caring for frail elderly parents compared to adult children whose aged parents are able to care for themselves. We might even be able to extend the argument to single-parent families. Children growing up in single-parent families are at greater risk than children growing up in two-parent families (i.e., in theory, two parents constitute twice the resources as one) and therefore should receive more if both families are to be treated fairly.

The use of the argument as a single rationale has some serious limitations because it is grounded in contract theory. Contract theory is appealing to most people, of course, since it is a long-standing part of our history. Beginning with the American Revolution, we have emphasized the *contractual rights* of people. This position was articulated initially in the Constitution and the Bill of Rights and has become the major emphasis in our approach to social policy. Important legal milestones in this policy include:

- the landmark 1954 Supreme Court decision (*Brown v. Board of Education, Topeka*) guaranteeing blacks and minorities educational rights;
- civil rights legislation beginning in the 1960s, guaranteeing voting rights, nondiscriminatory hiring practices, fair housing, etc.;
- PL 94-142, which guarantees mentally retarded and other handicapped persons access to the public school system.

Given our history, such an emphasis is understandable. The American Revolution was sparked, in part, because of oppressive measures introduced by the British government—measures that infringed on the rights of citizens. Rothman (1979) points out that most of the "rights" expressed in the *Bill of Rights* are written as negative statements, e.g., "Congress shall make no law. . . . No person . . . shall be compelled . . . " and suggests that this preoccupation with rights grew out of a profound mistrust of government.

Such an approach assumes an adversarial society, one in which people relate to others as competitors. Lowi (1969) describes this as "interest group liberalism." Furthermore, in emphasizing rights, we begin any problem-solving process with the position that some groups are being treated unfairly or unequally by others, whether these "others" are institutions such as government or educational systems, or individuals such as employers or landlords. Moreover, our policy instruments (e.g., laws, regulations, and sanctions), which are intended to coerce compliance, often end up being divisive and weaken feelings of community.

Rothman goes on to say that the expansion of rights only responds to a part of the problem, insofar as it does not address the equally important issue of needs:

> [There are] imbalances in economic and social power, in inherited physical constitutions, that demand redress. . . . To this end advocates of the liberty (rights) model are far more comfortable with an adversarial approach, an open admission of conflict of interest, than with equality with its presumption of harmony of interest. (1979:92)

Can we as a society continue to recognize and respect rights and ignore needs? Of what value is it to grant people rights to inadequate or nonexistent resources—a problem that is endemic when we analyze, for example, the needs of the chronically mentally ill in this country? A second troublesome point is the possibility that if used alone, this rationale could, like the economic rationality argument discussed above, lead to competition between groups claiming they more nearly comply with Rawls's principles compared to other claimants for these same scarce resources.

TOWARD A REFORMULATION: A SYNTHESIS OF JUSTICE AND NEED

In developing any rationale for intervening in the lives of families caring for dependent members and meeting the social, physical, and emotional needs of its members, we will, of necessity, begin with the notion of "community" and the idea that we have responsibility for each other's well-being.

If we were to apply this rationale, the argument would probably be as follows. First, a relatively small number of "families" are raising a majority of the children in our society. (In this country as in Western Europe, approximately one-third of the families are currently raising 70% of the children). Since children cause financial burdens on the families who raise them (it was Gunnar Myrdal, the Swedish economist who first pointed out that "children were the major cause of poverty") *and* since children are our "resources for the future" (the idea of intergenerational responsibility), all of us have some responsibility to support those parents who are actively raising children. If we were to continue to hold in this country that children are the sole responsibility of their parents who brought them into the world and that the rest of us have no responsibility in easing the financial burden, we should not be surprised when these same children, when they become adults, refuse to support us (through the Social Security system) who will then be retired and dependent on that system for our basic medical and financial support. They are *our* responsibility, whether they are being raised by two-parent families, single-parent families, or adolescent mothers who never marry; whether they are white, black, Hispanic, Native American, or Asian; whether they are handicapped or not.

Next, we need to reexamine the concept of justice. Rawls's concern for justice does allow for treating people equally, only if the beneficiary of such treatment is the least advantaged. This principle becomes clear when we apply it to the human services. To offer equal services to people in unequal situations is *not* to offer equality. Such an approach merely underwrites the existing inequalities between and among people. In Chapter 2, we introduced Titmuss's argument for "positive discrimination," a concept compatible with Rawls's position with one exception. Titmuss believed that such positive discrimination needed to be built on a universal infrastructure and not a separate system.

Principles drawn from comparative justice are helpful because this view holds that like cases be treated alike and different cases be treated differently (Watson 1980). Certain differences—those based on the notion that special needs, justified as societally important (MacIntyre's formulation of validation discussed earlier)—call for special help, which may result in policy-produced advantages that are warranted. In this case, however, *all* members of a justifiable special need group are entitled to this advantage. Income tax credits for child care may be an example of unwarranted advantages; persons not earning enough to pay taxes, but with equal or greater need than those of higher incomes, are denied the benefit. An example of a warranted advantage would be the children's allowances granted by most Western countries to families with children. All families, regardless of income, are beneficiaries.

If we were to move in this direction, we would begin to balance our preoccupation with rights with an equally important concern for need in the tradition of Tawney (1946), who argued for justice; of Marshall (1972), who suggests that citizenship be the basis for social policy; and Titmuss (1971), who argued for and demonstrated the societal value of altruism with its foundation in beliefs of shared common need and responsibility for others.

SUMMARY

By underestimating these stresses and risks encountered by all families in American society, the residual approach encourages stigmatization of families designated by public policies as needing special consideration. Since self-sufficiency and independence are powerfully sanctioned social values, the stigmatization related to being placed in a dependent position by these policies and programs is often accompanied by substantial loss of perceived status and self-esteem. In addition, families ignored for special attention are not likely to seek external resources and support, even when they experience the inevitable difficulties of American life. Reluctance to seek help is particularly strong among parents (regarding their child rearing responsibilities), who often view it as an admission of weakness or pathology

Kahn and Kamerman (1975) also argue against the residual approach and for universalist provision of services for all families. They point out that rich and relatively fortunate people also receive "benefits and services assigned for important public reasons, in the public interest, and not achieved through market place transactions" (p. ix). These social welfare benefits include agricultural subsidies, and tax deductions for interest on real estate loans and business expenses. In arguing for the concept of "public social utilities" they state:

> Society masks realities by distinguishing among what it calls public welfare and social services for the poor and troubled, and education and public health protection for everyone, and benefits for the affluent. It fails to recognize that, in a more basic sense, there are really two categories, not three: social services and benefits connected to problems and breakdowns (and these are not limited to the poor), and *social services and benefits needed by average people under ordinary circumstances.* (ibid.:x, emphasis in original)

This in no way argues against or diminishes the need to meet the needs of those families who are poor. The framework offered toward the end of the chapter, in fact, strongly supports the development of priorities based on need. It does, however, argue against the continuing strategy of establishing separate systems for the poor and the nonpoor. The issue of means testing, introduced at the beginning of this book, still needs to be addressed. Is it an essential component of the present-day concern to become more efficient and to reduce dependency, or can these objectives be achieved without this process, which so many argue is demeaning to a potential recipient? In separating we stigmatize no less than *Plessy v. Ferguson* did 100 years ago. By offering separate services we continue to divide an already fragmented society.

CHAPTER

7

Policies for the Elderly

In the last public speech of his life in 1977, Hubert Humphrey challenged us with the following:

> The moral test of a society is how it treats those in the dawn of life—its children; those in the twilight of life—the elderly; and those in the shadow of life—the sick, the needy and the handicapped. (*Washington Post*, May 13, 1977, p. 8)

While the evidence would suggest that our commitment to children and the poor has been mixed at best and negligent at worst, there is little question that the group of people referred to as the aged, the elderly, senior citizens, or retirees have not been neglected, nor have they been slighted. In the previous chapters we have seen that those "in the dawn of life" and those "in the shadow of life" have not been treated well, especially if they are doubly at risk, if they are in both groups.

Not only has there been a commitment to the elderly, but this commitment has not been made to any other population group within our society. We need only look to the Older Americans Act passed in 1965 for such an expression of this formal commitment. Title 1 of the act lists ten objectives Congress has established:

    1.   An adequate income in retirement in accordance with the American standard of living.

    2.   The best possible physical and mental health which science can make available without regard to economic status.

    3.   Suitable housing, independently selected, designed and located with reference to special needs and available at costs which older persons can afford.

    4.   Full restorative services for those who require institutional care.

    5.   Opportunity for employment with no discriminatory personnel practices because of age.

    6.   Retirement in health, honor, dignity, after years of contributions to the economy.

7. Pursuit of meaningful activity within the widest range of civic, cultural and recreational activities.

8. Efficient community service including access to low cost transportation, which provide social assistance in a coordinated manner and which are readily available when needed.

9. Immediate benefit from proven research knowledge which can sustain and improve health and happiness.

10. Freedom, independence and free exercise of individual initiative in planning and managing their own lives. (U.S. Department of Health, Education and Welfare 1974:2–3)

Congress not only established a set of principles or a philosophical position for this group; it has made a concrete commitment to achieving those objectives by consistently approving policies and programs and by appropriating the funds necessary for their implementation. Today, this population group, which accounts for 12.5% of the population, roughly 33.5 million people, consumes 30% of all federal expenditures (Schick and Schick 1994). Such, however, has not always been the case.

PRE-TWENTIETH-CENTURY ATTITUDES AND PRACTICES

Morris (1986) provides us with a fascinating historical analysis of the process and dynamics of caregiving. With a broad brush, he covers almost 3,000 years of societal responses toward the vulnerable, i.e., the elderly, widows and their children, and the handicapped. It is fascinating, because he combines the more recognizable approaches of policy analysis with methods drawn from the tradition of hermeneutics and exegesis. Based on his analysis of texts such as the Hebrew Testament; writers such as Homer, Plato, Aristotle, Demosthenes, Seneca, Cicero, and Marcus Aurelius of the early Greek and Roman worlds; the Christian Testament and writings of the Fathers of the Church; Morris concludes:

> Throughout this history it is possible to trace a continuing tension between the unfairness, the brutality and the injustices encountered in the real world on the one hand and the attempts to introduce and to impose more civilizing, humane ideals upon peoples and leaders struggling in an imperfect world. A moral code evolved about behaviors in relation to real life conditions. (p. 68)

What emerges in Morris's analysis is not a linear progression of the practices and dynamics of care to the vulnerable, nor a common rationale. Whereas the Jewish tradition emphasized justice as the guiding principle, the early Greeks stressed reciprocity, the Romans stressed citizenship, and the early Christians operated within a sense of moral and spiritual obligation. What is common to all is the apparent belief that dependency and therefore caring for dependent persons are not negative phenomena. Vulnerability was an all too common occurrence, and therefore the vulnerable needed protection and support. All of these societies seemed concerned with the issue of community and the importance of building and strengthening social cohesion.

This sense of responsibility took a sharp turn in the fourteenth century, when deep cracks began to appear in the feudal system. For over 700 years, the needs of most Europeans were met by the church and the manor. Serfs were required to give complete obedience to their masters, personal freedoms were nonexistent, mobility was unthinkable; but all physical (and spiritual) needs were met. The coming of the Black Death in 1348, however, forever changed this system. Between 1348 and 1471, the bubonic plague decimated the population of most European countries, creating a number of crises. The first, and probably the most important, was the erosion of authority. Authority figures, whether they were secular or religious, literally abandoned the estates and villages when the plague came. The hold that these leaders had over the serfs was broken. Second, with so many deaths, the serfs found that they were able to sell their labor services to the highest bidder. No longer were they tied to a particular place but were free to move about, and as importantly, they found themselves in a position to demand wages for their work and not depend on the good graces of the manor lord. Thus began a 200-year period of social instability. While men, women, and children were free to move about and work for whom they wished, these same people found that no one had responsibility to care for them when there was no work. When these "hordes of vagrants" moved from place to place, they created an atmosphere of fear, fear of violence, and fear of civil unrest:

> Poverty was a potential danger to the state, and was therefore, a peril to the King. At a time when no monarch was so firmly seated on the throne that he, or she, did not fear rebellion; persons went up and down the country side, starving and discontented, and linking up the country with a web of dissatisfaction. . . . [They] were regarded as a menace. . . . In short, the poor must be relieved, if not on religious grounds, then for the sake of ensuring political stability. (Marshall 1969:17)

During this period, numerous laws were passed that attempted to control wages and limit mobility (the Statute of Laborers enacted in 1349 was the first of a series of laws passed over the next hundred years). People were required to obtain "letters of authorization" if they were going to travel from one village to another, and those found without such letters were severely punished. The "ablebodied" were required to work, charity was banned, and begging became a crime.

The period up to the fourteenth century is characterized as an era when vulnerable individuals and families were cared for because they were members of a community and as such had legitimate claims for support. The period following the plague can be characterized as the beginning of an era when rationales such as community and social cohesion lost their significance, to be replaced with punitive legislation that coerced families to care for their vulnerable under the threat of harsh civil penalties.

Over the next four centuries, various amendments were made to the Poor Laws (the most noteworthy being the Elizabethan Poor Laws enacted in 1601) that attempted to resolve the problem of care for the vulnerable, apparently with little success:

> It appears from the whole Evidence that the clause of the 43rd Eliz., which directs the parents and children of the impotent to be assessed for their support, is very seldom enforced. In any ordinary state of society, we much doubt the wisdom of such an enactment. The duty of supporting parents and children in old age or infirmity is so strongly enforced by our natural feelings, that it is well performed, even among savages, and almost always in a nation deserving the name of civilized. (Report of the Poor Law Commission of 1832, 1905:43)

The nineteenth-century family, particularly three-generational families, had only the institution of the Poor Law—primarily the workhouse—to look to for assistance, and for a number of families, this was either not acceptable or they could not meet the strict eligibility criteria. Dependents were kept in the home but often at a high cost in both material and psychological well-being. Care was provided to the old and the handicapped: But what kind of care? Was it offered freely and with affection or was it perceived as something that had to be done, something to which there were no alternatives?

Testimony presented to the Royal Commission on the Poor Laws offers a rather bleak picture of the status of the elderly in that century:

> The large majority of those who endure biting poverty without seeking relief from Guardians are women. Men do not so frequently attain old age under disadvantageous circumstances as women do. Old men go more readily into the workhouse than old women. Women struggle longer and with greater determination with the difficulties of poverty and the incapacities of old age. Families in poor circumstances find it less possible to provide food and shelter for an old man who is a relative than for an old woman. He is more in the way, he expects not only a larger portion of the food, but to share in the better portions. He does not fit into the household

of a working family as an old woman does and is not as useful in domestic matters. His welcome is colder . . . a decent old woman will cling to a home where she may be regarded as a drudge . . . and she will exist on the plainer portions of the meals and will wedge in both day and night without encroaching much on the means of the family. (Report of the Royal Commission 1909:259)

Stephen Marcus (1979), in a fascinating essay, blends an analysis of historical documents and literature to describe the impact of the Victorian Poor Law on the lives of the average nineteenth-century family. His retelling of Wordsworth's story of the "Old Cumberland Beggar's" desire to stay out of the workhouse and of Betty Higden's (a character from Dickens's *Our Mutual Friend*) extraordinary efforts to die "free" are moving. One of Higden's final speeches is particularly insightful as to how the elderly felt about the Poor Law:

"Dislike the mention [of the poorhouse]?" answered the old woman. "Kill me sooner than take me there. Throw this pretty child under carthorse's feet and a loaded wagon sooner than take him there. Come and find us all a-dying, and set a light to us all where we lie, and let us blaze away with the house into a heap of cinders, sooner than move a corpse of us there. . . . Your old granny is nigher fourscore year than three score and ten. She never begged nor had a penny of the Union money in her life. She paid scot and she paid lot when she had the money to pay; she worked when she could, and she starved when she must. You pray that your granny may have strength enough left her at last . . . to get up from her bed and run and hide herself, and sworn to death in a hole, sooner than fall into the hands of those Cruel Jacks we read of, that dodge and drive, and worry, and weary, and scorn and shame the decent poor." (pp. 58–59)

During this transition from an agricultural to an industrial society there were bound to be casualties. The traditional extended family may have become nonfunctional, but the isolated nuclear family—although suited to the needs of the economic system—was probably as ineffective in meeting the new pressures. Anderson seems to support this notion of a period of uncertainty for families and suggests that families only became viable caregivers in the twentieth century:

It was probably only after the introduction of the old age pension had transferred much of the economic burden of old age from kin . . . that a really strong, effective and non-calculative commitment to the kinship net could develop and "traditional" community solidarity become possible. (1971:178)

He, like others, concluded that early developments of the welfare state in this century had a positive effect on the quality of life of the elderly. By removing the economic strain and establishing an income maintenance floor, families were finally capable of providing other forms of support.

SUPPORT FOR GOVERNMENT PROGRAMS
THAT TARGET THE ELDERLY

Since the middle of this century, the elderly as a constituency have enjoyed a relatively privileged political status. Efforts in the United States to extend government programs as a right of citizenship have not succeeded— with the exception of the elderly. In 1949, Harry Truman rejected a comprehensive national health insurance proposal and introduced a program targeted at the health care needs of the elderly. This began the process that eventually created Medicare in 1965 (Austin and Loeb 1982). Supplemental Security Income (SSI) grew out of an unsuccessful attempt to pass Nixon's Family Assistance Plan. Rather than the proposed guaranteed minimum income for families, SSI provides an income floor for low-income elderly, the blind, and disabled. The social policy distinction between "worthy" and "unworthy" has tended to favor the elderly. In 1995, the government spent approximately $450 billion on entitlement programs for the elderly, constituting about 30% of all federal spending that year. There are signs, however, that public support for the political privilege enjoyed by the elderly for the past 60 years might be eroding.

The image of the elderly as a "more" worthy constituency has come under attack in the latter part of this century. Age-based policies such as OASI and Medicare reinforce the notion that the elderly are a relatively homogeneous, classless group with similar characteristics and needs. While this may have been more or less accurate in the beginning of this century, it is not the case today. Our image of the elderly is no longer typified by Dickens's "old woman in the poorhouse." As a result of this changing image, continued support for entitlement programs has become one of the most hotly contested policy debates.

Those who argue a residual role for government promote a vision of the typical elderly person as an asset-wealthy senior who pays little in taxes and enjoys a long retirement on Social Security, financed on the backs of current employees. A logical extension of this vision is that entitlement programs are an appropriate place to "trim the fat."

In contrast, those who favor the institutional model of social welfare promote a vision of the elderly as isolated, physically infirm, and on the brink of poverty. The true status of the elderly, however, is likely someplace in the middle.

TOWARD A TWENTY-FIRST-CENTURY VISION
OF THE ELDERLY

Chapter 2 discussed the role of the policy analyst as raising the level of the policy debate by (1) debunking myths and stereotypes through the provision of data and (2) unearthing the normative questions. There are many factors, both complex and interrelated, that affect the elderly's need for services and their participation in government programs. The remainder of this chapter presents a historical and projected account of key demographic and economic variables that influence program participation and dependency among the elderly. Data are presented on population, life expectancy, gender, marital status, living arrangements, health, education, labor force participation, and income. Given this broad context of the elderly generated by data, we conclude with a discussion of the major entitlement programs and the implications changing them would produce.

The Aging of America

The one well-known fact about the elderly is that they are growing as a population. Two trends, a decline in fertility and a rise in longevity, have combined to increase the proportion of elderly, those over age 65 (see Table 7.1). The elderly, who comprised 1 in every 25 Americans in 1900,

Table 7.1. Elderly as a Percentage of the Total Population and Trends in Life Expectancy

Year	Population over age 65 (%)	Life expectancy (years)	
		Female	Male
1900	4.1	49.0	46.4
1910	4.3	53.6	50.1
1920	4.7	56.3	54.5
1930	5.4	61.3	58.0
1940	6.8	65.7	61.4
1950	8.0	71.1	65.6
1960	9.1	73.2	66.7
1970	9.7	74.9	67.1
1980	11.1	77.5	69.9
1990	12.3	78.8	71.1
2000[a]	12.4	79.7	72.6
2030	25.0	81.8	75.3

Source: Committee on Ways and Means (1994:855), Schick and Schick (1994).
[a]All data beyond 1990 are projections.

and 1 in 8 in 1994, are estimated to increase to 1 in every 4 persons by the year 2030 (Administration on Aging 1997). As the baby boomers—the 75 million people born in the United States between 1946 and 1964—reach age 65, growth of the elderly population will become rapid.

Age Distribution

In colonial times, most people never reached "old age" as we know it today. In the beginning of the nineteenth century life expectancy is estimated to have been approximately 35 years. At the beginning of this century, it had been raised to 47 years. As this trend continues those born in the year 2000 can expect to live to age 75. This dramatic increase is largely attributable to improved health behaviors such as reduced smoking and increased physical activity, and biomedical technological innovations such as the use of vitamin E to reduce circulatory disease risks and control adult-onset diabetes (Singer and Manton 1993).

While the total population will have increased by 270% during this century, the elderly population will have increased by 820%, the population over 74 by 1,529% and the population over 84 by a staggering 2,690% (see Table 7.2). In real terms, this means that by the year 2000 there will be 14 million people over age 74 (an absolute increase of 2.4 million) and 2.6 million people over 84 years of age (an absolute increase of 600,000). As life expectancy increases, so does the proportion of the "oldest" old, those aged 85 and over. The oldest old, who numbered 3 million in 1994, are expected to grow to 19 million by the year 2050 (U.S. Bureau of the Census 1995).

Gender Composition

Another facet of these demographic shifts worth noting is the gender composition of the elderly population (see Table 7.3). From 1910 until 1930, 50% of the aged were female. Among the elderly over age 74, there

Table 7.2. Increase of the Elderly Population (%)

	1900–1950	1951–2000	1900–2000
Total population	100	85	270
Over age 65	247	165	820
Over age 75	334	275	1,529
Over age 85	385	473	2,690

Table 7.3. Age and Gender Distribution of The Elderly

| Year | Population 65 and older (000s) | Distribution by age and gender | | | | | |
| | | 65–74 | | 75–84 | | 85 plus | |
		Female	Male	Female	Male	Female	Male
1940	9,556	35.8	34.8	13.4	11.9	2.3	1.7
1950	12,807	35.7	32.6	14.7	12.2	2.8	2.0
1960	17,268	35.7	30.2	16.3	12.2	3.5	2.2
1970	20,892	34.7	26.9	19.2	12.4	4.6	2.4
1980	26,125	33.9	26.3	19.3	11.3	6.5	2.8
1990	31,995	31.8	25.9	19.8	12.1	7.5	2.9
2000	35,170	28.5	23.9	21.4	13.8	9.0	3.5
2025	60,599	31.0	27.8	17.8	13.0	7.3	3.2

Source: Committee on Ways and Means (1994:854).

were approximately 92 males for each 100 females. By 1960, the ratio of males to females had dropped to 83 (75 for those over age 74), and by the turn of the century the ratio will have decreased to 65 and 52, respectively. Not only will there be more elderly women, but they are also likely to be older than elderly men. The more significant differences are found in the over-84 age group. By the year 2025, not only will there be over 6 million people this old, but over 4 million, or 7 of every 10 will be female.

Marital Status

Over the past few decades there has been a consistent shift in the marital status of the elderly. Longer life expectancies and higher rates of marriage have increased the likelihood of being married in old age for both men and women. Age and gender differences in mortality rates, however, contribute significantly to gender differences in marital status—particularly in later life (see Table 7.4). While most elderly men are married, most elderly women are not—an enduring pattern that is expected to continue for the next several decades. In 1960, elderly men aged 65 to 74 were almost twice as likely as their female counterparts to be married, three times as likely among those aged 75 and above. In 1992, 70.2% of men aged 75 and over were married, compared to 25.6% of women. Women aged 75 and older, because of their lower remarriage rates (elderly widowed men remarry about seven times more often than elderly widowed women) and the premature mortality of men, are almost three times as likely to be widowed. Thus, while most elderly men have a spouse to provide social support, most elderly women do not.

Table 7.4. Marital Status of the Elderly Population by Age and Gender (%)[a]

	1960		1980		1992	
	65–74	75 plus	65–74	75 plus	65–74	75 plus
Female (N)[b]	5,529	3,054	8,549	5,411	10,174	7,616
married	45.6	21.8	50.1	23.3	53.0	25.6
widowed	44.4	68.3	40.3	68.0	35.9	65.0
divorced	1.7	1.2	4.0	2.3	6.7	4.0
never married	8.4	8.6	5.6	6.4	4.4	5.4
Male (N)[b]	4,778	2,280	6,459	3,234	8,266	4,533
married	78.9	59.1	81.6	69.4	79.1	70.2
widowed	12.7	31.6	8.5	24.0	10.2	23.7
divorced	1.7	1.5	4.4	2.2	6.1	2.6
never married	6.7	7.8	5.4	4.4	4.6	3.5

Source: Committee on Ways and Means (1994:857).
[a]Civilian noninstitutional population only.
[b]Numbers reported in thousands.

Living Arrangements

Over the past 30 years, between 5 and 6% of the elderly population have been residents in institutions at the time of the decennial census. Most of these people are in nursing homes, homes for the aged, and mental hospitals. Institutionalization is clearly related to age. Since 1950, the rates of institutionalization for the younger elderly have actually decreased, while the major increases have been in the older groups, especially among those over 84 years of age. From Table 7.5 we see that it is the oldest elderly group that is the fastest growing nursing home population. While 1% of those aged 65 to 74 years lived in a nursing home in 1990, nearly one in four aged 85 and over did (U.S. Bureau of the Census 1995). Between 1980 and 1990, the nursing home population increased by 24%, from 1.4 million to 1.8 million (U.S. Department of Health and Human Services 1997). The number of nursing home residents between 1985 and 1995 was up only 4%, despite an 18% increase in the population aged 65 and over. Prior to 1995, utilization rates had kept pace with the increase in the elderly population. This recent shift is attributed to the growth in home health care as well as advances in medical technology.

These numbers and rates must, however, be put in perspective. All too often policy analysts emphasize the negative aspects of conditions, providing a somewhat distorted picture of reality. This approach assumes that since the acceptable paradigm of social welfare in this country is residual, and since most people, including elected officials, support the

Table 7.5. Institutional Population by Age (%)

Age	1950	1960	1980	Change 1950–1980
65–69	1.78	1.77	1.67	−6
70–74	2.55	2.64	2.68	+5
75–84	4.73	6.89	7.96	+49
Over 84	9.41	12.63	18.0	+191

Source: Adapted from U.S. Bureau of the Census, *Census of Populations,* 1953, 1963, 1984.

belief that government should not become involved in the lives of individuals and families until there is evidence of pathology, policy analysis and policy proposals should be limited by these parameters. A major proponent of this view is Steiner, who discusses this emphasis in his studies of public welfare (1971), child welfare (1976), and family policy (1981). Given this view, many analysts and advocates, wittingly or unwittingly, argue as convincingly as they are capable that the problems and needs of a target population are overwhelming and that action to ameliorate the situation should be taken. The distortion arises when these same analysts and advocates deemphasize the positive aspects. To some degree such has been the case with regard to the elderly.

And yet, the quality of life for most elderly has improved considerably, not only since the Poor Law began to be dismantled with the passage of the Social Security Act of 1935, but even more so over the past 30 years. During this period, most of the elderly—between 94 and 95%—lived in noninstitutional settings.

Adult children represent an important source of noninstitutional care for the elderly. Approximately 12.5%, almost 4 million elderly persons, were living as dependents with their children or other relatives in 1992, down from 17% in 1980. Of this group, 52% were aged 75 and over and 76% were women. Most of these persons are severely handicapped and incapable of living independently.

The availability of adult children varies by age and race. For persons aged 85 and over, the percentages of men and women married with children are much lower than for the age group 65 to 84. The proportions, however, of married and unmarried persons with at least one child are projected to increase markedly between 1990 and 2020. The increase in the proportion of elderly with an adult child is affected by the higher survival rate for women who have children and the general rise in marriage and fertility since the 1930s. African-American elderly, however, are more likely than their white counterparts to be childless, and Hispanic elderly are less likely than whites to be childless. Overall, only about 8% of the aged 85 and over group will be unmarried and without children by the year 2020 (Administration on Aging 1996). This means that in the near future a smaller proportion of the elderly will be without an adult child or a spouse as a potential source of support.

The majority of elderly do not live in institutions or with their children, but live in self-maintained residences. In fact one-fifth of all households are maintained by a person or persons aged 65 years or over, and this proportion is expected to increase between now and the year 2010 (Administration on Aging 1996). The households of elderly persons are mostly maintained by married couples (45%) or by older women (35%). As the age of the householder increases to 75 and over, the proportion of married-couple households decreases (34.9%), and the number of lone female households increases (44.6%) (see Table 7.6). Projections indicate that 45% of elderly householders aged 85 and over will live alone by the year 2020. Single-male households are much less common, accounting for approximately 10% of the total of all elderly households. Elderly female householders are more than three times more likely to have relatives living with them than are elderly male householders.

By and large, the increase in the percentage of the elderly living alone can be interpreted as a positive trend. Of the elderly who need long-term care, more are able to receive the care they need in their homes. Unlike the picture of the nineteenth-century elderly offered earlier in the chapter, 75% of the elderly today are not impaired and 90% are not handicapped. Older persons today are more independent than in the past, possibly because of better health status, more adequate housing, higher incomes, and expanding community support services. While most of the elderly live alone or with their spouses, most do so by choice, finances and health permitting. Their preference has been and continues to be to live near their families but not with them.

Table 7.6. Distribution (%) of Households Maintained by Persons Age 65 and Older

Type of Household	1995		2010	
	Age 65–74	Age 75 plus	Age 65–74	Age 75 plus
All households (N)	11,849	9,454	13,298	11,821
Married couple	52.8	34.9	54.1	38.8
Female householder with other family	7.8	7.6	7.2	7.1
Male householder with other family	2.2	1.9	2.5	1.9
Lone female	27.3	44.6	25.1	41.5
Lone male	10.0	10.9	11.2	10.8

Source: Administration on Aging (1997:7).

Health Status

Self-assessed health is a common method used to measure health status. In 1992, about three in every four noninstitutionalized person aged 65 to 74 considered their health to be good. Two in three aged 75 and over felt similarly (U.S. Bureau of the Census 1995).

With age, however, comes the increasing chance of being dependent. In 1984, over 5 million elderly Americans required assistance with the tasks of daily living (dressing, eating, bathing, using the toilet, walking, getting in and out of a bed or chair, and getting outside), and that number is expected to rise to over 13 million by the year 2030 (Schick and Schick 1994). The need for assistance is directly correlated with age (see Figure 7.1). Among those who were not institutionalized in 1990, 50% of those aged 85 and older needed assistance performing the tasks of daily living,

Percent

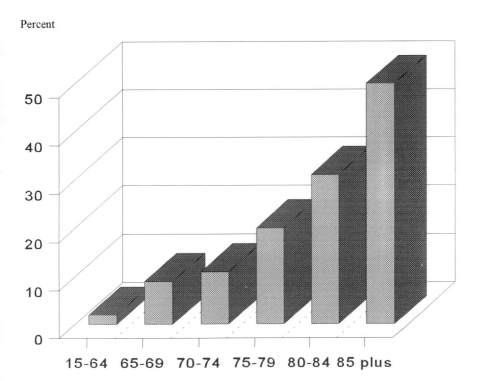

Figure 7.1 Need for assistance with the tasks of daily living by age. Source: U.S. Census Bureau, "Sixty-Five Plus in the United States,"www.census.gov/ socdemo/www/agebrief/html, p. 5, July 16, 1977.

compared to less than 10% of the elderly under age 70. Considerable assistance and social support is provided through contact with relatives. Having children living nearby significantly increases the likelihood that an aged parent receives help with life's daily activities.

As more people reach increasingly old age, issues surrounding the care of the "frail" elderly are becoming more prevalent. At the turn of the century, acute and infectious diseases were the elderly's number one health problem; today it is chronic diseases and disabilities. Roughly 20% of the elderly suffer from at least a mild degree of disability and 80% have at least one chronic condition such as diabetes, hypertension, heart disease, and arthritis. These conditions result in people becoming dependent on others for help.

While it is generally agreed that the elderly are more likely to be disabled and have higher rates of handicapping conditions than the general population, it is difficult to locate comparable time series data to measure historical patterns. In 1990, a total of almost 1.9 million elderly were appreciably handicapped, 1 million were severely handicapped, and 542,000 very severely handicapped. Two of every three impaired elderly were female and over half were 75 years of age or older. By the year 2000, the severely and very severely handicapped elderly will have increased by 65% or an additional 700,000 persons, of whom 550,000 will be women. These are people who, by definition, will be either bedridden or confined to a chair (Harris 1971; Moroney 1986a).

Education

Research has shown that the better educated tend to be healthier longer (U.S. Census Bureau 1995). The elderly of the next century will be better educated as younger cohorts age. In 1995, 64% of the elderly were high school graduates. This proportion is expected to increase to over 75% by 2010 (Administration on Aging 1996). While only 12% of the elderly had college degrees in 1993, 20% of those 55 to 59 years old, and 27% of those aged 45 to 49 did.

Economic Status of the Elderly

The income situation of the elderly is relatively favorable, and the extent of poverty, about 13%, is less than among other age groups. The percentage of the elderly living below the poverty line has decreased significantly since 1960. Furthermore, if the market value of noncash goods and services were included, the percentage of the elderly living in poverty would be even lower. As the elderly of the future have higher average levels of education, their relative affluence should also increase as education is positively correlated with income.

While income has increased, we have also experienced a sharp reduction in the percentage of the elderly who are employed. Before the passage of the Social Security Act in 1935, more than one half of men over the age of 64 were employed—they had no choice but to work. The passage of the Social Security Act both made it possible for many of the elderly to retire at the age of 65 and made it less attractive to continue working for those who wanted to. In Chapter 3 we discussed the importance of the 1974 amendments to the Social Security Act when Congress made benefits inflation proof by providing an automatic cost of living increase in benefits when the Consumer Price Index rose by a certain percentage. This allowed more people to stay retired once they began receiving benefits. There was an equally important, and still somewhat controversial, component of the act: the "work test" or the "retirement test" was implemented to ensure that beneficiaries were actually eligible, i.e., that they were really retired.

In the early 1960s, for example, retirees under the age of 72 would receive the full benefits they were entitled to if their earnings were less than $1,200 a year. If earnings were more than this amount, the benefit would be reduced by $1 for each $2 earned up to $1,700. For all earnings above $1,700, $1 of benefits would be withheld for each $1 earned (Schottland 1963).

By 1994, retirees between the ages of 65 and 70 were allowed to earn $11,160 before losing benefits, and an exemption of $8,040 was allowed for beneficiaries under age 65 (Committee on Ways and Means 1994). The retirement test does not apply to beneficiaries over age 70. Furthermore, changes to the Social Security Act in 1983 required some retirees to pay taxes on their benefits. Beginning in 1994, earnings up to $44,000 for a couple and $34,000 for an individual were exempt from taxes. After this, one-half of the social security benefit is taxable.

Because of the cost of living adjustments, we have experienced a steady decrease in employment among male retirees since the 1950s (see Table 7.7). Currently, less than 16% of elderly males are employed, compared to 65.5% of males aged 55 to 64. Women of retirement age, on the other hand, had relatively low participation rates throughout this century. In 1994, 53.4% of women aged 55 to 64 were employed, compared to 13.6% of those aged 65 to 74, and 3.5% of those over age 75. According to the latest projections from the Bureau of Labor Statistics, labor force participation rates for men will either remain unchanged or decline slightly, discontinuing the long downward trend in retirement age. For elderly women, however, labor force participation rates will continue to rise (Administration on Aging 1996).

Table 7.7. Labor Force Participation Rates of the Elderly by Gender

Year	Males	Females
1900	68.3	9.1
1910	58.1	8.6
1920	60.1	8.0
1930	58.3	8.0
1940	41.5	5.9
1950	41.6	7.6
1960	30.5	10.0
1970	25.8	9.1
1980	19.1	8.1
1990	16.3	7.4
1993	15.6	8.2

Source: Committee on Ways and Means (1994:856).

The prospective increase in the proportion of the elderly population, and the stabilization of employment rates among the elderly, will lead to shifts in the balance of employees to Social Security beneficiaries. The ratio of beneficiaries to employees is expected to increase from 31 beneficiaries per 100 employees in 1995 to 51 beneficiaries per 100 retirees in 2050 (Administration on Aging 1996). This phenomenon, as discussed in Chapter 3, has caused considerable concern over the sustainability of the Social Security system as we enter the next century.

Lower labor force participation rates for the elderly do not seem to place the average retiree at financial risk. Radner (1989) reports that if income were used as the single indicator of economic status, the elderly would appear to be at risk relative to other age groups. In 1994, the median income of households maintained by persons aged 65 and over was $18,095, compared to the median for all households of $32,264 (Administration on Aging 1996:9).

Assets

Despite the fact that the elderly have relatively low incomes, the point is often made that they are "asset" rich. Financial assets are another measure of economic well-being used to compare the relative economic status of the aged with other groups. As can be seen by examining Table 7.8, the average elderly person, even the average older elderly, has a net worth greater than the average for all households. The average elderly person's position is superior, even when home equity is excluded.

Table 7.8. Net Worth of the Elderly by Income Quintile and Age, 1991

Household income	All households	65 and over	75 and over
Lowest quintile (N)	18,977	7,266	3,939
Median net worth	$5,224	$32,172	$32,946
Excluding home equity	$1,144	$3,577	$4,570
Middle quintile (N)	18,969	3,523	1,075
Median net worth	$28,859	$154,203	$171,032
Excluding home equity	$8,661	$68,372	$83,472
Highest quintile (N)	18,905	1,751	522
Median net worth	$123,166	$424,721	$485,557
Excluding home equity	$48,893	$299,679	$399,301

Source: Adapted from Moon and Mulvey (1996).

Haves and Have-Nots among the Elderly

Despite the advances for the average elderly person, not all the elderly are enjoying their retirement years. The problem in dealing with averages is that while statistics are useful in providing a single measure of the financial status of the elderly, they can lull us into a sense of complacency. By focusing on the average elderly person, we lose sight of the fact that all retirees are not average.

Financial assets, like other sources of income, are very unequally distributed among the elderly population. The lowest income quintile has only $3,577 worth of assets (excluding home equity), whereas the highest quintile has $299,679 in comparable worth. Discrepancies in assets by gender, race, and marital status mirror those found in income (Moon and Mulvey 1996).

For instance (see Table 7.9), elderly women have a higher poverty rate (16%) than elderly men (9%) (U.S. Bureau of the Census 1995:5). The data also reveal a decline in income and an increase in poverty with advancing age. The 1992 poverty rate was 11% for those aged 65 to 74, 15% for those aged 75 to 84, and 20% for elderly aged 85 and older. African-American (33%) and Hispanic elderly (22%) had higher 1992 poverty rates than whites (11%). The 1992 median income of elderly white men ($15,276) was more than double that of elderly African-American ($6,220) and Hispanic ($5,968) women.

In addition, many elderly fall just below the poverty level, or have incomes only slightly above. The total 1994 poverty rate without Social Security would have been about 54% as opposed to the actual 12%. Figure 7.2 shows the percentage of the elderly by marital status and race that remain poor with Social Security benefits, and that were kept out of poverty because of it.

Table 7.9. Poverty Rates of the Elderly by Age, Gender, and Marital Status, 1992

| | Percentage poor | | | |
	65 and over	65–74	75–84	85 and over
Total	12.9	10.7	15.3	19.8
Female total	15.7	12.7	18.9	22.7
married	6.4	5.6	8.0	NA[b]
widowed	21.5	18.9	23.2	23.8
other[a]	26.0	25.6	27.0	NA
Male	8.9	8.1	9.7	13.2
married	6.6	6.0	7.5	10.5
widowed	15.0	13.7	15.7	16.7
other[b]	17.6	18.1	16.5	NA

Source: Committee on Ways and Means (1994:860).
[a]Other includes the categories of divorced, separated, and never married.
[b]NA, not available due to unreliability of estimate. Percentage base represents fewer than 250,000 persons.

The importance of Social Security benefits as a percentage of income declines as we move up the income distribution. Table 7.10 shows the percentage that each income source contributes to the total income package for poor and nonpoor elderly. As can be seen from Table 7.10, Social Security benefits constitute the greatest percentage of total income, almost 68%, for those elderly classified as poor. Public assistance, i.e., means-tested programs such as AFDC, SSI, GA, food stamps, and housing assistance constitute the second largest share of income for the poor, almost 19%. For the nonpoor, Social Security makes up a much smaller share of the total (31.3%), and is less than earnings, interest, and dividends combined (48.9%). The distribution of income among the elderly is highly slanted in favor of the upper-income elderly, who receive a disproportionate share of total income, including government benefits, the majority in OASI and Medicare.

Pensions

In 1935, approximately 1% of all retired persons had pensions and only 15% of workers were employed in jobs offering pensions. Today, private pensions constitute an important source of income for the elderly: 16.4% of the income package for the nonpoor. Most women, however, find themselves at a disadvantage when they join the retirement population. Many have limited employment histories and are dependent upon their husbands for retirement income. If their husband has participated in a

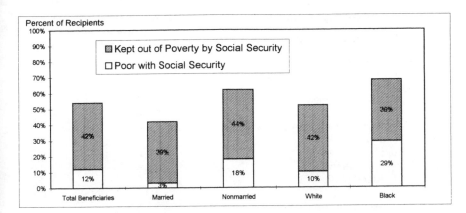

Figure 7.2 The role of Social Security in reducing poverty. Note: This figure represents the percentage of elderly in various categories who are still poor with Social Security and that percentage who are kept out of poverty by Social Security. The remainder are those whose incomes places them above the poverty line. Source: ssa.gov / statistics / income__aged / 1994/p10.pdf.

pension plan they are more fortunate than those whose husbands did not, but for many women, the benefits cease upon their husband's death, or run out after so many years. In 1994, 44.7% of whites, 42.7% of African-Americans, and 25.6% of Hispanic male workers under 65 years of age had pension plan coverage. This compares to 39.6% of whites and African-Americans, and 27.3% of Hispanic females of the same age (Committee on Ways and Means 1994).

Other women have participated in employment, but given the historical practice of labor market segregation (see Chapter 8 for a more detailed discussion of this issue) found themselves in secondary labor markets that provided few benefits, let alone pensions. The only group of women who had higher rates of coverage than their male counterparts were never married women (see Table 7.11). These were the women who were likely to have been career employees and professionals. Still, while men may have been better off than women, two of every three male retirees did not have pensions, a percentage that changed only slightly, dependent on marital status.

Income has important implications for health. About 26% of elderly with incomes over $35,000 per year describe their health as excellent compared to others their age, while only 10% of those with incomes less than $10,000 per year report excellent health (Schick and Schick 1994).

Table 7.10. Percentage of Total Income from Each Source for Poor and Nonpoor Elderly, 1992[a]

Income Sources	Poor	Nonpoor
Number of elderly (%)	3,983 (15.2)	26,887 (84.8)
Earnings	5.0	30.9
OASDI, railroad retirement	67.7	31.3
Pensions	2.6	16.4
Unemployment, workers compensation, veterans payments	1.6	1.5
AFDC, SSI, GA	10.0	0.7
Child support, alimony	0.6	0.9
Interest, dividends	3.5	18.0
Food stamps[b]	3.1	0.1
Housing assistance[b]	5.8	0.2

Source: Committee on Ways and Means (1994:863).

[a] Based on census poverty levels.

[b] The cash values of food stamps and housing assistance were estimated using their market values. Their cash values are excluded from total incomes for purposes of determining poverty status, but included as a percentage of the total share of income.

Summary of Elderly Characteristics

This brief demographic and economic analysis has highlighted a number of changes that have taken place over the past century and those that will lead us into the next. In 1900, the elderly represented about 4% of the total population. By 1995, the elderly constituted 12.5% of the population, an increase in absolute numbers of almost 30 million. Moreover, this shift has been accompanied by a significant growth of the very old, those aged 85 and older. Both of these trends are likely to continue as the baby boomers age and the outlook for longevity and health are optimistic.

Currently, approximately 6 of every 10 elderly persons are women.

Table 7.11. Percentage of Retirees with Private Pensions

Marital Status	Women	Men
Married	11	29
Widowed	14	38
Divorced	19	35
Never married	43	29
Total	14	34

Source: Woods (1988:5).

Women not only make up more of the elderly population, but they are likely to be older than elderly males. While more elderly are married than in the past, three of every four women over 74 years of age are single, widowed, or divorced. Widowed women will continue to constitute the greatest proportion of the oldest elderly because the high premature death rate of men and the very low remarriage rate of elderly women are expected to continue.

Reductions in mortality and increased longevity are inevitably accompanied by higher rates of chronic illness and disability. The elderly are more likely to be disabled and have higher rates of handicapping conditions than the general population. As the proportion of oldest old increases, more persons will be facing chronic illnesses such as Alzheimer's disease, hypertension, and diabetes. Despite these conditions, improvements in income, modern health care, and home health services have resulted in more elderly maintaining their own residences, and a decline in the proportion of elderly living with adult children or seeking nursing home and institutional care. The two most important factors related to the elderly being able to maintain their own households into old age are marriage and the presence of children living nearby. The likelihood of being married and having adult children is on the increase. Undoubtedly, the demand on family members as caretakers and to provide assistance with the tasks of daily living can be expected to increase in the coming years.

Income is highly variable among the elderly. Social Security is an important source of income for all elderly. Without Social Security the 1994 elderly poverty rate may have been as high as 54%. The poor elderly receive more of their income from social assistance, whereas the nonpoor are more likely to rely on earnings and private pensions for the bulk of their income. The employment rate for elderly men is likely to remain stable, at around 16%, while the employment rate of elderly women will continue to increase in the coming years. Changes in the age structure of the population will decrease the ratio of employees to retirees, which will negatively tax the Social Security system. In the future we can look to a more highly educated group of elderly, a factor positively impacting income and health.

Along with the general increase in the elderly population, there will be increases in vulnerable subsets of the elderly, the "oldest" old, women, racial minorities, and unmarried persons with no children or siblings. These are the groups with high poverty rates, low incomes, and poorer health. These demographic and economic characteristics are important because they impact needs in the areas of health care, income support, and personal social services. Knowledge of these trends is essential for policy design.

POLICIES AND PROGRAMS: AN ISSUE OF EMPHASIS

Earlier in this chapter, we suggested that we have reached a point in the evolution of our welfare state where the status of the elderly has improved significantly compared to other age groups. Thirty percent of all federal expenditures target the elderly—a population group making up just over 12% of the total population. Furthermore, during the three-year period 1981–1983, a period of high inflation and budgetary short-falls, expenditures not only grew but also exceeded increases in the CPI by considerable margins. While the average annual rate of inflation was 4.8% during this period, federal government outlays increased by almost 13% from 1981 to 1982 and by over 7% from 1982 to 1983.

Wilensky (1975) has suggested that this phenomenon is not unique to this country but has occurred in most mature industrial nations and is a major factor in understanding the overall growth of the welfare state (in expenditures) and the proportion of that growth going to the elderly. This section will identify and discuss the types of policies and programs that have been implemented.

Federal outlays for the elderly over the recent past have been distributed over nine major program areas: income maintenance, health, housing, social services, community support, food and nutrition, home energy assistance, planning and research, and other miscellaneous expenditures (see Table 7.12). Ninety percent of these outlays can be classified as *social insurance* expenditures and 10% as social assistance expenditures. As discussed in greater detail in Chapter 2, social insurance—the institutional approach—incorporates such concepts as universal provision, entitlement, and needs-based benefits, which recipients receive as a matter of right and citizenship. Two of these programs are income maintenance programs (OASDI and other retirement/disability programs such as the Railroad Retirement Program and the Military Retirement Program) and one is a health insurance program (Medicare).

Social assistance—the *residual approach*—is built on a different set of assumptions, i.e., selective provision to the really needy as determined by their ability to pass a means test. Benefits are not provided as entitlements, although once an individual or family successfully completes the eligibility process, they are entitled to receive "available" benefits. These programs include Medicaid, Supplemental Security Income, subsidized and section 202 housing, Food Stamps, and low-income energy assistance.

It needs to be emphasized that 64% of all expenditures went to income maintenance programs, an additional 32% to pay for medical care services, and approximately 4% for housing, social services, community support services, food stamps, home-energy assistance, planning, and

Table 7.12. Federal Outlays Benefiting the Elderly, Fiscal Year 1991

Type of Outlay	Dollars in Millions	Percentage of Total
Medicare	101,949	26.3
Medicaid	16,975	4.4
Other federal health	6,698	1.7
Health subtotal	125,622	32.4
Social Security	207,329	53.5
Supplemental Security Income (SSI)	5,345	1.4
Veterans pensions	5,313	1.4
Other retired, disabled, survivors benefits	30,506	7.9
Retirement/disability subtotal	248,493	64.2
Older American volunteer programs	121	<1
Senior community service employment	359	<1
Subsidized housing	6,078	1.5
Section 202 housing loans	401	<1
Farmers Home Administration housing	633	<1
Food stamps	1,385	<1
Older Americans Act	819	<1
Social Services (Title XX)	588	<1
Low-income home energy assistance	468	<1
Other miscellaneous	2,375	<1
Other subtotal	13,277	3.4
Total outlays	387,342	100
Percentage of total federal outlays	30	

Source: Table adapted from Schick and Schick (1994:261).

research. This distribution can best be understood by returning to our earlier discussion in Chapter 1 of appropriate roles of government. Our capitalist system is built on the assumption that competitive markets will produce socially optimal results, i.e., when there is a demand for a specific service or good, some one will produce it. Furthermore, a competitive market will be characterized as one in which there will be a reasonable balance between consumers and producers (demand and supply), and products of different value and quality will be available for consumers with differing ability to pay.

The passage of the Social Security Act of 1935 was a clear reaffirmation of this belief. By providing cash grants to beneficiaries, the federal government underscored the importance of its laissez-faire role in the marketplace. Individual recipients could spend the money however they wished, and it was assumed that they would be able to meet their basic needs. *Implicit in this formulation was the belief that the major problem being experienced by the elderly was financial.*

The giving of pensions also met another of our strongly held beliefs. In the early years of the depression, it cost, on the average, $28 per month to maintain an individual in one of the thousands of county homes or poorhouses (this amount covered only operating costs). At the same time, the average state pension was only $14 per month. Pensions were cheaper and thus cost-effective. It was fortunate for the needy aged that a more humane treatment was also more economical (Rimlinger 1971).

While income maintenance and medical programs represent the major expenditures for the elderly (we have dealt extensively with those programs in Chapters 3 and 5), we will restrict our analysis in this chapter to other policy areas affecting the elderly.

The Older Americans Act

The year 1965 was a watershed year not only because of the enactment of Medicare and Medicaid, but also for the passage of the Older Americans Act. While this legislation never came close to matching the financial commitment Congress and the administration made in the medical-care field, it did have a broad impact on state and local services for the elderly. The purpose of the act was

to provide assistance in the development of new or improved programs to help older persons through grants to the states for community planning and services . . . and to establish within the Department of Health, Education and Welfare an operating agency to be designated as the Administration on Aging. (U.S. Department of Health, Education and Welfare 1974:1)

Initial efforts under the legislation had two primary emphases: (1) the development of state planning capabilities, and (2) the provision of nutritional services to undernourished and malnourished frail elderly. States were required to establish State Units on Aging (SUAs), which were to be responsible for developing a comprehensive statewide plan to meet the needs of the elderly; to establish a participatory and open process that would determine priorities within that plan; to coordinate the existing service delivery system; and to stimulate the development of new services and the expansion of existing services. (The 1973 amendments added another planning layer with the establishment of local planning and coordinating agencies know as Area Aging Agencies—AAAs.) The 1965 act, appropriating $7.5 million, funded these activities from existing social-service grants and research funds.

For the remainder of the 1960s, the program's budget stayed relatively small. Planning systems were established and specialized service delivery systems evolved. Early priorities were on establishing programs that would address problems of fragmentation in the human service delivery system. Given this, communities were encouraged to develop (1) information and referral services, (2) outreach, and (3) transportation services.

The 1972 amendments established a national nutrition program for the elderly and provided funds for the development of centrally located and physically accessible centers responsible for providing hot, nutritional meals at least five days each week. These programs had multiple purposes. The obvious one was to improve the nutritional status of the elderly. Other objectives were concerned with the problem of social isolation many elderly were experiencing and the need to identify and deal with the array of social, physical, and emotional problems in their early stages rather than waiting until they became serious. The center was viewed as an ideal vehicle to achieve these objectives. A considerable amount of the social services were funded first through Title XX (passed in 1974), and later through the Social Services Block Grant passed in 1981.

By 1974, approximately 26% of all funds were used for planning and the provision of social services, 36% for nutrition services, and 29% for community service employment programs. Under the legislation, the following services were required:

- home health/homemaker,
- information and referral,
- nutrition,
- outreach,
- transportation,
- home repairs/renovation,

and the following services encouraged:

- education,
- employment,
- energy,
- financial assistance,
- housing,
- mental health,
- rehabilitation,
- senior centers.

Over 30 years after its passage, the OAA has resulted in an infrastructure of home and community-based services in every state. The bulk of OAA funds are targeted toward elderly nutrition. In 1995, 123.4 million congregate meals, and 119 million home-delivered meals were provided at a cost of $250 million and $134 million, respectively (Administration on

Aging 1995). Three services, congregate meals, home-delivered meals, and transportation account for the majority of OAA federal expenditures. Transportation is the third largest service in terms of OAA federal funding, accounting for $63 million in 1995. Transportation programs, found in most communities, include services such as specially designed vans and buses that pick individuals up at their home and drive them to community agencies and other providers of human services. Together these three services account for 66% of the Title III federal funding. Title III federal funds comprise 39% of the total service expenditures reported by the Area Aging Network in 1995.

States have different service priorities for federal funding under the OAA, so the mix of services and levels of funding vary from state to state. Table 7.13 presents 1995 state participation rates in the 14 service reporting categories under OAA, as well as an additional service category that states can provide at their discretion.

In 1995, programs and services supported by OAA served an estimated 7.5 million persons aged 60 and over. Twenty percent of program participants were members of a minority, and 30% had incomes at or below the poverty level. Thirty-five percent of the participants in 1995 lived in rural areas. While the OAA programs are available to all elderly, they do appear successful in reaching the most vulnerable sub-groups.

Table 7.13. State Participation in Selected Services with OAA Funding, 1995

Home and Community-Based Service Categories	Number of States Participating[a]	Percentage of All States Participating
Personal care	41	78.8
Homemaker	47	90.4
Chore	38	73.0
Home-delivered meals	52	100.0
Adult day care/health	40	76.9
Case management	41	78.8
Congregate meals	52	100.0
Nutrition counseling	17	32.7
Assisted transportation	31	59.6
Transportation	50	96.2
Legal assistance	50	96.2
Nutrition education	29	55.8
Information and assistance	48	92.3
Outreach	45	86.5
Other services[b]	46	88.5

Source: Administration on Aging (1995).
[a] Includes the District of Columbia and Puerto Rico.
[b] The other category includes such services as benefits counseling, senior center activities, health promotion, home repair and modification, telephone reassurance, friendly visiting, and volunteer services coordination.

Catastrophic Illness

The Medicare Catastrophic Coverage Act, which was enacted in 1988 with the wholehearted endorsement of the American Association of the Retired Persons (AARP), is discussed in detail in Chapter 5. Basically, it was designed to protect elderly and disabled OASDI beneficiaries from catastrophic medical expenses due to illness or injury. Here we wish only to discuss the significance of its repeal one year later in 1989.

In great part the bill was repealed because of the intense lobbying activities of a vocal minority group of the aged who were angry that they, the elderly, would have to pay for the benefits (as in Part B) rather than receive them as an extension of Part A, which is financed by current workers. Their position was unequivocal: they argued that they were entitled to the benefits because they were retirees but that they should not have to pay for them.

We use the term "vocal minority" in the sense that a small group convinced the larger group of OASDI recipients that they would have to pay higher "taxes" for these questionable benefits. The reality was that 58% of the elderly would not have had to pay the surcharge—their total cost would have been the additional $4 monthly premium—and an additional 12% would have paid less than $100 beyond the $4 monthly charge. This meant that 7 out of 10 OASDI recipients would have had significant increases in benefits at minimal costs. Only about 6% of Medicare recipients would have had to pay the maximum surcharge. It was this group—the more affluent elderly, those with high incomes and retirement plans that already included most of the benefits to be covered under catastrophic illness—that initiated the pressure to repeal the program. Less than 2 million retirees who already had coverage did not feel it fair that they should be required to support the remaining 31 million Medicare recipients.

Crystal (1982) has argued that the gap among the elderly is, in fact, widening. While the data in Table 7.8 document the relative financial worth of the average elderly person and the data in Table 7.12 identify the considerable effort on the part of the federal government to support this population, the distribution of income among the elderly is highly slanted in favor of the upper-income elderly, who receive a disproportionate share of total income including government benefits:

> [O]ne world is inhabited by those who are poor, sick and incapacitated; the other by those who are economically and physically well off. Much of aging policy subsidizes the latter at the expense of the former. (ibid.:30)

Housing

One other service important when analyzing services to the elderly is housing. While we devoted Chapter 4 to housing policies, it is important to point out that low-income elderly persons are major beneficiaries of these means-tested programs. It is reassuring to see that 80% of the elderly own their own homes. Still, approximately 6% of the elderly receive housing benefits. Forty percent of all public housing units (over 500,000) are lived in by retirees, 357,774 elderly are receiving rent subsidies under the section 8 program (this represents 50% of the total), and over 45,000 units for the elderly were built under the Mortgage and Construction Assistance program (Section 202).

UNRESOLVED ISSUES

While this chapter described medical, environmental, and social advances that in some degree might be viewed as indicators of overall improvement in standards of living in a developed nation, these changes have brought with them the need to develop a new social infrastructure to maintain the quality of life of these persons. Our analysis of policies for the elderly brings us to an interesting juncture. We see that the federal government has made a significant and lasting commitment to insuring a reasonable quality of life for individuals over the age of 65. A relatively small percentage of the population receive a disproportionate amount of available resources, a share that is likely to grow still higher as the elderly increase in number and live longer.

This commitment is not only greater than that given to any other age group, but it differs on two other dimensions. First, most of the benefits are provided from a social insurance perspective. Major programs such as OASDI and Medicare, and smaller but extremely important programs such as various transportation, nutritional, and social services, are available to all elderly persons (universal provision), are not means-tested, and are entitlement programs. These programs are the clearest statement we have that a "total" population group is potentially at risk and therefore should be supported.

Second, most of the benefits and services are not only available to all elderly, but the package itself is the closest we have to a comprehensive service delivery system. The foundation was laid in 1935 with the passage of the Social Security Act, which guaranteed a source of income for virtually all retired persons. Later blocks, such as Medicare and the services provided or stimulated by the Older Americans Act of 1965, completed the structure. Elderly persons are provided income maintenance, medical care, services in the community, and institutional care when necessary. No other age group has such an infrastructure available to it; no other group has the equivalent of the "Elderly Bill of Rights" expressed in Title 1 of the Older Americans Act of 1965.

This same commitment, however, may have created a series of problems we will need to face over the next two to three decades. Currently, 12.5% of the population are allocated 30% of the federal budget. Is this reasonable? Is it too much? Should it be more? As the aging population increases [by the year 2030, it is projected that the population over 65 will reach 25% (Schick and Schick 1994)] should this ratio be maintained? By the turn of the century, almost 45% of the elderly population will be over 75 years of age and 11% will be 85 years of age or older.

It is this last group, the older elderly, the frail elderly, that causes us to pause. Not only is this the fastest growing age group, it is the age group that is more likely to be handicapped, more likely to need institutional care, and more likely to require assistance with the tasks of daily living. And therefore it is more likely to need still more resources. Will we accept the reality that the ratio of expenditures will need to be increased? In 1995, the Congress passed a budget resolution to reduce spending on Medicare by $270 billion and Medicaid by $182 billion (Moon and Mulvey 1996). How will priorities be established? What criteria will be used to determine the distribution of resources among age groups? Who will be involved in setting those criteria? What are the opportunity costs involved? Should the ability to keep people alive longer than ever before in our history be balanced with the issue of the quality of that life?

In 1991, the federal government expended almost $390 billion on the elderly. Of this amount, 53.5% was for Social Security ($207 billion), 1.3% for Old Age Assistance or SSI ($5 billion), 26.3% for Medicare ($101,949 million) and elderly recipients under Medicaid ($16,975 million), and $6,698 million for other federal health. Another $13 billion was spent for programs under the Older Americans Act, Food Stamps, low-income energy assistance, and the other service programs discussed earlier in this chapter. In 1995, federal government spending on the elderly reached $450 billion (Moon and Mulvey 1996), and still we are experiencing serious shortfalls in this area. Approximately 12% of elderly persons are poor and 8% have incomes under $5,000. The poverty threshold in 1993 was set at $6,930. Fifty-two percent of all elderly persons eligible for Supplemental Security Income (SSI) were actually receiving benefits, and only 30% of poor elderly had Medicaid coverage. In the housing field, while 6% of all elderly are receiving benefits, as many as 20% need housing services. Given the current federal deficit of $55 billion, how much more can we afford to spend?

The juncture we have reached is critical. To protect a cracking infrastructure and to ensure that the elderly in the greatest need will have their income, health, housing, and service needs met, we are likely to see a greater consensus among the nonelderly to transfer more and more of the benefits and services to the residual model—to introduce the means test as the major criterion for eligibility. Such a solution is appealing to many in that its purpose is to target those in the greatest need. Such a solution, however, would have considerable long-term effects on the shape of our social-welfare system and the humane qualities of our society. These issues will be addressed in the final chapter.

Demographic pressures in the near future will force further debate on entitlements for the elderly. Any decisions to retrench on our social commitment to the elderly need to be based on facts. Taking the polar positions of "no change" or "dramatic retrenchment" is neither realistic or desirable given the relative vulnerability of the elderly. In addition, it is important to recognize that Social Security, Medicare, and Medicaid are inextricably linked, and that changing one will undoubtedly affect changes in the others (Moon and Mulvey 1996). Given the increase in demand from a growing elderly population, and an increasing dependency ratio, how can we maintain the integrity of these programs? This could prove to be the greatest policy challenge of the twenty-first century.

8

Employment

In a market economy the relationship between employment and social policy is reciprocal, i.e., changes in one influence the other. For instance, when soaring rates of unemployment left workers unable to meet their needs for food and shelter in the 1930s, the government expanded employment opportunities by creating millions of public service jobs. In other instances, the government attempts to influence the employment market—as opposed to reacting to changes in the economy. For example, in 1993 President Clinton signed the Family and Medical Leave Act (P.L. 103-3). This act offers employees unpaid, but job-guaranteed leaves for up to 12 weeks per year for family and medical emergencies. Consequently, parents who have a terminally ill child can now take time off from work to attend to their child without risking their health insurance or job security.

Government's need to look after the interests of both the employment market and the employee can create a difficult balance. An inherent tension exists between (1) the needs of the employee for economic security and workplace benefits such as family leave, and (2) the needs of the employer to generate profit and remain competitive. In recent years factors such as the globalization of the economy—increased foreign trade and the migration of industry in search of cheap labor, the need for flexibility as businesses respond quickly and cost-efficiently to the demands for new products and services, and the costs of modernization— have increased this tension.

On one hand, the employment scene has never looked brighter. Corporate profits rose by 127% from 1980 to 1995 (Johnston 1997). The size of the labor force grew 73% between 1966 and 1994 (Slater 1995). The national unemployment rate dropped to 4.8% in July 1997, its lowest point since 1973. Women accounted for 46% of the labor force in 1995, representing a 132% increase since 1966. Production workers in July 1997 earned an average hourly wage rate of $12.14. The percentage of teens who drop out of high school is on the decline, from 11% in 1985 to 9% in 1994. And many employees have a variety of workplace benefits available to ensure their long-term health and economic security. These benefits include pensions and stock plans, retirement accounts, health insurance, life insurance, paid leaves, child care, vacation, and counseling for personal problems such as depression and alcoholism.

In a recent effort to increase the flexibility of the labor market, President Clinton signed the Health Insurance Portability and Accountability Act. The 1996 act guarantees small businesses access to health care. Insurance companies are required to renew coverage and cannot deny a business health care insurance because of any employee who may be considered a "bad risk." Individuals who lose their group coverage because of a loss or change of jobs will be guaranteed access to coverage in the individual market or in an alternative program created by the state. Failure of insurers to follow this law can result in monetary fines. In theory, this act will increase the flexibility of employees to move to better job opportunities and make employers more able to attract new workers.

On the other hand, even with these gains, the employment picture is not so bright. There has been an involuntary growth in temporary and part-time labor. A wage gap persists in which men earn more than women and whites earn more than nonwhite minorities. In 1995, the ratio of women's median weekly earnings to men's was 75.5%. Even in traditionally female-dominated occupations such as teaching and social work, women still earn less than men. A wage gap also persists by race and ethnicity. In 1995, the median hourly wage of whites was $8.32, while African-American workers earn an average of $7.66 per hour and Hispanics $7.00. The overall unemployment rate in 1995 was 5.6%. White women are, however, less disadvantaged by unemployment (4.8%), than African-American (10.2%) or Hispanic (10%) women (DOL 1996). Workers with low levels of education are earning less. Between 1973 and 1995, the average hourly wage (adjusted for inflation) of high school dropouts fell by 23% (Annie E. Casey Foundation 1997). High-paid manufacturing jobs are being replaced by low-paid service jobs and the growth in low-wage employment has resulted in greater poverty among families with an employed adult. Either social policy has not dealt effectively with these problems or they are yet to be addressed.

In Chapter 1 we introduced the idea of social policy as a response to social problems. While employment-related social policies have been important in securing many workplace benefits, some blame these same policies for perpetuating gender and racial inequalities, decreasing the global competitiveness of U.S. businesses, and encouraging individuals to choose public assistance over paid employment. This mixture of success and criticism leads us to ask: (1) How have social policies addressed employment problems? and (2) How should government respond to employment problems in the future?

EMPLOYMENT-RELATED THEORIES

The way a problem is understood has important considerations for social policy design. Our understanding of employment-related problems has been dominated by four theoretical explanations: market failure, discrimination, individual deficiency, and human capital.

1. *Market Failure*

In a free market economy a number of structural problems can occur that create problems for both the employer (the producer) and the employee. For example, price is determined by the supply of a good or service and the corresponding demand. When the quantity of a good or service supplied is equal to the demand, the market is said to be perfectly competitive. However, perfectly competitive markets seldom endure. The desire for new products and services causes prices to fluctuate. Price constitutes the best source of information for producers, indicating when it is time to increase, decrease, or abandon production. A producer's ability to meet new market demands and remain competitive depends on (1) prompt and reliable information, (2) the level of investment required for new capital such as buildings and machinery, (3) the availability, cost, and skill level of labor, and (4) the ability to liquidate high-cost capital that is no longer required. Any of these four factors can influence the producer's flexibility and cause a time lag in meeting new market demands. In the meantime, the supply of the former good or service will outpace demand and prices will fall, resulting in layoffs and lower wages, which in turn lead to unemployment. Until the supply and demand of the new good or service reach equilibrium, prices will be inflated and wages will be high, providing an incentive for producers to invest and workers to attain marketable knowledge and skills. Thus, free market capitalism is characterized by cycles of growth and decline. Some analysts argue, therefore, that the role of the welfare state is to (1) ensure that the education, health, and welfare of the work force are sufficient to meet the demands of labor— social reproduction, and (2) smooth out economic business cycles through policies that buffer the costs of lost or inadequate employment opportunities when the economy contracts, and that discourage reliance on government benefits when an expanded labor force is required.

2. *Discrimination*

Discrimination theory views some individuals as disadvantaged by their life circumstances. The concept of the dual labor market refers to the separation of employment into two classes. The primary labor market is characterized by full-time jobs that provide high wages, benefits, on-the-job training, and a career track. In contrast, the secondary labor market is characterized by irregular, low-paid employment with no benefits, security, or hope of career advancement. Through no fault of their own, those who are subject to discrimination by age, physical or mental disability, gender, or race are overrepresented in the secondary labor market. A body of empirical research provides support for this theory by showing that differences in occupation and pay are not merely products of education, experience, or family roles and responsibilities (Doeringer and Piore 1971; Kominski 1991; Russo and Green 1991). Supporters of this position contend that government's role is to (1) promote primary labor market opportunities for members of discriminated groups, and (2) sanction employers who engage in discriminatory practices.

3. Individual Deficiency

Most individuals who experience employment problems do so only temporarily. These individuals are usually able to mobilize their internal and external resources and resume self-sufficiency. For a residual of the population, however, the problems of unemployment and poverty are chronic. Proponents of the individual deficiency theory view the chronically unemployed as personally deficient. There are two schools of thought as to why this deficiency exists. One, with its roots in the Poor Laws and personality theory, focuses on the negative experiences of childhood and emotional maladjustments in shaping behavior. Problems are viewed as the effects of conscious and unconscious psychological processes on an individual's motivation. The role of government, therefore, is to cure these individuals of the psychological defects that are prohibiting them from attaining "productive" lives.

The second view of individual deficiency is informed by behavioral theory. This view considers deviant behavior as self-reinforcing and as passed on from generation to generation through socialization. By giving ablebodied individuals money the government is believed to be fostering dependency. Behavior theory suggests that behavior change can be motivated in two ways: by punishing negative behavior or by rewarding the desired alternative—employment. From this view the role of government is to force behavior change through punishment or positive reinforcement.

4. Human Capital

The human capital explanation views income as a function of productivity, and productivity as a function of human capital, i.e., education, training, and health. By investing in human capital, productivity and income are expected to increase. Better health is associated with more time and energy available to invest in education, training, and employment. In the 1960s, research examining employment outcomes focused on individual factors such as education, skill, training, health, and attitude (Iatridis 1994). As a result of this research, differences in individual earnings were attributed almost solely to differences in human capital. Thus, the role of the government under this approach is to improve the education and training of the poor in an effort to increase their productivity, which will thereby increase their earnings.

THE NATURE OF GOVERNMENT INTERVENTION

Government has at its disposal a number of different ways to intervene in employment problems. The more common of these are:

- assuming the role of employer by hiring workers to fulfill a variety of tasks such as providing medical care, cleaning parks, and policing the streets;
- stimulating the private sector employment market by paying employers to hire welfare recipients;
- providing incentives to employers to relocate to areas of high unemployment;
- imposing regulations on employers, for example, by setting a minimum wage and enforcing safety standards;
- paying for the provision of a resource in whole or in part such as providing child care subsidies to low-income, single-parent women to facilitate their entry into the labor force;
- directly providing goods and services such as an employment service that operates as an information and referral source to connect workers with employment opportunities and vice versa; and
- directly providing cash benefits such as Social Security, which exempts the aged, blind, and disabled from employment expectations.

These options vary in the extent that they intrude on the operations of the free market economy.

In the remainder of this chapter we look historically at employment-related social policies. We use the four employment-related theories as an organizing framework to illustrate the relationship between the understanding of an employment problem (e.g., market failure, discrimination, individual deficiency, or human capital) and the corresponding social policy response. Included in each section is a critique of the theory, especially as it relates to resolving the employment problems facing us as we enter the twenty-first century. The danger in presenting the history of employment-related policies by theory, as opposed to a chronological account, is that we overdifferentiate. However, we chose this presentation format to illustrate the sense of direction and continuity that can exist in social policy, which is shaped by a few basic attitudes or values that are not necessarily empirically validated. Some of these guiding theoretical frameworks tend to be more consistent with the residual model of social welfare, whereas others are more consistent with the institutional model.

BEGINNING FEDERAL INVOLVEMENT

Since the beginning of this century, the U.S. government has involved itself in the employment sector. Until the Great Depression, government's role in employment could be described as minimal or residual. The government tended to react to crisis situations rather than involve itself proactively. Such was the case in 1908 when President Roosevelt responded to the large number of industrial accidents by enacting the first workmen's compensation law.

The Department of Labor (DOL) was created in 1913 to formulate and implement employment-related social policy at the national level. Its official purpose is to "foster, promote and develop the welfare of working people, to improve their working conditions, and to enhance opportunities for profitable employment" (DOL 1997a:1). The DOL was comprised of four preexisting bureaus: Labor Statistics, Immigration, Naturalization, and the Children's Bureau. In its early days, it played a rather unobtrusive role, finding jobs for workers and workers for jobs. It was not until World War I that the DOL established itself as an essential arm of government. As the need for war production flourished, the DOL engaged in extensive efforts to meet the demand for labor. It began a clearinghouse for female labor, bringing 110,000 workers into the country from Puerto Rico and the Virgin Islands (DOL 1997). The DOL makeshift employment offices registered 7 million workers, took requests for 12 million positions, made more than 6 million referrals, and placed almost 5 million workers between January 1918 and June 1919 (Schottland 1963).

The war also created another important role for the DOL. The mass labor shortages gave labor unions optimal conditions to press for better wages and working conditions. The DOL intervened to provide conciliation services in labor-management disputes and thereby avoid costly strikes that would undoubtedly harm the war effort. By the end of the war, the DOL had carved a niche for itself: (1) matching employees with employment opportunities, (2) mobilizing reserve sources of labor for seasonal work and crisis situations, and (3) mediating labor-management disputes. Government intervention in employment did not really take stride, however, until the onset of the Great Depression.

SOCIAL POLICIES CREATED IN RESPONSE TO MARKET FAILURE

The post–World War I period witnessed an unprecedented rise in prosperity and plunge to disparity. As unemployment skyrocketed in the early 1930s, private savings were exhausted and hundreds of thousands of unemployed workers wandered the country in search of employment. As the depression worsened, stores closed, farmers faced foreclosures, banks failed, bread lines appeared in every major city, and the resources of local relief efforts were exhausted. By 1933, industrial production fell by 44% of what it had been four years earlier, creating a huge labor surplus (DOL 1997). The DOL intervened to bring the supply of workers in line with the demand. Nearly every state introduced bills to prevent the employment of married women in the context of safeguarding the family and protecting women's fertility (Abramovitz 1988). Restrictions on immigration virtually cut off newcomers from anywhere but Western Europe. Spurred by a national atmosphere of social and economic uncertainty, the Bureau of Immigration, which at the time was consuming three-fourths of the DOL's total budget, began a high-profile and questionable crusade to deport "undesirable" aliens.

The government also attempted to stimulate employment opportunities through a "trickle down" economics approach. This approach advocates supporting business over individuals with the belief that businesses will use the support to generate increased opportunities for individuals. In 1932 President Hoover established the Reconstruction Finance Corporation (RFC) to aid failing businesses—a supply-side strategy. Later that same year, realizing the failure of this approach to achieve adequate employment opportunities, the RFC appropriated $300 million for loans to the states. These loans were to be used for public works projects and direct relief for the unemployed. The states, however, already facing financial hardship, were reluctant to participate in the program because the money was offered as loans rather than grants. By the end of 1932, only $30 million, or one-tenth of the appropriated funds had been awarded, while Congress had spent more than three times that amount to aid a single Chicago bank (Trattner 1989).

Franklin Delano Roosevelt succeeded President Hoover in 1933 on promises of federal participation in relief, public works projects, and unemployment insurance. Upon election to office, President Roosevelt appointed Francis Perkins, the first female in the cabinet, as secretary of labor. By this time the economy had virtually collapsed. Perkins, a social worker with experience in lobbying for factory legislation and workmen's compensation, successfully promoted many elements that became part of the New Deal. These included direct relief to the unemployed, a public works program, unemployment and old age insurance, the abolition of child labor, and the establishment of a true federal employment program. The United States Employment Service (USES), established under the Wagner-Peyser Act of 1933, built on the existing 150 employment offices to create a formal nationwide employment service.

President Roosevelt also initiated the Federal Emergency Relief Administration (FERA), which provided grants to states to feed and clothe the needy. FERA was headed by Harry Hopkins, a social worker dedicated to the cause of the underprivileged. Under Hopkins's leadership an alphabet soup of work relief programs was conceived in an effort to get the unemployed back to work. The Rural Rehabilitation Program provided work relief to rural families, gave advice on agricultural problems, and issued farm loans. The Civilian Conservation Corps (CCC) sent young unemployed men from the cities to work on conservation projects in rural areas at a dollar per day. A Federal Surplus Relief Corporation purchased surplus food from farmers and distributed it to the needy. The Public Works Administration (PWA) was established to stimulate large, state-administered public works projects. The Civil Works Administration (CWA) was created in November 1933 as the first national works program. The CWA employed more than 4 million persons in its first two months. The Works Progress Administration (WPA) replaced the CWA in 1935 and employed more than 8 million people over the next five years in activities ranging from road-building to painting murals on government buildings.

Although the work relief efforts did not totally solve the unemployment problem, they did create support for a federal role in ensuring the economic security of the nation. This newfound acceptance of government intervention into the economy and private lives of its citizens paved the way for the most important of the New Deal reform programs, the Social Security Act of 1935 (the Social Security Act programs are discussed in greater detail in Chapter 3). The Social Security Act created the Unemployment Insurance Program to provide temporary and partial wage replacement for the involuntary unemployed and to help stabilize the economy. Mothers' Pensions were nationalized through Title IV of the Social Security Act as Aid to Dependent Children (ADC). Both the Mothers' Pensions of 1913 and its successor ADC were means-tested, residual programs intended to assist widowed women meet their basic needs without resorting to employment. The Social Security Act also provided direct aid for the destitute elderly and the blind. Not only did these programs provide income support, they exempted a substantial number of would-be participants from the employment market.

The government took on an even more intrusive role in employment in 1935. The National Labor Relations Act, known as the Wagner Act, gave federal sanction to the right of workers to organize and bargain collectively. This gave labor unions a tremendous boost. After passage of the Wagner Act, union membership soared from 3.8 million in 1935 to 12.6 million in 1945 (DOL 1997). A second piece of legislation, the Fair Labor Standards Act of 1938, established a minimum wage of 25 cents per hour and a maximum work week of 40 hours for most workers in manufacturing (ibid.). These two pieces of legislation marked the realization that government intervention into the free market economy was necessary to prevent the instability that would occur if wages and working conditions were to be determined solely by market forces, especially in times of high unemployment and depression. Historically, the United States has opted for less employment—an accepted level of involuntary unemployment—and greater price stabilization, with the creation of jobs being second to managing inflation (Iatridis 1994). By exempting certain groups from employment and thereby decreasing the pool of eligible workers, enforcing a wage floor, and allowing workers to bargain collectively and strike, the government assumed a much more intrusive role in the free market, one that attempts to balance the needs of the worker with the economic cycles of capitalism.

The unemployment problem of the depression was resolved with the entry of the United States into World War II. During the war, women were expected to occupy paid positions left vacant by men. Married women with young children were recruited as a last resort and child care was provided as a "war emergency measure" with funding from the Lanham Act. Two months after the end of World War II the gains made in female employment were curtailed by the termination of federally subsidized child care. The repeal of the Lanham Act ensured that women would return to the home, making the paid jobs available for returning men. The struggle for public child care continued, however, and in 1971 Congress proposed the Comprehensive Child Development Act, which sought to expand child care services to middle-income families. This act proposed federal expenditure to provide preschool children from low- and middle-income families with education, nutrition, and health services in return for a sliding income-tested fee. President Nixon vetoed the Comprehensive Child Development Act and called for a return to family-centered child care, once again impeding the entry of women into paid labor (Tuominen 1992). That same year, $1 billion was provided under the Emergency Employment Act to create nearly 170,000 temporary, public service jobs (DOL 1997).

In this brief historical sketch we observe a tendency of the federal government to define and respond to employment problems structurally. From the Great Depression until the expanded labor efforts of World War II, government experimented with a variety of strategies to deal with market failure. Government's initial efforts were relatively unobtrusive. Matching labor seekers with labor opportunities through the creation of an employment service was, and remains today, a valuable public service that helps employees reduce the cost of unemployment and employers respond more quickly to market demands.

Government's role became more intrusive with the contraction of the economy. When supply-side strategies failed to provide adequate employment opportunities, the government stepped in as an employer of last resort. The massive public works programs helped stabilize the economy. In the years since the Great Depression, public employment has proven to be an easy target for budget cutting and is therefore only an interim measure.

Perhaps one of the most important realizations of the early era of government intervention into employment was the necessity of direct relief. Programs under the 1935 Social Security Act relieved certain populations of paid-labor expectations, some permanently—the aged, the blind, and later the disabled—and others temporarily. Public protection buffered the most vulnerable from the brute forces of the free market—a practice we continue today. Ablebodied women, on the other hand, have been forced in and out of the labor force as the market required. Immigration policies, including those governing deportation, have been used to create a flexible source of reserve labor. For example, the Bracero Program temporarily imported migrant farm workers from Mexico to be hired by eligible growers during the harvest season. Although these policies appear successful when judged on their ability to respond to market failure, they are questionable when judged on criteria of equity and fairness. Market-failure theory tends to emphasize the neutral nature of economic processes and ignores the potentially discriminatory nature of social policy. Social policies, however, in design or implementation can perpetuate inequities along the lines of class, gender, race, and disability (Gil 1973).

Many early efforts to intervene in employment began at the state and local levels, e.g., workmen's compensation and unemployment relief. A federal presence has proven necessary, however, to expand such efforts equitably throughout the nation and to stabilize the economy. Current trends in social policy that give more power to the states and restrict the federal role to funding seem to ignore the important role federalism has played in balancing the interests of both the employer and the employee.

SOCIAL POLICIES CREATED IN RESPONSE TO DISCRIMINATION

By 1955 the U.S. economy was booming, employment was at a record high, wages were healthy, and prices were stable. Union membership decreased as did the number of labor strikes. Labor movement efforts turned from economic gain to employee benefits, health insurance, life insurance, and retirement programs. Beneath this veil of prosperity, writers such as Michael Harrington, author of *The Other America: Poverty in the United States,* found poverty and gave it a face. As social scientists and writers of the 1960s illustrated the relationship between poverty and the lack of civil rights, employment disadvantage came to be viewed as a result of negative treatment and blocked opportunities due to discrimination.

A massive agricultural revolution was at least partly responsible for the poverty following World War II. Rapid mechanization and modernization lessened the need for agricultural labor by about 45% after the war (Trattner 1989). Similar developments occurred in the rural industries of mining, forestry, and fisheries. Displaced rural workers began a massive migration to the cities, where the demand for unskilled labor was already declining. About one-fifth of the American population, including nearly one-half of the nation's African-American people, were estimated to be poor in 1964 (ibid.). As the literature documenting poverty in America exploded, civil rights demonstrations erupted around the nation. Black activism and the women's liberation movement paved the way for other disadvantaged and unsatisfied groups to unite in protest.

J. F. Kennedy was elected president in 1960 on the promise of a "New Frontier" of domestic social and economic reform. Arthur Goldberg, secretary of labor under President Kennedy, focused his term on improving equal employment opportunities and taking steps to abolish the segregated facilities that were widespread in Washington's government offices. These efforts became models for the rest of government and the private sector.

Prior to 1961, antidiscrimination programs were voluntary and the nondiscrimination clause in government contracts was virtually unenforced (Leonard 1991). Executive Order 11246 (1961) was the first legislation to go beyond antidiscrimination to require contractors receiving public funds to take affirmative action. Affirmative action is formally recognized as a policy to enable discriminated minorities and other population groups to achieve full equality with majority groups (Dubey 1991). Affirmative action policy considers individuals to be deserving of admission and employment on the basis of what their qualifications would have been if they had not been subject to past injustices. Thus, to ensure that injustice does not continue, a program of reverse discrimination, preferential as opposed to equal treatment, is required. This order was also the first to establish specific sanctions such as the termination of, and debarment from, federal contracts (Duke 1992).

The Equal Pay Act of 1963 made it unlawful to pay different rates for equal work on jobs that require equal skill, effort, and responsibility under similar working conditions in the same establishment. Pay equity defends such sources of wage differences as merit, seniority, and quality or quantity of production, while prohibiting pay disparities based on gender and race. Pay equity rests on two assumptions: (1) that discrimination by gender in the world of employment and pay ought to be illegal; and (2) that equal access to all jobs and equal pay for equal work is a constitutional right of all citizens (Dubey 1991).

Title VII of the Civil Rights Act of 1964 made discrimination in employment based on race, color, religion, sex, or national origin unlawful. The affirmative action provisions of the Civil Rights Act were further operationalized under Executive Order 11246 in 1965. President Johnson, who had declared an unconditional War on Poverty, directed government contractors to actively seek out African-American candidates for jobs; colleges and universities to recruit African-American faculty members, promote those already there, and to recruit African-American students (Dubey 1991). On October 13, 1967, Executive Order 11375 amended Order 11246 to expand its coverage to women. Employment discrimination based on age was forbidden through the Age Discrimination in Employment Act, Executive Order 11441. Detailed regulations, including numerical goals, were introduced in 1969 after the Supreme Court ruled that affirmative action legislation was too vague to fulfill its intent (ibid.). In the early 1970s, Congress, President Nixon, and the courts intervened to promote affirmative action practices. In 1971, the DOL issued regulations directing government contractors to adopt goals and timetables, to hire minorities and women, and to end underutilization in all areas of employment. Underutilization, an important concept in affirmative action policy, is defined as employing fewer members of a protected group than would be reasonably expected from their availability in a given field (ibid.). Affirmative action goals generally aim at equivalence between the percentage of a protected group in a given organization and the percentage on the local market. An employer must make efforts to recruit, employ, and promote members of groups formally excluded, even though their exclusion cannot be traced to particular discriminatory actions on the part of that employer.

Despite this entirely new body of law, regulation against discrimination did not reach full stride until the Equal Employment Opportunity Act of 1972. The Equal Employment Opportunity Act extended federal prohibitions against discrimination in hiring, firing, promotion, compensation, and other conditions of employment to state and local governments. The act further required systematic data collection and reporting on the employment of minorities and women and gave the Equal Employment Opportunity Commission (EEOC) power to bring enforcement actions in the courts.

In 1973, the Rehabilitation Act required affirmative action for those with handicapped status. The Vietnam Era Veterans Readjustment Assistance Act of 1974 provided an employment preference for disabled veterans and veterans of the Vietnam War era. In 1990, the Americans with Disabilities Act (ADA) extended the federal Rehabilitation Act of 1973 for persons with handicapped status. The ADA prohibits private employers, state and local governments, employment agencies, and labor unions from discriminating against qualified individuals with disabilities and also requires employers to make reasonable accommodations in the workplace. Accommodations could include anything from improving the physical accessibility of a building to modifying work schedules, or acquiring special equipment such as voice-activated computers. Consistent with the 1973 legislation, the act defines an individual with a disability as someone who has a physical or mental impairment (including psychiatric disorders), or who has a record of such impairment, that substantially limits one or more major life activities. Employers are not allowed to ask job applicants about the existence, nature, or severity of their disability and applicants may only be asked about their ability to perform specific job functions. The principal agency for implementing these laws is the EEOC.

Wherever regulations exist, resistance is a key factor, making policy implementation difficult and expensive to achieve. The ADA has been described as the "EEOC giving workers a license to behave badly" (Hagen 1997:A13). Policies that rely on enforcement, as opposed to widespread understanding and acceptance, are difficult to police and can easily be sabotaged by succeeding administrations that do not share the same values or priorities. Pay equity and affirmative action legislation are classic examples of faulty implementation. Problems with these policies have ranged from scarce funding and personnel, to decentralized administration, unclear goals, weak enforcement, and a lack of political support. Employers must document good-faith efforts to meet affirmative action goals and negotiate suggested changes; however, no automatic penalties are in place for noncompliance.

In practice, affirmative action policies have sometimes operated like quota policies and preferential hiring practices. Once affirmative action goals are met, employers can overlook subsequent applicants. Preferential hiring provides affirmative action candidates token status, and tokens are subject to increased scrutiny, stereotyping, and hostility (Russo and Green, 1991). Recent research shows that (1) most people have no idea or are misinformed about affirmative action, (2) women who feel that they have been hired based on gender tend to devalue their performance, and (3) there is a stigmatization effect attached to affirmative action that results in candidates being viewed as less competent by their colleagues (DeAngelis 1997). These and other problems have prompted intense political debate over the myriad of laws, orders, and regulations intended to deal with discrimination, and the government agencies involved in enforcing them.

As evidence of the success of affirmative action policies, the employment of women and minorities grew significantly faster in federal contract affiliates that were subject to the legislation than in noncontractor affiliates. Women and minorities have also made progress in obtaining managerial and professional jobs. In 1995 women held 48% of managerial jobs and 52.9% of professional jobs, compared to the respective rates of 35.6 and 49.1% 10 years earlier. In typical business, law, and medical schools, 20 to 40% of the students are female, whereas 20 years ago the percentage was closer to 2% (Lazear 1991). However, the actual number of managerial and professional jobs is relatively low and subsequently the largest proportion of employed women still work in technical, sales, and clerical occupations—the secondary labor market. The labor force participation rate is higher for whites than it is for African-Americans or Hispanics, as is the median hourly wage rate. In 1995, unemployment rates were lower for whites (4.3%) than for African-Americans (7.7%) or Hispanics (8%).

Despite three decades of pay equity legislation, wage inequities have also endured. In 1991, highly skilled and educated women aged 24 to 35 earned 80 cents for every dollar earned by men in the same age group. Older and less educated women earned only 70 cents for every dollar earned by men (Wilson 1993). Efforts in the public sector to eliminate the gender-based pay gap have been more successful than in the private sector. In 1980, however, the mean earnings of women at the federal level of government were still only 62.8% of that for men. In comparison, the average woman employed full-time and year-round in the private sector earned only 56% of the 1980 salary earned by the average man employed full-time and year-round (Aitkenhead and Liff 1991). While affirmative action and pay equity policies have been met with some success, there is still a long way to go.

In sum, government's role in response to discrimination has been to voluntarily encourage public and private employers to take remedial action, and to set forth regulations and create an infrastructure to enforce reverse and antidiscrimination legislation. This strategy has been met with limited success, at least in part because of the lack of resources to implement the maze of new laws and regulations, and also the lack of attention to enforcement.

SOCIAL POLICIES CREATED IN RESPONSE TO INDIVIDUAL DEFICIENCY

As AFDC caseloads climbed in the 1950s, a new approach that promised to bring financial independence to the poor was implemented. Social workers and other experts argued that what the poor needed was not merely financial aid, but psychological assistance and other forms of counseling to deal with emotional, personal, and behavioral problems that prohibited them from attaining economic independence. This was a clear shift from the cash and public works programs of the New Deal era. It was argued that public assistance combined with social services would provide welfare recipients the opportunity to learn how to make friends, develop self-esteem, gain housekeeping and money management skills, and facilitate adjustment to life as a single parent or inner-city dweller. President Kennedy, convinced by social service advocates, increased federal support to the states to add social services to AFDC. The social services amendments of 1962 gave the federal government responsibility for 75% of the cost of social services. The money was to provide casework, job training, job replacement, and other direct services to public assistance recipients. The Kennedy administration changed the name of ADC to AFDC and extended benefits to two-parent families. In 1961, Aid to Families with Dependent Children–Unemployed Parent (AFDC-UP) broadened public assistance eligibility to two-parent families whose heads of households were out of work and whose unemployment benefits were exhausted (because of the permissiveness of the legislation, all states did not propose an AFDC-UP program until it was made mandatory in 1990). AFDC-UP was enacted to prevent men from deserting their families so that women and children could qualify for public assistance. Juvenile crime and mental health also received attention from the Kennedy administration through the funding of prevention and treatment projects that addressed delinquency in inner-city neighborhoods and the construction and staffing of mental health centers throughout the country (Trattner 1989).

The fact that the New Frontier and Great Society programs did not solve the problem of poverty left many of the poor angry and dissatisfied and the public critical of social services. As a result, when Richard Nixon entered office in 1969 he began to move away from the so called "soft" services such as long-term therapy in favor of more concrete services such as day care, housing, vocational rehabilitation, and drug rehabilitation centers.

The perceived failure of the Great Society programs foreshadowed a surge of neoconservatism. AFDC recipients were promoted as deviant, cheating, malingerers. If services or money could not help the poor, the government would force them to change their dependent behavior. As a first step in 1967, Congress imposed a freeze on the number of children under age 21 who would be allowed to receive AFDC because of the absence of a parent from the home. Also in 1967, the Work Incentive Program (WIP), an acronym that was later changed to WIN, was established. WIN disqualified adults and older, out-of-school children receiving AFDC if they refused to accept employment or participate in training programs. States could, at their option, exclude mothers with young children from the work requirements. This shift away from a child's right to public support and his or her mother's care was a major change in philosophy. In addition to its punitive aspects, WIN also included a financial employment incentive. Instead of taxing earned income at 100%, AFDC recipients could keep $30 and one-third of their remaining earnings before their welfare grant was reduced, effectively lowering their tax rate to 66%. Work-related expenses such as the cost of child care, union dues, lunch, and transportation were deducted before calculating the welfare payment. Women who had been off welfare for more than four months and new applicants were not eligible for the $30 and one-third disregard— this was to discourage women from applying for AFDC merely to qualify for the financial incentive. Data on the effectiveness of "work for welfare programs" like WIN have not been positive. Of the welfare recipients enrolled in WIN, approximately one-fourth completed the training, and few could find or were placed in jobs. Studies indicate that WIN cost more to operate than it saved in reduced AFDC expenditures (Trattner 1989).

The Earned Income Tax Credit program (EITC) was introduced in 1975 to support families with an employed adult and to make employment more attractive than public assistance. The EITC is a wage subsidy for workers from low-income families who have low wages. Offering the wage subsidy as a refundable tax credit avoids the problem of employment reductions that may result from increasing the minimum wage. A "refundable tax credit" means that families can receive the full amount of the credit even if it is greater than their tax liability.

Under the Reagan administration the War on Poverty was replaced with a War on Welfare. In 1981, the Omnibus Budget Reconciliation Act (OBRA) set into motion a series of AFDC retrenchment policies. Under OBRA, the government reduced the $30 and one-third financial incentive benefit to four months and states were free to design their own employment-related programs for AFDC applicants and recipients. Despite these efforts at reform, the welfare rolls continued to increase and in 1986, 3.7 million families were receiving AFDC, only 10% of whom were eligible due to unemployment (Gornick 1992). The next major revision to AFDC came in the form of the Family Support Act (FSA) in 1988. The FSA transformed AFDC into a mandatory welfare-to-work program. The Job Opportunity and Basic Skills Training Program (JOBS) was a central feature of the 1988 legislation. Mothers with children as young as age three were required to participate in JOBS, and those with children as young as one could be included at the state's option (Naples 1991). To help AFDC recipients become independent of welfare through employment, the JOBS program could provide services such as resume writing, job readiness training, child care and transportation costs, training and unpaid work experience, and support for those who needed a high school diploma, GED, or postsecondary education. Some states imposed time limits on postsecondary education and denied JOBS benefits to recipients enrolling in college. A major obstacle to implementing the FSA was the lack of affordable and available child care. Like the Great Society approach, the War on Welfare focused on the individual at the expense of structural factors such as the rate of involuntary unemployment and the lack of jobs that paid a living wage. One Chicago mother participating in the JOBS program commented:

> It was disgusting. Here were these women getting jobs at McDonald's for $4.25 an hour and people were clapping and cheering. And then they would find out that they couldn't make it on that amount, so they would just come right back on welfare a month or so later. And that was the best they seemed to do. They didn't offer any really good jobs to anyone. (Edin 1995:5)

The most recent welfare to employment legislation came in the form of the Personal Responsibility and Work Opportunity Reconciliation Act (PRWORA) of 1996. PRWORA continues the state's emphasis on moving welfare recipients off the rolls and into paid labor. Under PRWORA, the AFDC program was replaced with the Temporary Assistance to Needy

Families (TANF) program. This new welfare legislation requires states to have an adult employed in 25% of all TANF single-parent families and 75% of TANF two-parent families in 1997 (a minimum of 20 and 35 hours per week, respectively). States have the option to exempt single parents with children under age one from the employment requirement. The required employment participation rates increase each year, culminating at 50% of all single-parent TANF families and 90% of two-parent families by the year 2002. A limited number of TANF recipients can meet the employment requirement by participating in vocational and high school education programs (TANF is discussed in greater detail in Chapter 3). The new welfare law eliminates the Community Work Experience Program (CWEP), which provided unpaid volunteer employment experience, and the JOBS program. The federal government will instead provide grants to the states and allow them to determine what programs they will offer to meet their employment goals. The federal funds could be used in a demand-side approach to improve the skills and training of individuals, or alternatively in a supply-side approach to encourage businesses to relocate and provide incentives to hire welfare recipients.

In this section we observe a tendency to explain employment disadvantage as a function of individual deficiency, and thereby a focus on reforming the individual. Initially, the individual was to be reformed through therapy, but when that failed to produce the desired results, more punitive measures were introduced. These latter government efforts attempted to reform the individual by narrowing the choice between employment and the social wage through increasingly restrictive eligibility criteria. This shift in philosophy is reflected in the titles of programs such as WIP, PRWORA, and TANF. Current welfare reform efforts aimed at eliminating dependency are significant in the sense that they bring to a close a 40-year history that acknowledges government responsibility for those who are unable to find adequate employment, or those for whom employment does not pay because their family responsibilities are too great.

Research on behavioral theory supports the effectiveness of techniques that positively reinforce the desired behavior over those that punish. Proemployment financial incentive programs like the EITC and the $30 and one-third disregard have been positively reinforcing. To their credit, these programs do not stigmatize low-income families and can be evaluated on their ability to raise families out of poverty. Since 1993, the EITC has been responsible for raising 1.38 million families out of poverty (Scholz 1993). In 1996, families with children who had 1995 incomes up to $22,370 were eligible for the EITC; however, families do not receive the tax credit unless they file a tax return and apply (Karger and Stoesz 1994). It is estimated that anywhere from 14 to 20% of eligible taxpayers failed to receive the credit in 1990 because they did not apply. Still, the EITC has a higher participation rate than other programs like AFDC or Food Stamps that are directed toward the poor (Scholz 1993). It is debatable whether these programs are targeting the same population with different philosophies, or, if they are really aimed at two different groups.

SOCIAL POLICIES CREATED IN RESPONSE TO HUMAN CAPITAL

In the 1960s a lack of adequate employment opportunities, the discovery of massive poverty, and widespread fear that automation would eliminate low-skill jobs precipitated a series of efforts to better prepare the poor for the labor market. In contrast to the previous approach, which was focused on a deficit model of social welfare, the human capital approach had more of a value-added or investment philosophy. As the national unemployment rate hit 7% in 1961, the Area Redevelopment Act (ARA) was passed to provide retraining and allowances for unemployed workers in areas of serious unemployment (DOL 1997). A second effort, the Manpower Development and Training Act (MDTA) of 1962 was much broader than the ARA. The MDTA gave the Department of Labor major responsibility for identifying labor shortages, training the unemployed, and sponsoring a comprehensive program of social research. The budget for the MDTA grew rapidly from $93 million in 1964 to $358 million in 1973 (ibid.).

The ARA and MDTA were only two of the many employment development programs aimed at populations with different needs. The Neighborhood Youth Corps (NYC) was set up under the Economic Opportunity Act of 1964 to help unemployed youths aged 14 to 21 from poor families gain work experience and earn income while completing high school. By the end of 1968, the NYC had served just over 1.5 million youths, largely employed in public service jobs such as libraries, schools, and museums. The Bureau of Work Training Programs replaced the NYC and a number of new programs were developed. For instance, the Special Impact Program was created for people in very poor neighborhoods, New Careers trained poor persons of all ages at a preprofessional level in public service fields, and Operation Mainstream helped older people and workers with outdated skills by providing work experience on community projects that would improve the local environment. The Job Corps Program was developed to provide job training for needy youths at residential centers, usually in rural areas. The Upward Bound Program encouraged children living in urban slums to go to college, and Operation Head Start was developed to give preschool training to children from low-income families. These programs differ from those discussed under market failure because they are directed toward a specific population.

The cost of job training programs and the "New Federalism," which promoted an equal partnership with the states through block grants, prompted the Nixon administration to consolidate the MDTA and other job training programs under the Comprehensive Employment and Training Act (CETA) in 1973. By 1978, CETA was budgeted at $11.2 billion and enrolled 3.9 million persons (DOL 1997). During the recession of the late 1970s, CETA began filling civil service positions left vacant because of local government retrenchment. Under President Carter's Economic Stimulus Act, about $8 billion was appropriated for public service employment and other programs under CETA. Public service jobs increased from 310,000 in 1976 to 725,000 in 1978 (ibid.). The job training needs of veterans were addressed via the Hope Through Industry Retraining and Employment Program. A Skill Training Improvement Program provided retraining for displaced workers to prepare them for employment by giving them skills that were in short supply. Accused of neglecting the chronically unemployed in favor of the more skilled workers, CETA was revised with a focus on placing the unemployed in the private sector. The Private Sector Initiative Program (PSIP) was developed to help private firms provide job training for disadvantaged persons and the long-term unemployed.

When Ronald Reagan became president he cut CETA's budget from $8 billion per year to $3.7 billion, largely through the elimination of public service employment jobs (DOL 1997). In 1983, President Reagan replaced CETA with the Job Training and Partnership Act (JTPA), which attempted to focus training on the hard to employ. Private Industry Councils were created to synchronize job training with job opportunities. The DOL also implemented legislation requiring state and local sponsors to provide literacy training under JTPA. As unemployment rates hit double digits, the appropriation for JTPA in its first year was $2.8 billion, about three-quarters of what had been spent on CETA in 1980 when unemployment rates were three to four percentage points lower (ibid.).

In 1997, the House passed comprehensive job training reform legislation that would consolidate more than 60 federal programs into three block grants to states and would allow adult workers to purchase training services using a voucher system. What the new job training measures will look like remains to be seen.

What data we have to date, however, provides evidence that these programs have had some success. Studies of preschool education have shown that programs like Head Start more than pay their way for low-income preschoolers (Gramlich and Long 1997). The random assignment evaluation of JTPA programs found positive impact for adults but not for youths who have dropped out of school. Job Corps is the only program for out-of-school youths demonstrating positive results (Osterman 1996). A study of single-mother AFDC recipients shows that women with job training are more likely to obtain paid employment, and full-time over part-time work. However, the differences in job status and wages are insignificant. As the states grapple with designing their individual approaches to job training under the new block grant program, they will confront the quality versus quantity dilemma. In the past, relatively cheap interventions have been supported in order to spread the existing resources over as many recipients as possible. This guarantees limited results and may not be cost effective.

There is no doubt that the skills and knowledge needed in the employment market are increasing at a rapid pace. A lot of traditional jobs have disappeared. Young adults who drop out of school are not as likely to find employment as easily as their parents did. The fastest growing occupations from 1994 to 2005 are estimated to be low-paid service jobs such as personal and home care aides (up 119%), and high-paid technical jobs such as systems analysts (up 92%) and computer engineers (up 91%) (Bureau of Labor Statistics 1996). For people to obtain better paying jobs, advanced education has become more important. The median earnings of those with a high school degree are almost twice those who dropped out, and those with a degree can expect to earn three times the amount of high school dropouts (Annie E. Casey Foundation 1997). Census data from 1995 show increasingly pronounced differences in average earnings by education, $508 per month for high school dropouts compared to $5,067 per month for a professional postgraduate degree. The difference between high school graduates and graduates of training programs that provide vocational certificates is around $300 per month, while the difference between high school and a college degree is about $1,000 per month (U.S. Bureau of the Census 1995).

The percentage of the civilian labor force with less than a high school education fell from 36% in 1970 to 13% in 1991 (U.S. Bureau of the Census 1996b:395). The 1994 high school dropout rate was 9% (Annie E. Casey Foundation 1997). This is good news for society as employment participation rates increase with education. In 1991 the participation rates were 60.7% for those with less than a high school education, 78.1% for high school graduates, 83.2% for those with one to three years of college, and 88.4% for those with four or more years of college (ibid.).

Rural Americans have fewer average years of education and higher school dropout rates than the urban-based population. On average, students from rural high schools score lower on the Scholastic Aptitude Test

(SAT) than other students. College completion rates are about 10% higher in metropolitan areas than in rural areas (Dudenhefer 1993). However, education and work experience are compensated at lower levels in rural than in metropolitan regions, making the investment in human capital less attractive. Human capital, therefore, is only one part of the equation for improving the employment status of the rural poor; the other part concerns low wages and inadequate employment opportunities.

Investing in human capital is expensive. The current employment market demands an approach to learning and investment in human capital that is lifelong. Those in the primary labor market are more likely to receive training opportunities from their employers. And yet, research comparing matched firms in the United States, Germany, and Japan has consistently shown that American firms provide the least training to workers (Osterman 1997). For those entering the secondary labor market, not only has training been isolated from the employment needs of industry, but industry has not been an effective partner. While important, training and education cannot be viewed as a panacea. Human capital theory is flawed in assuming that an increase in productivity (employment) will lead to increased income. Investments in human capital do influence employment rates, but do not influence the low-paid, dead-end opportunities of the secondary labor market. This forces the questions (1) Who should human capital efforts target? and (2) How should the population for whom employment does not pay a living wage be supported?

UNRESOLVED ISSUES

As we prepare to enter the twenty-first century there are several employment problems that are yet to be addressed. For instance, the value of the minimum wage has decreased over the years and its ability to foster self-sufficiency is far from adequate (see Table 8.1). In July 1997, the hourly minimum wage rate was equivalent to 39% of the average production worker's wage. Fortunately, only 5.3% of hourly paid workers earn the minimum wage or less. We find, however, that more women (6.8%) than men (3.9%) had earnings at the minimum wage or less in 1995, and a greater proportion of Hispanics (7.4%) than African-Americans (5.6%) or whites (5.3%) (U.S. Bureau of the Census 1996).

On the other side of the debate, the minimum wage is criticized by employers for being too high. Employers argue that they would be able to make more jobs available to inexperienced, relatively young, unskilled workers if the minimum wage were lower. The entry of former welfare

Table 8.1. The Minimum Wage

Year	Nominal Dollars	1995 Dollars
1956	1.00	5.60
1966	1.25	5.88
1968	1.60	7.01
1976	2.30	6.16
1986	3.35	4.66
1995	4.25	4.25

Source: DOL, *Value of the Federal Minimum Wage 1954–1996.* www.dol.gov/dol/esa/public/minwage/chart2.htm (1997).

recipients into the labor market as a result of welfare reform will likely increase the supply of minimum wage earners because welfare recipients and minimum wage earners show marked similarities. For instance, over one-half of welfare recipients and 39% of minimum wage workers lack a high school diploma (Employment Policy Foundation 1997). Both groups tend to be relatively young with few employment skills.

The loss of manufacturing jobs in U.S. cities to other markets has shifted jobs away from the well-paid, low-skill manufacturing sector to low-paid, low-skill service jobs or high-paying, high-skilled technical jobs. The concept of spatial mismatch refers to the lack of congruence between jobs and workers that has evolved in Northeastern and Midwestern cities with the change from a manufacturing-based economy to a high technology, service economy (Johnston 1995).

In addition to the shift from manufacturing to service jobs, there is an increased use of "nonstandard" labor. The nonstandard labor force includes the self-employed, contract, part-time, and temporary work force. In 1995, almost one in three workers was in a nonstandard job (Woodward 1997). Business advocates claim that this is a response to the need for flexibility in the marketplace. There is a tension, however, between the employees' need for economic security and the employers' need for flexibility. Part-time labor tends to exist in low-wage, gender-segregated sectors of the labor market with few, if any, employee benefits and relatively little opportunity for training or advancement. Some 68% of all part-time workers are women (DOL 1996). In 1995, 13.6% of part-time wage earners were paid the minimum wage or less, compared to 2.6% of full-time workers (U.S. Bureau of the Census 1996). Women doing part-time work earn 20% less than full-time women with similar jobs and experience, and men working part-time make 24% less than full-time men. Self-employed women make 25% less than full-time women and self-employed men 13% less. Many of the new jobs are on-call or temporary. From 1989 to 1994, the number of workers employed by the nation's temporary help supply firms rose by almost 43% (Bureau of Labor Statistics 1997). Workers in temporary help firms are more likely than workers in traditional jobs to be women, young, and African-American. In contrast, total nonfarm employment grew by about 5% overall (Hoyle 1995). While nonstandard employment may enable some employees to combine employment and family responsibilities, it can also function to trap workers in the secondary labor market.

The history of supportive family policies in the United States is largely one of omission. Labor force participation rates of married women with children under age six have increased from 18.6% in 1960 to 63.5% in 1995. Of all women, those who are divorced have the highest participation rates, mainly because they are the sole wage earners for their families. Despite assertions by the business community prior to the enactment of the Family and Medical Leave Act that family and medical leave was nearly universally available, at least in large firms, the Employee Leave Survey conducted in 1990 found otherwise. The Employee Benefits Survey of 1989 found that unpaid maternity leave was available to only 33% of employees in medium and large firms. Paid maternity provisions are rare and include some form of disability and sickness insurance benefits providing income replacement for about six to eight weeks (Marlow 1991). Public child care in the United States is often discussed solely as an antipoverty program for lower-income groups to ensure child development or to enable welfare women to participate in employment. This means low benefit levels, applicable to a narrowly defined population. While this encourages low-income women to seek paid employment, it discourages middle-income women who cannot afford to purchase child care services. With increased life expectancy, care for the dependent elderly is also threatening women's employment participation. Employees who have difficulty meeting family commitments often find it difficult to give their best at work. Policies like the Family and Medical Leave Act (P.L. 103-3) signed by President Clinton in 1993 are a step in the right direction, but are limited. The act only covers employees who work for employers with at least 50 employees and the act excludes part-time, temporary, and contractual workers.

Workplace injuries represents a substantial burden in health care costs to the nation, not to mention the costs to the individual, costs that may be largely preventable. In 1971, the DOL was given the responsibility to implement the Occupations Safety and Health Act. This law required the secretary of labor to set and enforce safety and health standards for almost all of the nation's workplaces. The Occupational Safety and Health Administration (OSHA) was created to implement the law. As new health standards were developed, the costs of compliance created opposition from manufacturers and OSHA was redirected toward "the more serious workplace problems" (DOL 1997a). However, we find that in 1992 about 6,500 Americans died and 13.2 million were injured from employment-related causes. That same year occupational illnesses such as lung disease and lead poisoning caused 60,300 deaths and 862,200 illnesses. The direct cost of injuries and illnesses totaled $65 billion in 1992, and $106 billion in indirect costs including lost wages—a total of $171 billion for 1992 (Coleman 1997:A1).

And finally, union membership is on the decline. Union members accounted for 14.5% of wage and salary employees in 1996; three-fifths were in private industry, down from 14.9% in 1995 and 20% in 1983 (Bureau of Labor Statistics 1997). This decrease is important as union membership has been, and continues to be, an important source of protection and benefit for laborers in this country. Between full-time wage and salary workers, union members have higher median weekly earnings, $615 in 1996 compared to $462 for nonunion workers (ibid.). This pattern of higher median earnings for union versus nonunion employees is consistent among the categories of gender, race, and ethnicity, full-time and part-time, private and public sector employees. With the exception of African-Americans, union membership is becoming less likely to cover those who need it most. For instance, union membership is higher among men than women, and among African-Americans (19%) than whites (14%) or Hispanics (13%). Full-time workers are more than twice as likely as part-time workers to be union members, as are public sector versus private sector employees (U.S. Bureau of the Census 1996).

SUMMARY

There has been a steady stream of government intervention to influence employment since the beginning of this century. These efforts have developed in response to social, political, economic, and philosophical considerations that have sometimes spurred and at other times retarded their evolution. Despite social policy efforts aimed at improving wages and working conditions, the increase in service-oriented and nontraditional employment and the decrease in industrial jobs have meant an overall increase in poverty rates for paid workers, rural and urban alike. The percentage of workers employed full-time but remaining poor increased from 12% in 1978 to 18% in 1990 (Ozawa 1994). While investments in human capital can make the difference between employment and non-employment, part-time and full-time work, they do not translate into higher pay for those in the secondary labor market.

While those in the primary labor market enjoy increasing workplace benefits, the portion of the population that has tended to rely on public assistance to supplement or replace its employment earnings is being virtually shut off from this source of support. In the past, the minimal subsistence level of public assistance provided to these individuals was considered to be in the protection of the public interest, to prevent greater social problems that would result from an inattention to parenting and participation in illegal activities to provide an alternative source of income. Recently, however, the choice between the employment wage and the social wage has been narrowed to such an extent that it represents, at least for this population, a virtual return to the Poor Laws. No longer will social policy assist these individuals when jobs that provide a livable wage are not available. No longer will these families be subject to a federally defined minimum standard of protection. Under the current legislation, support for child care and health insurance are treated as transitional needs, even though full-time labor at a minimum wage job pays about $9,880 per year. For a family of three, this is equivalent to 76% of the poverty level—not enough to pay for health insurance, transportation, child care, clothing, food, and shelter. History tells us that low-paid jobs for this population are more likely to be a fact of life than an initial employment experience.

We might wonder how we arrived at this juncture, given the growing attention of social policy to fight discrimination, promote child well-being, advance civil rights, and decrease poverty. Recent policy changes that mandate employment over welfare for all "ablebodied" adults are supported by the individual deficiency theory. Individual deficiency theory provides a very limited definition of poverty, and as such it fails to acknowledge that the profit-driven enterprise of capitalism creates low wages and cycles of unemployment—market failure theory. Nor does it acknowledge that the likelihood of employment disadvantage is linked with factors such as race, class, disability, and gender, factors outside of the individual's control—discrimination theory. Perhaps even more importantly, it fails to acknowledge that the long-term costs associated with the stress and poverty that accompany low-wage labor, inadequate health benefits, and insecure child care arrangements may actually be greater than the approximate 5% of the federal budget currently spent on AFDC, food stamps, and Medicaid for the "ablebodied" poor. While the punitive policies of welfare reform will undoubtedly decrease the welfare rolls and increase the number of single mothers and mentally and physically unstable individuals available for low-wage labor, we must ask ourselves at what cost—to these individuals, their children, and society?

We have seen throughout this chapter that the way employment disadvantage is explained has important implications for the social policy response. Many expensive and well-intended social policies have failed to achieve their desired outcome because they were based on an overly simplistic view of the problem. We have not had a coherent set of policies that clearly builds on any one employment-related theory. Policies dealing with discrimination, market failure, individual deficiency, and human capital appear to run in fads and are not well integrated. As we have seen by this historical review, acceptance of one theory over another leads to radically different explanations for poverty and dependency, as well as to different solutions. However, efforts that ignore the importance of both structural and individual factors are limited in success. This would suggest the adoption of an integrated theory of employment. A multitheoretical approach would be informed by knowledge from a wide range of disciplines, including economics, human behavior, child development, and psychology. The bottom line underlying any attempt to influence employment is (1) Are there jobs? and (2) Are these good jobs that pay a living wage?

If we accept the idea that social policy not only reflects values, but can shape values and enforce behavior, we must reflect on the values that are implied by our current social policy approach to employment. Are people merely things to be employed in the market, regardless of the wage, the conditions, or the needs of their families? Do the values of employment-related social policies foster a sense of community, shared responsibility, equality, or freedom? We have also seen by this review that national goals require a federal presence that extends income support—the opposite of our current direction.

Successful policy implementation depends on voluntary compliance, and as we have seen in our discussion of policies dealing with discrimination, well-intended policies are likely to be sabotaged when they are not well understood or accepted. The entire social policy approach to employment has become more punitive. The poor are increasingly punished and business is increasingly regulated. Research on behavioral techniques informs us that punishment is not the most effective strategy. This challenges us to find new ways to work together to find solutions or resolutions that all parties can accommodate.

CHAPTER

9

The Poor and the Permanent Underclass

Since the early 1980s we have seen the publication of a number of books and articles that have helped fuel a growing and often bitter debate about the welfare state. These publications, some with more fanfare than others, have been used by proponents and opponents of welfare expenditures to "prove" their point—that governmental intervention has or has not been effective in promoting individual self-sufficiency and social well-being. This debate revolves around the general issue of poverty and the more specific question of whether efforts over the past 60 years have assisted people to become independent or whether they have created a permanent underclass.

At one end of the continuum are the analyses of Murray (1984), Gilder (1981), and Mead (1992). Charles Murray has argued that as social welfare expenditures grew, the incidence and prevalence of poverty and related phenomenon such as out-of-wedlock births have increased dramatically. Based on the analysis of secondary data, he concludes categorically that if AFDC were eliminated, poverty, especially as it relates to female-headed households, would disappear. In more general terms, he argues that poverty increases when benefit levels rise, and conversely, that poverty decreases when benefit levels contract.

Gilder's conclusion is similar to Murray's. Based on a number of "case studies" he argues that anyone who wants to work can, and if they are willing to make sacrifices like the earlier immigrants did, they can succeed in our capitalist economy. Welfare, on the other hand, erodes the work ethic without which people will always be dependent. Mead argues that welfare has failed to integrate the poor because it was permissive and did not set behavioral standards that would require work in exchange for economic benefits.

Walter Williams, a noted African-American economist and columnist, has been arguing for years that minorities are in a worse position today than they were before the social programs of the 1960s were initiated, which unleashed billions of dollars for ill-advised efforts to increase self-sufficiency. His position is simple and closely mirrors the New Right's position on the family (see Chapter 6). If high levels of expenditures had not been so readily available, minorities would have sought and found jobs, participated in the nation's economic growth, and developed their skills as entrepreneurs. Instead, they are even more dependent on the public sector and even further removed from the American mainstream than they were 30 years ago.

At the other end of the continuum are the works of Kahn (1984) and Schwartz (1983), who offer an entirely different view of that same system. In *America's Hidden Success*, Schwartz documents major improvements in the lives of many Americans as the direct result of existing social welfare measures. Specifically, he points to the diminishing levels of hunger and malnourishment among the nation's children, declining levels of poverty among the elderly, and an overall reduction in the general population's morbidity and mortality rates.

Between these two positions are the studies of researchers who have been systematically grappling with these issues for a long time. Based on their analysis of a panel study of 5,000 families, Duncan and his colleagues (1984) have concluded that poverty is a dynamic and not a static condition. Poverty was a temporary state for most people and only 2.6% of the total population were continuously poor between 1971 and 1978. However, equally reputable scholars such as Garfinkle (1985) and Bane and Ellwood (1983), using the same data, argue that such conclusions are misleading in that 60% of those who were poor in 1971 were still poor in 1978. More recent data from the "Survey of Income and Program Participation" (SIPP) found that about 21.6% of people who were poor in 1992 moved out of poverty in 1993 (Eller 1996). However, the proportion of the population who were chronically poor, i.e., poor in all 24 months of 1992–1993, was 4.8%, and one-half of all poverty spells lasted 4.9 months or longer.

For decades policymakers have been debating the merits of the AFDC program. Critics of the program argue that the system creates intergenerational dependency, while proponents point out that the average length of stay in the program is two years. Welfare dependency, like poverty, tends to be a static condition for some and a chronic condition for others. Corbett (1993) concludes from his analysis of the welfare dynamics literature that of all new entrants to the welfare system, 30% will be short-term users (less than 3 years), 40% will be intermediate users (3 to 8 years), and the remaining 30% will become chronic persistent users.

We find these same contradictory views of welfare emerging in the popular press and on television. In 1986 Bill Moyers presented a documentary on African-American families living in New Jersey, a documentary that seems to affirm the Murray and Gilder position. Based on a number of interviews with young adults, the viewer is forced to conclude that liberal public-welfare provisions were highly correlated with the young person's unwillingness to seek employment and were the "causes" of increased teenage out-of-wedlock pregnancies. At the same time, the author of an article published in the *Atlantic Monthly*, using anecdotal material, argues that families can rise above poverty if they want to (Lemann 1986). Similar to Gilder, he offers examples of families who have succeeded and examples of those who have failed. The key, he argues, is that successful families believe in the work ethic and failures do not. At the heart of his argument is a reaffirmation of the culture of poverty theory.

In opposition to the culture of poverty theory, Michael Harrington (1975) has argued that the American welfare system has created and perpetuated poverty by collecting the poor and separating them from the mainstream of economic life by providing them with subsistence-level and stigmatizing benefits. Frances Piven and Richard Cloward argue in their 1971 book, *Regulating the Poor: The Functions of Social Welfare*, that rather than address the real poverty producing factors such as racial discrimination and structural unemployment, the state chose to pacify the poor with money.

One has to conclude that all of these seemingly contradictory positions and findings are, in fact, reflections of reality. It all depends on the data used by the individual author.

The problem with these arguments and debates, however, is that some of the authors are attempting to explain a complex problem with simple linear causal models. In doing so, they divert attention from more fundamental issues—one of which is the possible existence of a permanent underclass in this society. This chapter will explore a number of issues key to this phenomenon including:

- the relationship between poverty, social welfare, and dependency;
- whether a permanent underclass actually exists as defined by persistent poverty; and
- the success of general antipoverty strategies, including the potential of current welfare reform.

ECONOMIC POLICY AND SOCIAL WELFARE: THE THEORY

What is important to note is that both proponents and opponents of the welfare state either ignore or reject the possibility that long-term welfare dependency is a function of the economic system. In fact, both agree that the major concern for this government is to support and strengthen the existing economic system. As discussed in Chapter 1, this position is grounded in the belief that our competitive market system is and will continue to be an efficient and just allocator of resources. Economic growth, it is argued, will create new jobs and, in time, double the standard of living for every one. Poverty will disappear.

Those who argue for a government role in combating poverty believe that, given market imperfections and the tendency of the market system to experience natural and unavoidable contractions, government has some responsibility to intervene, when necessary, to protect the well-being of those whose quality of life is threatened. Social policies are important in that they humanize the potentially harmful consequences of economic policies. Short-term unemployment is a fact of life in this society, but its effects can be mitigated by such mechanisms as temporary unemployment insurance and (re)training programs for adults as well as social insurance for those who are unable to work, i.e., the aged and the disabled. This is the position held by the Progressives at the turn of this century and of theorists such as Marshall, Briggs, Titmuss, and Keynes, whose ideas were introduced in earlier chapters.

Those who argue for massive government retrenchment, on the other hand, while agreeing that continuous economic growth is the key to eradicating poverty, believe that government intervention, especially through social welfare measures, inhibits economic growth, destroys the incentive to work, creates greater dependency, and eventually will drastically reduce the quality of life for all people. This is the position held by the leading theorists of the nineteenth century such as Bentham, Pareto, Malthus, and Spencer.

Most conservatives and some liberals in this country assume that the trickle-down economics approach has been successful in the past and will continue to be successful in the future. In a previous chapter we discussed trickle-down in the housing market. In that market, it is assumed that as some people are able to afford more costly housing, the houses that they sell become available to those in a lower income bracket and so on down the chain, until even the poor have housing available to them.

When we introduce the term in the context of poverty, we use it in a different way. In general, we assume that as the economy grows, people are able to purchase more goods, and thus more jobs are created to produce those goods. This argument has taken a number of forms over the years.

Keynes ([1936] 1973), for example, offered this basic strategy as a way out of the world depression of the 1930s. As we pointed out in Chapter 3, he argued that excessive savings and low levels of investment and spending would decrease the demand for goods and services, which in turn would increase unemployment. Instead, he proposed that government should increase its spending levels, even if this were to result in deficit spending, and should lower its taxes on consumers so that their purchasing power would be increased. The net effect would be the creation of new jobs.

The Townsend Movement, in the 1930s, offered a similar though somewhat unique formulation of the trickle-down theory. Francis Townsend, a charismatic California physician, proposed that all elderly persons be given an outright monthly grant with the simple provision that they spend that money during that month. The assumption in this case was that those people who were too old to be actively involved in the work force could have an effect on the unemployment rate by creating a demand for products that would generate new jobs for those who wanted employment.

The most recent version of the trickle-down theory is quite different in form but still draws on the same assumptions. Rejecting the Keynesian notion of deficit spending and the idea of giving one group an out-and-out grant of money, the decade of the 1980s introduced the idea of supply-side economics. Supply-side economics proposes that if taxes are lowered, most people will be in a position to purchase more goods and services. Furthermore, most will also have an incentive to save money, thus generating a pool of additional monies that will be invested in industry, which, in turn will, in producing those goods and services, be required to hire more people. Given this, the unemployment rate will decrease and dependency on social welfare programs will become even more of a residual approach as initially intended. President Clinton and the Republican Congress reflected this belief when they proposed tax relief for the middle class as a major goal for 1995 (Danziger and Gottschalk 1995).

The reality is that while the trickle-down theory is attractive there is little evidence that many of the poor have benefited. To address this, let us examine the experience of the past 35 years.

Poverty first became a national policy issue in the 1960s. This does not mean that the prevalence of poverty was not of concern to the federal government before that decade. There was a concern for the poor in earlier periods, usually during the ever-recurring depressions during the latter half of the eighteenth century and the first third of this century. What was different during the 1960s was not only the interest on the part of government and those in human service agencies dealing with poverty, but also the growing interest on the part of social and behavioral scientists, who found poverty—its nature, causes, and solutions—to be an acceptable area of academic inquiry.

ECONOMIC POLICY AND THE DISCOVERY OF POVERTY

Poverty existed before the 1960s, but it was never discussed, analyzed, or "treated" to the same extent. Moreover, poverty had become a media event. Just as the Vietnam War entered family life through nightly news programs in the latter part of the decade, depicting the extent and ravages of poverty was commonplace in the first part of the 1960s. We were exposed to the conditions of coal miners, poor elderly, sharecroppers, and children living in slums. Phenomena that were hidden in the past could not be swept away in the emerging telecommunication era, and documentaries such as "Harvest of Shame" narrated by Edward R. Murrow were singled out for honors. Poverty had become an industry.

One of the first tasks in the early 1960s was to measure poverty. How many people in the country were poor? Whereas President Roosevelt might have been comfortable in using Edith Wood's finding that one-third of the nation were poor (see Chapter 4) policymakers in the early days of the Kennedy administration demanded more accurate data on the incidence and prevalence of poverty and more information on the characteristics of the poor.

Initial efforts by the Council of Economic Advisors (1964) using the figure $3,000 for a family and $1,500 for an individual living alone as the poverty line, estimated that between 33 and 35 million people were poor in 1962, of whom 11 million were children. This represented 20% of the total population. The council also provided information on the incidence of poverty and argued that some groups were at greater risk than others. For example,

- 44% of minorities were poor;
- 17% of whites were poor;
- 45% of farm families were poor;
- 84% of farm families headed by a minority person were poor;
- 18% of nonfarm families were poor;
- 74% of families headed by a domestic worker were poor;
- 37% of families headed by a person with less than an eighth-grade education were poor.

In 1963, the definition of poverty moved from the somewhat crude single figure (i.e., $3,000 for a family) to a more flexible poverty line—one that made allowances for different needs of families with varying numbers of children and adults. Building on a previous study carried out by the Department of Agriculture in 1955 that identified the amount of food required by adults and children to maintain their health and the costs of that food, DHEW developed an "economy budget" that became the basis for determining whether a specific family's income was above or below the amount needed to meet basic needs. While the agency eventually provided estimates of 124 different kinds of families, the common denominator was the rationale that low-income families spent one-third of their posttax income on food (Orshansky 1965a, 1966).

Using this method of counting the poor, DHEW estimated that approximately 35 million people were poor in 1963, of whom 15 million were children. Further, with these refined measures, more accurate estimates were possible. While the earlier risk estimates of the Council of Economic Advisors were supported by the new analysis, the new analysis added the aged (25% were poor) and families headed by a female (48% were living under the poverty line). Based on the most recent update of the census available, Orshansky also reported that of children:

- over 20% of all children were poor;
- 38% of poor children were minorities;
- 60% of minority children were poor;
- 43% of the poor were children;
- 40% lived in households in which the head of household worked full-time;
- 67% of all children living in a female-headed household were poor.

Of the aged:

- 25% of the aged were poor; and
- the aged make up 25% of the poor.

Of adults:

- 20% of poor adults worked full-time;
- 40% of poor adults worked part-time;
- 15% of the poor were disabled.

The emerging profile of the poor in the early 1960s suggested that they were likely to be old, disabled, or children (83% of all poor persons). Furthermore, individuals were more likely to be poor if they were minorities, living in the South, or members of a farm family or of a female-headed household. And finally, as Moreau, David, Cohen, and Brager (1962) pointed out, the poor were likely to be uneducated or poorly educated—they had failed to improve their status relative to previous generations and had fallen behind relative to the current generation.

The Council of Economic Advisors (1964) argued that if we were to begin dealing with the problem of poverty we would need to implement a three-pronged strategy:

1. An economic strategy to:

    *   accelerate economic growth;
    *   fight discrimination;
    *   improve regional economies;
    *   rehabilitate urban and rural communities; and
    *   improve labor markets.

2. An employment strategy to:

    *   expand educational opportunities;
    *   enlarge job opportunities for youth;
    *   improve the nation's health; and
    *   promote adult education and training.

3. An income maintenance strategy to:

    *   assist the aged and disabled.

It is interesting to note that these prescriptions are a sharp departure from the theory discussed earlier in this chapter—that economic growth alone will successfully deal with the problem of poverty. As a general strategy, the council assumes, as a given, the appropriateness of direct and active state intervention in the economy. The first set of recommendations targets policies to strengthen the economic system (the creation of jobs), while the second set of recommendations is concerned with improving the qualifications of those in the work force (the fit between jobs and workers). This goes far beyond the argument that the reason people are poor is that they lack the skills, motivation, or personal habits necessary to obtain and hold jobs. Finally, the council recognized that some people, specifically the old and the disabled, were not likely to be affected by these strategies and would need more direct assistance.

Anderson and Locke (1964), however, provided us some insights into who would more likely benefit from which of these three basic strategies. From a historical perspective they argued that different strategies are needed for different groups, and that these strategies depend upon the nature of poverty in a society at a particular time. When a society has large numbers of people who are poor, few individuals find their way out of poverty regardless of economic growth. This happens because a few people control or have access to most of the society's wealth. As a society becomes more egalitarian and as a significant portion of the population begins to increase its skills and/or gain political power, a large number of people move out of poverty quite fast. Finally, they describe a third phase in which only a residual few remain in poverty. In this phase, as the masses become more affluent, fewer and fewer of the poor are able to leave poverty.

Following this, they divided the unemployed/poor population into three groups:

Group 1:   White, nonfarm families headed by a male under the age of 65. This group, they suggested, responds quickly to economic growth.

Group 2:   Nonwhite, nonfarm families headed by a male under the age of 65. This group responds to economic growth but not as quickly as group 1.

Group 3:   Predominantly farm families, female-headed families, people over age 65. These people are isolated from economic growth and income does not trickle down.

Based on their analysis of the 1959 census, they concluded that 65% of the poor were in the second phase and that steady economic growth would move most of them out of poverty. In fact, they predicted that for every 2.5% increase in the GNP, we would experience a corresponding 1% decrease in the poverty population. Their analysis would suggest that the first set of recommendations (the economic strategy) would probably assist groups 1 and 2 and the third strategy (income maintenance) would benefit the aged and disabled, but that the remainder in group 3 clearly needed services identified under the second strategy (the human capital strategy).

ECONOMIC POLICY: THIRTY-SIX YEARS OF GROWTH

The theory of economic growth and its trickle-down effects discussed in the previous sections not only support most of our theoretical assumptions of a free market economy, i.e., capitalism, it has been the foundation of most of our antipoverty efforts. Furthermore, it is so much a part of our individual and collective belief system that we rarely ask for empirical evidence that demonstrates its efficacy. We assume that it must work because we believe that it works.

Table 9.1 offers 36 years of data on five critical variables: (1) each year's GNP in constant 1992 dollars (this reflects "real growth" controlling for

Table 9.1.   Economic Growth and Poverty

Year	GNP (Current 1992 $, Billions)	Change in GNP from Previous Year (%)	Increase in Jobs (%)	Unemployment Rate (%)	Poverty Rate (%)
1960	2,276.0	2.4	1.0	5.5	22.2
1961	2,329.1	2.3	1.2	6.7	21.9
1962	2,471.5	6.1	0.2	5.5	21.0
1963	2,577.3	4.3	1.7	5.7	19.0
1964	2,727.8	5.8	1.7	5.2	18.0
1965	2,910.4	6.7	1.9	4.5	16.6
1966	3,087.8	6.1	1.7	3.8	15.4
1967	3,166.4	2.5	2.1	3.8	14.7
1968	3,314.5	4.7	1.8	3.6	12.8
1969	3,413.3	3.0	2.5	3.5	12.1
1970	3,417.1	0.1	2.5	4.9	12.6
1971	3,532.1	3.4	1.9	5.9	12.5
1972	3,726.3	5.5	3.1	5.6	11.9
1973	3,950.1	6.0	2.7	4.9	11.1
1974	3,930.2	−0.5	2.8	5.6	11.6
1975	3,903.3	−0.7	2.0	8.5	12.3
1976	4,118.8	5.5	2.5	7.7	11.8
1977	4,314.5	4.8	3.0	7.1	11.6
1978	4,543.7	5.3	3.3	6.1	11.4
1979	4,687.4	3.2	2.6	5.8	11.7
1980	4,670.8	−0.4	1.9	7.1	13.0
1981	4,769.9	2.1	1.6	7.6	14.0
1982	4,662.0	−2.3	1.4	9.7	15.0
1983	4,844.8	3.9	1.2	9.6	15.2
1984	5,178.0	6.9	1.8	7.5	14.4
1985	5,346.7	3.3	1.7	7.2	14.0
1986	5,501.2	2.9	2.0	7.0	13.6
1987	5,658.2	2.9	1.7	6.2	13.4
1988	5,878.5	3.9	1.0	5.5	13.0
1989	6,075.7	3.4	1.0	5.3	12.8
1990	6,157.0	1.3	1.5	5.6	13.5
1991	6,094.9	−1.0	0.9	6.8	14.2
1992	6,255.5	2.6	1.0	7.5	14.8
1993	6,408.0	2.4	1.1	6.9	15.1
1994	6,619.1	3.3	1.0	6.1	14.5
1995	6,748.7	2.0	0.9	5.6	13.8

Sources: For data on GNP, *Survey of Current Business,* www.bea.doc.gov/bea/data-n2.htm; for employment data, U.S. Department of Commerce, *Statistical Abstracts of the United States* (1989), *Economic Report of the President,* 1997, p. 347; for data on poverty, *Social Security Bulletin, Annual Statistical Supplements, 1962–1989, Economic Report of the President,* Washington, DC: USGPO, 1997, p. 336.

inflation), (2) the annual percentage change in GNP, (3) the annual percentage change in the number of new jobs, (4) the annual unemployment
rate, and (5) the annual poverty rate.

With all of its limitations, the GNP is the single best statistic to measure a
nation's economic growth. The major methodological and conceptual problems arise when we attempt cross-national comparisons (Myrdal 1966).
Given the theory we have discussed in this chapter, we would expect to see
an increase in the number of new jobs, a decrease in the unemployment rate
and a decrease in the poverty rate as the GNP increases. Correspondingly,
we should see a decrease in the number of new jobs and an increase in
unemployment and poverty when the GNP decreases.

Over the 36 years from 1960 to 1995 the GNP increased 197% in constant dollars and the poverty rate decreased by 38% (from 22.2 to 13.8%).
The average annual percentage point increase in the GNP over this period
was 3.2%, the average annual increase in new jobs was 1.8%, and the
average annual unemployment rate was 6.1%. Did the theory hold up?

From Figure 9.1 we see that the poverty rate decreased sharply during
the 1960s, leveled off during the 1970s, increased in the early 1980s, and
held relatively steady through the mid 1990s. To what extent do the
predictor variables explain this pattern?

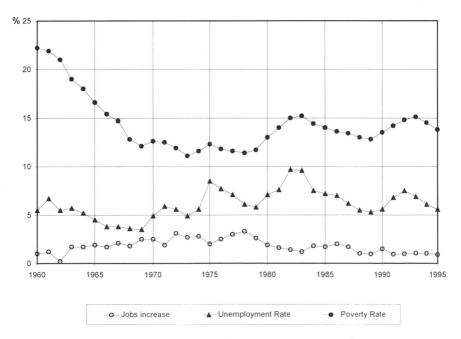

Figure 9.1   Economic development–poverty correlation.
Note: These Data from Table 9.1.

Figure 9.1 also shows the relationship between unemployment and an increase in jobs. We do see somewhat of an inverse relationship between job increase and unemployment. When job increase is greater, unemployment is generally lower. However, this trend becomes less pronounced after 1980. After 1970, the poverty curve also conforms with the trends in unemployment, but the variance in poverty rate is fairly narrow. Changes in the unemployment rate correspond as hypothesized in the 1960s (i.e., as poverty rates decreased, unemployment rates also decreased). However, unemployment rates showed increases in the 1970s while the poverty rates stabilized.

Looking at Figure 9.2, we see the relationship between change in the poverty rate and change in GNP. The average change in GNP shows considerable fluctuation, with the possible exception of the 1960s, and the slow-growth economy of the past decade. It is in the 1960s, however, that we see a steady decline in the poverty rate. In the 1960s, the average annual increase in jobs was 1.58% (range of 0.2 to 2.5%); lower than in the 1970s, 2.64% (range of 1.9 to 3.3%); and similar to the 1980s, 1.67% (range of 1.2 to 2.0%). Unemployment did increase in those years when there were sharp downswings in the GNP, e.g., 1970, 1974–1975, 1980–1982,

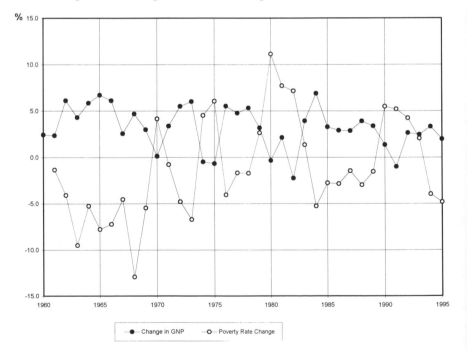

Figure 9.2   Economic growth–poverty correlation.
Note: Data from Table 9.1.

and 1991. Therefore, we can conclude that we do have one portion of the poverty population that responds to changes in the economy and another portion that remains poor despite economic growth.

As mentioned earlier, the poverty rate decreased by almost 8.5 percentage points, from 22.2% in 1960 to 13.8% in 1995. This represents an overall decrease of 38%. However, this figure is somewhat misleading in that most of the decrease occurred in the 1960s (see Table 9.2).

While there are any number of possible explanations for these unexpected trends, our purpose here is only to examine the hypothesis that economic growth is the most important factor in solving the problem of poverty in our society. One could argue, for example, that the poverty rate has dropped almost 8.5 percentage points, from 22.2 to 13.8%; another might argue that the number of poor was about 36.4 million persons in 1995—more than the estimated 34 million of 1963. What is clear, however, is that we do not see the predicted correspondence between increases in the GNP, increases in employment opportunities, and decreases in unemployment and poverty. The improvements in poverty reduction we have experienced occurred in the decade of the 1960s, and since then we have attempted, with mixed success, to maintain that level.

Earlier we discussed the characteristics of the 35 million people who were poor in the early 1960s. What are the characteristics of the approximately 37.6 million who were poor in the early 1990s? We find that there have been some shifts in the distribution of poverty.

The percentage of persons and families living below the poverty line was reduced significantly in these years, but the probability of escaping was not one of random chance, nor were the odds equal for all families. Families headed by white males (and a growing number of minority families headed by males who are graduates of high school) who have been temporarily displaced because of market disturbances continue to

Table 9.2. Changes in Poverty Rates[a] (%)

Years	Change
1960–1965	−25
1965–1970	−24
1970–1975	−2
1975–1980	+1
1980–1985	+7
1985–1990	−3
1990–1995	+2
1960–1995	−38

[a] These percentage changes are calculated from the data in Table 9.1

find employment when the economy improves. This explains the correspondence we see among poverty rate, unemployment, and job increases in Figure 9.1. These are Anderson and Locke's groups 1 and 2—the transitional poor.

Rural families, female-headed families (especially minority families), the elderly, and the disabled, on the other hand, did not find themselves affected by economic growth over the past 35 years. As discussed in Chapter 3, advances in the social insurance programs have dramatically helped the elderly (whereas 25% of the elderly were living in poverty in the early 1960s, approximately 13% had incomes below the poverty line in 1992) and the disabled. The others, however, have remained in poverty.

In 1963, 20% of all children were living in poverty. In 1994, 21.2% of all American children were still living in poverty. The statistical likelihood of a specific child being in poverty was, however, related to the type of family he or she was living in. In 1963, 66% of all children in families headed by a female were poor—a percentage four times higher than for children living in a male-headed household (Orshansky 1965a, 1965b). Almost 30 years later, the disparity still held (see Table 9.3). Nonwhite children growing up in families headed by a female had higher rates than those in white female-headed families (see Table 9.3). Living in a rural area increases the likelihood of poverty for all groups, female-headed households, married-couple families, whites, African-Americans, Hispanics, the elderly, and the disabled (Dudenhefer 1993).

Finally, while these statistics are informative, they are primarily a static description of a population at one point in time and, as such, tell only part of the story. Ellwood's 1987 panel study fills a much-needed gap in our understanding. After following a cohort of 3.5 million children born in an average year in the early 1970s, he concluded that 8 of every 10 children raised in a two-parent family, 2 of every 3 children raised part of the time in a single-parent family, and less than 1 of every 10 children raised entirely by a single parent escape poverty.

Conversely, while 2 of every 3 children raised entirely in a single-parent family experience long-term poverty, 12% of children raised part of the time in a single-parent family and only 2% of children raised in a

Table 9.3. Poverty Rates (%) among Related Children, 1990

Family Structure	White	African-American	Hispanic
Related children under age 18	15.1	44.2	37.7
In female-headed families	45.9	64.7	68.3
In male-headed families	9.2	18.1	26.5

Source: Devine and Wright (1993).

two-parent family experience long-term poverty. Furthermore, almost half of all the children living in poverty were raised entirely by a single parent.

Ellwood then concludes that while 20% of all children may be poor at any one time (the census data), 7.6% of all children experience 50% of the poverty years (the panel data). Here he makes the point that we need to distinguish between one child living in poverty for ten years (long-term poverty) and ten children living in poverty for one year (short-term poverty) (see Table 9.4).

POVERTY, THE WORK ETHIC, AND DEPENDENCY

The notion of the work ethic has been so ingrained in people that it has assumed the aura of natural law—a principle that has transcended time and is believed by most people to have been a part of the human existence. We need to be reminded, however, that the work ethic is the product of the early nineteenth century. As discussed earlier in Chapter 3, the emerging economic system of capitalism needed a mobile supply of labor and the ability to convert large numbers of agricultural workers into disciplined factory workers. To accomplish this, the state developed a number of social policies such as the principle of less eligibility and created institutions such as the poorhouse or "house of industry." Finally, the work ethic assumed not just moral and theological dimensions, it became an intrinsic part of the total human being.

Table 9.4. Poverty Rate (%) for Children in Different Family Types[a]

	Two-Parent Families	Part-Time Two-Parent	Single Parent
Never poor	80	67	7
Temporarily poor	18	21	31
Long-term poverty	2	12	62

Source: Adapted from Ellwood (1987).

[a] *Temporarily poor* is defined as 1–6 years; *long-term poverty* is defined as 7–10 years. *Two-parent family* is defined as growing up with two parents present for the entire period; *part-time two-parent* is defined as being raised partly in a single-parent family and partly in a two-parent family; *single parent* is defined as being raised entirely in a single-parent family.

Christopher Lasch (1977) in his provocative work *Haven in a Heartless World*, however, has argued rather convincingly that the work ethic, to be successfully implemented, had to go beyond employment issues:

> Ever since Max Weber showed the connections between Protestantism and capitalism, and demonstrated, moreover, that the connections lay at the level not of formal religious doctrine but of "psychological sanctions," it has been clear that modern civilization requires among other things, a profound transformation of personality. The Protestant concept of the calling not only dignified worldly life, insisted on the moral value of work . . . it also upheld the spiritual dignity of marriage and domesticity. (p. 4)

As the nineteenth century evolved, the "ideal" family type to meet the needs of the prevailing economic system was systematically redefined. This new concept of the family held that the father had to be the head of the house, that the mother was responsible for the care of the house and the children, and that, in return, the children owed their parents honor and obedience. Parents had the responsibility to produce authority-oriented children—children who would meet the requirements of the labor market.

Donzelot (1979), a French social scientist and colleague of Michel Foucault, is penetrating in disclosing what he terms the latent functions served by societal institutions. Writing within the same general perspective as Lasch, he argues that human service professionals should be more appropriately labeled "social pathologists"—a cadre of professionals who have undermined the family through social control mechanisms. In *The Policing of Families*, he writes of the "colonization of the family" by the helping professions, of their "full penetration into family life," of their "ceaseless technocratic interventionism," of the "continuous surveillance they exercise over domestic life," and of the "transfer of sovereignty to the corrective system that never stops swelling."

The term *policing* used in the title of the book comes from Foucault's emphasis on the biopolitical dimensions of society. Policing, he suggests, is not to be understood in the limiting repressive sense we give the term today, but has a much broader meaning that encompasses all the methods for developing the "quality of the population and the strength of the nation." Not trusting the family to carry out these necessary functions—the shaping of values and behavior required to meet the needs of the industrial revolution—extrafamilial organizations assumed responsibility.

Focusing on family type ignores the fact that by the second half of the twentieth century, fewer workers (especially those who were unskilled) were required by the labor market. The work ethic, so important a century ago, has become less important. This is the crux of the current dilemma. Individuals are still being socialized to believe that they can achieve personal satisfaction only through their attachment to the work force, and then they are systematically denied the possibility of finding a job—especially if they are young, rural, a member of a minority group, or a single mother. They are also socialized to believe that a two-parent, father-headed family is superior to other family forms.

The impression given is that the problem of persistent poverty resides in the family and is not to be found in structural factors. This thesis has led to one of two conclusions: (1) Because poor families are not like the ideal family they are not governed by the work ethic. (2) Because they lack the work ethic they have experienced family deterioration. Both conclusions, however, are built on two assumptions: that poor families do not work, and that either the individual or family is at fault and is exhibiting pathology.

The ability of the single mother to educate her children and instill in them the habits of persistence and hard work has been undermined by her own frustrations and economic deprivation. The children raised in many female-headed families that are poor learn how to survive but pay a great price in doing so. As the youth goes through the development process, he or she becomes disabled for life in other surroundings, especially in school and the workplace. Piven and Cloward (1971) pointed out almost 20 years ago that poverty and family deterioration are usually accompanied by the spread of certain types of behavior in youth, including failure in school, crime, addiction, and increased out-of-wedlock pregnancies. These findings have been reaffirmed by McLanahan and Garfinkel (1986) and McLanahan and Sandefur (1995).

While the trend among families is to have fewer children than previous generations, more and more families are deciding not to have children. Although we see this occurring in all families, it is most pronounced in white families, where 52% did not have any children in 1995, compared to 42% of African-American families and 36% of Hispanic families (see Table 9.5).

When we couple this with the fact that increases in birth rates are found among younger women (ages 10 to 19; see Table 9.6), and that these increases are likely to be associated with single, never-married, female-headed households, we are faced with the reality of a growing underclass.

Although divorce continues to be the major route into single parenthood, a growing contributor is the increase in births to never-married women. In the United States, 40% of the increase in single-mother families from 1970 to 1984 has been attributed to births outside marriage (Ermisch 1987). While some have defended the female-headed household as a healthy adaptation to inner-city life and domestic violence, the high incidence of poverty with its associated consequences make this family type a growing policy concern.

Table 9.5. Presence of Children and Family Size by Race[a] (%)

	1970	1980	1985	1990	1995
Families with no children	44	48	50	51	51
White	45	49	52	53	52
African-American	39	38	43	41	42
Hispanic	30	31	34	37	36
Average number of children per family					
White	na	1.03	na	0.95	1.02
African-American	na	1.51	na	1.26	1.27
Hispanic	na	1.56	na	1.37	1.50

Source: U.S. Bureau of the Census (1989:50, 1996:64).
[a]na, not available.

Today, more than one million teenagers become pregnant each year, and half of these choose to deliver and keep their children. A disproportionate number of these mothers are from minority groups, and most are from poor families. Finally, two of every three teen mothers will not graduate from high school. The child poverty rate for children whose parent(s) are high school dropouts is 57%, compared to 24% for those whose parent(s) are high school graduates, and 4% where a parent(s) has a college degree (Annie E. Casey Foundation 1997). Research shows that children born to single teenage mothers are more likely to drop out of school, to give birth out of wedlock, divorce or separate, and become dependent on welfare (Annie E. Casey Foundation 1997). Given the higher birth rates among younger, minority, never-married women, we are faced with the prospect that the chronically poor will produce a significant percentage of the future's adults, who in turn will be poor also.

What possibly distinguishes the current generation of the chronically poor (especially the youth and young adults) from their parents and grandparents is a rejection of the work ethic. The work ethic makes no sense whatsoever when there are no jobs available or if the only jobs available are in the secondary labor market, paying marginal wages, with

Table 9.6. Trends in Birth Rates by Age of Mother[a]

Age in Years	1960	1970	1980	1993
10–14	0.8	1.2	1.1	1.4
15–19	89.1	68.3	52.7	59.6
20–24	258.1	167.8	115.1	112.6
25–29	197.4	145.1	112.9	115.5
30–34	112.7	73.3	61.9	80.8

Source: U.S. Bureau of the Census (1989:61–62).
[a]Rates are per thousand live births.

no hope of advancement, and characterized by continuous fluctuations that result in a revolving-door experience with the welfare system. In addition, these poor lack positive role models, in that they tend to live in neighborhoods that reinforce their reality. As Merton (1957) pointed out, if traditional channels are closed, some youth will find alternative pathways to success. While society may label these behaviors as deviant and irrational, for the youth they are the only meaningful avenues open, since the work ethic has little meaning. This sense of hopelessness is the major difference between the temporary and permanent underclass. This is, and will continue to be, a major stumbling block for future policy initiatives.

THE PERMANENT UNDERCLASS

Whereas in the 1930s there was *mass* unemployment, in the postwar period we have been experiencing *class* unemployment. In 1947, 32% of all families were poor. By 1956 there had been a reasonable economic recovery and this percentage had dropped sharply to 23%. Over the next six years, the percentage of families escaping poverty had slowed and by 1962, 20% of all families were still poor. Presently, almost 14% are living in poverty.

These advances, however, were not equally experienced by all. Special groups have been singled out by the workings of the economy to suffer, while all others have experienced increasingly improved standards of living. As Harrington argues, "America for the first time in its history has a hereditary underclass. Most of the children of the poor have become the fathers and mothers of the poor" (1975:111).

The weight of evidence would suggest that the existence of a permanent underclass—the permanently poor—was inevitable given our economic system. Over 60 years ago, in forecasting the economic and social order of the postdepression era, Tugwell attempted to warn the country of the dangers of emerging industrial trends:

> We now know that there are millions of workers, formerly employed by industry, who cannot be reabsorbed by our present industrial system, assuming it to remain unchanged, even if the volume of physical production is brought back to the levels of the turbulent twenties. In 1932, I am told, industry could produce as much as in 1923 with one-third less labor. . . . When new machines forced the workers out of jobs, they were expected to applaud the spirit of progress and find other jobs if they could. . . . [T]he millions out of work were expected to resign themselves to industrial bad luck. (1934:36–37)

In time, and mainly because of the war, many eventually did rejoin the labor force and Tugwell's warning was muted. These new jobs, however, required much more education and higher order skills. Those without skills found themselves restricted to the economic underworld—to low-paying industries or industries requiring lower levels of skills.

Over the past 20–30 years, technological advances and automation were instrumental in enlarging the underclass, because they destroyed tens of thousands of unskilled and semiskilled jobs that had been the major source of employment for minorities. With few skills and poor educational background, they found themselves totally unprepared for this new environment with its highly sophisticated labor market requirements.

Stoesz (1985), in reviewing the experiences of the past 25 years, documents the extent to which these events have affected the prevalence of poverty. He cites the earlier study of Piven and Cloward (1971), who pointed out that between 1950 and 1969 one million farms were lost to mechanization; the works of Robbins (1983) and Benjamin (1983) who described the hardships experienced by coal miners and their families in West Virginia when the extractive industries mechanized; and the deep and enduring poverty of the inner cities experiencing economic displacement and creating an underclass of millions of workers who were left in regions without a need for their "skills" (Garreau 1981; Dorfman 1982). Roughly 25% of the poor live in rural areas and the rural poor are more likely to be chronically poor, regardless of race.

Kuttner's recent study (1984) also supports Tugwell's prediction. While most argue that shifting from a manufacturing economy to a service economy is a sign of progress, Kuttner disagrees:

> In theory . . . just as mechanization of agriculture freed human workers to do more industrial tasks, the automation of industry should free workers to do more highly refined jobs and enjoy leisure time. Unfortunately the workings of the market do not necessarily produce that happy outcome. (p. 169)

Kuttner points out, contrary to the theory, that a postindustrial economy employs a large number of relatively well-paid production workers in industries such as manufacturing and construction, while a service or high-technology economy may employ a small number of highly paid professionals at one extreme, but a large number of poorly paid workers at the other end. Furthermore, the number of high-paying jobs in previously high-paying industries has decreased over the past 20 years. Kuttner concludes that "technological advances are not translating into gains for the blue collar worker. . . . [T]he work is becoming more routinized and lower paid" (ibid.:174).

A growing number of people—referred to by some as the permanent underclass—have become a "surplus population" in that they are only marginally useful to the economy. Some people, as discussed further in Chapter 8, are not employed because they lack the necessary skills, education, or experience; or because of their color, the place they live, or technological changes that are making their skills obsolete.

Despite the evidence that the underclass are victims of an economic system that has little or no use for them, the historical response has been to turn the argument around and suggest that the reason lies not in the economy, but in the individuals themselves. While the language may be different, the analysis is the same as that offered by Bentham in the nineteenth century: the poor have lost the work ethic (see Chapter 3). In the view of many, therefore, the task facing the country is similar to that facing the theorists of the early decades of the previous century—to offer explanations that are grounded in the ideology of the work ethic and to develop social programs that will rekindle the drive to work.

DEPENDENCY:
A CRITIQUE OF SOCIAL WELFARE STRATEGIES

Social welfare programs in capitalist societies do not cause dependency, nor are they responsible for the existence of a permanent underclass any more than social welfare measures caused cyclical downturns in the economy, obsolete capital in certain industries, automation, structural unemployment, or the decay of the inner cities. Despite this, the welfare system continues to be blamed for the persistence of seemingly intractable problems.

Social welfare measures have been created to solve crises and problems created by a market economy with its inevitable hot and cold cycles, but the measures can only modify the system since they are only peripherally related to the causes. The overall social welfare strategy attempts to identify an appropriate equation made up of three components: (1) income maintenance, (2) employment training, and (3) social services. This search has proven over time to be not so much elusive, but more a problem of adequacy given society's concern to eradicate long-term dependency and to (re)instill the work ethic.

Income maintenance programs, as discussed in Chapter 3, provide a family with a subsistence level of support and then penalize them if they are able to supplement this with even minimal employment opportunities. Employment training programs, as discussed in Chapter 8, showed short-term results for some (usually white males) but for the permanent underclass, "success" was usually a short-term job with a high probability of returning to the welfare rolls. While there was significant movement from welfare to work, there was significant movement from work to welfare.

In areas with large-scale structural unemployment, welfare recipients were being trained for jobs that either did not exist, or if they did, paid less than the poor could obtain from welfare. Quite simply, the employment programs were powerless since they could not create jobs. In fact, they have had the unintended effect of convincing many that the work ethic is an irrelevant concept.

As Ginsburg (1976) argued, every administration since the passage of the Full Employment Act of 1946 has refused to consider supporting a program that actually creates jobs, e.g., a public jobs program. There have been, of course, limited efforts to deal with the job side of the equation, e.g., tax breaks for private employers who hire the "hard to employ" and some emergency efforts through public service strategies. Both of these have been viewed as temporary or emergency efforts dealing with cyclical unemployment and not with the permanent unemployment of the underclass. He concludes that "the country has yet to move up to the starting line" (p. 2) in implementing the promises of the 1946 act. Instead, our employment policies have been primarily focused on the training and placement of the unemployed into the existing labor markets.

We see, then, that our government's overall approach in this area is similar to its response to the housing problem (see Chapter 4). It can be characterized as a supply-side strategy, because it assumes that economic growth by itself will create new jobs, which will in turn be filled by the currently unemployed. To understand this belief is to understand this society's approach to solving most social problems. It reinforces the dominant view that markets, whether these are the housing, employment, medical care, or educational markets, work most efficiently if government does not interfere with them.

The overriding assumption has been and continues to be that employment opportunities exist—the solution being one of identifying and removing barriers some people experience in finding appropriate jobs. In part, these barriers were assumed to be market imperfections and discriminatory practices on the part of employers and, in part, deficits on the part of the unemployed. Efforts to address each of these barriers are discussed in Chapter 8.

Current government efforts to move recipients from welfare to employment rest on three premises: (1) that welfare recipients do not value employment over welfare and therefore must be coerced into employment, (2) that welfare recipients have little or no work experience, and thus any job will do, and (3) that employment at a low-wage job will lead to a better job (Edin 1995). The rhetoric of welfare reform, however, has little to do with reality.

While it is difficult to evaluate these efforts in their totality, it is clear that the permanent underclass was not being helped. Critics continue to point out that "creaming" occurred in employment training programs, and with reduced funding levels the existing programs are likely to exacerbate this practice.

On the other hand, our competitive market system has not proven to be an efficient and just allocator of resources and economic growth has not doubled the standard of living for everyone. Poverty remains with us and the numbers are growing.

WELFARE REFORM

In Chapter 3, we discussed this country's major income maintenance programs in some detail. In this section, we will discuss those aspects of those programs as they relate to the issue of dependency, poverty, and single-parent families. The Council of Economic Advisors assumed that effective job creation and job preparation policies would meet the income needs of most Americans. Those unable to participate in the labor force—the elderly and the disabled—would be supported through a reasonably generous income maintenance program.

The council's position was similar to those who drafted and implemented the Social Security Act of 1935. The Social Security program offered a two-pronged system: one for labor force participants and one for those who were unable to work. For the former group, a combination of employee benefits and government social insurance provided protection against illness, disability, and unemployment and funds for retirement. For the latter group (i.e., children, the permanently disabled, and the elderly) government provided a safety net. Congress and the administration believed that the social insurance program would, in time, meet most people's needs and only a small group—a residual population—would need social assistance. Unfortunately, both were only half right. The social assistance population has not dwindled and women heading families with children have not been able to achieve and maintain economic independence.

As early as 1966, in their report to the secretary of DHEW, the Advisory Council on Public Welfare pointed out: "Public assistance payments are so low and so uneven that the Government is, by its own standards and definitions, a major source of the poverty on which it has declared unconditional war" (1966:5).

At any one time, only 50% of the poor receive welfare benefits, and as discussed in Chapter 3, even those who received social assistance benefits (e.g., SSI and AFDC) did not receive enough to raise them above the poverty level.

Enforcement of the child support obligations of noncustodial parents is another strategy the government has used to reduce dependency. The earlier Child Support Enforcement Program was not very successful in collecting awards over the period 1980–1994 (see Table 9.7). Successful collections in AFDC cases never exceeded 12.5% in any single year and the amount recovered was approximately 7% of the AFDC monies spent in those cases. The success rate was significantly higher in non-AFDC cases, but still amounted to only 30% of the cases. Increased efforts as a result of amendments that aimed to increase paternity establishment, withhold wages, make regular adjustments in the award amounts, and create a national system of enforcement have been met with mixed success. In 1991 the average annual child support award was $2,961, but even this average was lower for African-American families ($2,079) and Hispanic families ($2,165) (U.S. Bureau of the Census 1996:385). Only 27% of women who had never married were awarded child support awards, compared with 73% of divorced women. Never-married women receive on average the lowest amount of child support payments. African-American and Hispanic mothers are much less likely than their white counterparts to be awarded child support (ibid.). Finally, mothers who are not high school graduates and younger mothers are less likely to have a child support award, and their support payments are on average less than better educated and older women (Committee on Ways and Means 1994. While child support is an important source of income for some low-income families, it is less likely to assist the chronically poor.

Table 9.7. Trends in Child Support Collections

Year	Cases with collections (%)		
	AFDC cases	Non-AFDC	AFDC recovered
1980	11.0	28.7	5.2
1985	11.0	30.3	7.3
1989	11.5	29.2	10.0
1990	11.9	28.1	10.3
1991	12.2	28.9	10.7
1992	12.3	27.1	11.4
1993	11.7	26.1	12.0
1994	11.6	26.5	12.5

Source: U.S. Bureau of the Census (1996:386).

Policies created under the individual deficiency approach can be criticized for being overly simplistic. Many welfare recipients have received training for jobs that did not exist. Others ended up in dead-end, low-paid jobs in the secondary labor market. Needs such as child care and health insurance have been defined as transitional, making families worse off by participating in employment. Other needs such as transportation and well-paid jobs have been completely ignored. The success of "workfare" programs have been judged narrowly by their ability to reduce the welfare rolls, as opposed to their ability to raise families out of poverty through stable employment.

In August 1997, President Clinton declared PRWORA a success, citing a 27-year low in the AFDC/TANF population (Phoenix *Tribune* 1997). What Clinton failed to mention, however, was the impact on employment of the strongest economy since World War II, and more importantly, what happened to the 1.4 million people who have dropped off the welfare rolls in the nine months since the enactment of PRWORA. Accounting for the success of welfare reform needs to go beyond a reduction in the welfare rolls.

These efforts at reducing dependency will fail if the federal government does not assume a more proactive and more aggressive role in the economy and in the employment sector. To train people for jobs that do not exist or are dead-ended is not a solution to the problem of dependency.

Ellwood (1987) argues that our income maintenance programs are built on a questionable set of assumptions, the most troublesome one being the implicit belief that the poor are a homogeneous population. He comes to this conclusion by pointing out that we have only one antipoverty program. The reality is, however, that we have a large number of families experiencing short-term poverty and a small number experiencing long-term poverty. Each requires different solutions. The three-pronged proposal from the Council of Economic Advisors 30 years ago is as valid today as it was then because it does differentiate and it links dependency to more structural issues that must be dealt with if the problem is to be ameliorated.

In conclusion, we are not suggesting that social services and employment training are irrelevant. While we have argued that they cannot solve the problem in the absence of more proactive economic policies, we would also argue that the latter will not produce the desired effect without the former. Whatever it is that is supposed to trickle down with economic growth does not reach those on the bottom. Unskilled and semiskilled workers who had been able to find and hold jobs in the industrial sector do not have the skills required in a growing service economy. Social skills may not have been important on an assembly line, but they are essential in jobs requiring social interactions. As long as we refuse to reexamine the meaning and value of the work ethic, and as long as we define an individual's worth in terms of his or her employment, we have the responsibility to provide them with meaningful, well-paid employment and the skills required for these jobs.

TOWARD A REFORMULATION

It would seem that we are faced with a number of options. If we continue to separate social and economic policies and treat dependency only as a social and not an economic problem, and if we further look to a solution in traditional social services, employment training, and income maintenance programs, we will continue to treat the problem through historic Poor Law provisions. The choice is between the more humane Poor Law strategies of the twentieth century or the more orthodox and punitive nineteenth century Poor Laws. Neither course, however, will solve the problem of dependency nor will it (re)instill the work ethic into this population.

If we are convinced that the work ethic is still important for other than just economic reasons (our economy might not need all adults in the work force if production is the objective) and we are unwilling to provide a reasonable level of guaranteed income support to female-headed families, the unemployed, and the underemployed, then the only rational strategy is to create meaningful jobs.

The strongly held belief that government should be the employer of last resort does not mean that government should only take a reactive role in the employment sector. The federal government can and should create jobs in the public sector similar to those initiated in the New Deal and those created by programs of the 1960s such as the Appalachian Regional Commission ($4.5 billion) and the Economic Development Commission ($4.8 billion), through which funds were channeled to sagging local economies. If, as we have argued, the youth of the permanent underclass have rejected the work ethic (or at least that version of the work ethic that mainstream society accepts) because of a sense of hopelessness that has turned to anger, they need to be resocialized. It follows that if the private labor market continues to ignore these youth, a public labor market has to be created to provide opportunities for paid employment, combined with relevant education and vocational training for those who are not able to find work in the private sector.

As we reexamine our policies and look for new ways to solve seemingly intractable problems, we need to sift carefully through proposals that have already been offered but never acted on. A number of these were developed in the 1960s during that period when we seemed to make a national commitment to eradicate poverty. We do not argue that we should continue or expand the initiatives of that period. We are not even arguing that they were a success or a failure. What is important now is to seek solutions that can deal with present problems. A number of analysts during the 1960s did provide critiques and directions that, if acted upon, might have eased the situation.

The insights offered by Titmuss (1966) are as relevant today as they were 30 years ago. First, he argued that the theory that economic growth would solve the poverty problem was really an assumption that had not been tested.

Second, Titmuss contended that the position that economic growth needs to precede social growth—that without economic growth we cannot afford social programs—is a simplistic solution to a complex problem. He predicted that we were underestimating the extent and rate of obsolescence of much of our social capital, especially schools and housing. He suggested, further, that we were also underestimating the rate and effects of scientific, technological, and economic changes and were ignoring the impact they were having on the poor and the unskilled. We were underestimating the cumulative effects of discriminatory school systems and housing and labor markets. And finally, we were overestimating the potentialities of the poor and the permanent underclass to understand and participate fully in an increasingly complex society, and the will of all people to move toward a more equal society. Titmuss concluded his argument with the charge that we were exaggerating the capacity of private markets to resolve social problems.

In an earlier article, Titmuss (1968) suggested that we take our lead from Myrdal (1966), who offered a number of proposals in his *Beyond the Welfare State*. These included:

- aggressive economic development;
- full employment;
- equality of opportunity for youth;
- social security; and
- protected minimum standards of health, nutrition, housing, and education.

What is notable is Myrdal's insistence that while economic prosperity is essential to eradicating poverty and improving the standard of living for all, a deep and abiding political commitment to these goals is even more important.

Galbraith (1984) and Schorr (1963), two of the more prolific analysts of poverty during this period, severely criticized existing and proposed policy initiatives on the basis that, with the exception of the emerging civil-rights efforts, solutions to poverty assumed a case-by-case, family-by-family approach. While the programs of the 1960s focusing on individual deficiency were likely to have been more humane than those of the nineteenth century, they were similar in philosophy to institutions such as the earlier Charity Organization Societies—the poor were responsible for their poverty and they, the poor, had to change. For Galbraith and Schorr, this residual approach had to give way to a more institutional formulation if we as a nation were serious about dealing with poverty.

Finally, Miller and Rein (1964) are representative of a large group of analysts who maintained that poverty was not a condition that lent itself to short-term investments. They were critical of existing efforts (especially the expanding demonstration programs) as forms of "ad hoc tinkering" that would not be successful. Instead they argued for sustained and comprehensive long-range efforts.

STRATEGIES FOR THE NEW MILLENNIUM

The directions offered by the above critics found their way into much of the work of the Council of Economic Advisors in the 1960s. Earlier in this chapter we outlined their proposals as falling into three major categories: (1) an economic strategy, (2) an employment strategy, and (3) an income maintenance strategy.

Of the three general strategies the council identified, most of the effort to date has focused on the second and third, with little real effort in the area of economic development. And yet, it is only in the first that a nation deals with the creation of jobs. The second attempted to prepare individuals for jobs and the third attempts, in theory, to provide the individual with income when he or she is no longer able to work.

ECONOMIC DEVELOPMENT AND EMPLOYMENT

These three interdependent strategies are basically concerned with two issues: full employment for those who can work and protection for those who cannot. It is only through full employment, moreover, that we can directly deal with the fundamental issue of poverty. The Council of Economic Advisors in its 1964 report was reiterating the promise of the Full Employment Act of 1945 and the earlier statement by Roosevelt, who introduced the concept in his 1944 State of the Union Address, his "Economic Bill of Rights." Even this was preceded by the president's assertion in the height of the depression that Americans wanted jobs and not the dole.

Kuttner considers that Beveridge's (1944) report on employment "remains the definitive exposition on why full employment must be the centerpiece of social citizenship. Without it, the social fabric of the welfare state falls apart" (1984:32). In Chapter 3, we pointed out that Beveridge considered income maintenance to be one of the pillars of a caring society. For Beveridge, full employment was the foundation upon which all other social polices are built. Beveridge, like Roosevelt, saw unemployment in more than economic terms, and, in commenting on the potential adverse affects on those who were not employed, both were unwilling to deal with the issue only as a macroeconomics issue (i.e., the balance between employment and inflation). Unemployment was a human and personal problem to be resolved by society:

> Unemployment remains a personal catastrophe . . . even if an adequate income is provided by insurance or otherwise. Idleness, even on an income corrupts; the feelings of not being wanted demoralizes. . . . As long as there is long term unemployment not due to personal deficiency, anybody who loses his job fears that he may be one of the unlucky ones who will not get another job quickly. The short term unemployed do not know that they are short term unemployed until their unemployment is over. (Beveridge 1944:19)

Beveridge, like Roosevelt, believed in the work ethic, but went beyond the rhetoric that has mesmerized so many. To hold individuals to the work ethic without making it possible for them to get jobs was contrary to what Beveridge believed a modern society to be. In allowing unemployment to be used as an economic tool to fight inflation, our society becomes more and more divided; that is, the employed are pitted against the unemployed, the haves against the have-nots.

Full employment will not solve the total poverty problem, but without full employment it will get even worse. First, the future stability of our economic system requires full employment. Second, a national commitment is built on a society that is not divided but, in Boulding's (1967) terms, a society that is integrated and, in Titmuss's formulation, an altruistic society that fosters a sense of community. Third, while we have presented data in this chapter that shows the risk of being poor to be higher among single-mother families, among minorities, and among rural families, of the two-parent families who are living below the poverty level, 33% of these families were "headed" by a male who worked full time and 33% by a male who could not find work. Even among single-parent families headed by a woman, 13% were employed and 22% tried to find employment but could not. These are the individuals and families who would benefit from the reality of a full-employment society. Income maintenance programs are not the long-term solution to their problems. Still, even full employment must be put in perspective. One-half of the 17 million new jobs created in the 1980s paid a year round full-time equivalent of less than $11,611, which is just about equal to the current, officially defined poverty level. Almost 11% of the mothers of poor children in single-mother families are employed full-time, year-round. This is not the type of full employment proposed by Beveridge, Roosevelt, or the Council of Economic Advisors.

To deal with the growing problem of regional unemployment in this country, we might learn from the experiences of a number of European countries where national governments actively become involved in macroeconomic policies and employment sectors. Kuttner (1984) provides an interesting contrast to our economic policies and the role of government in his study of a number of other countries, including, Sweden, Austria, the former West Germany, Norway, and Japan.

All of these countries have a fairly large public sector (with the noted exception of Japan) and more direct government involvement than we do and yet have been able to strike a balance between relatively low unemployment rates, a more equal distribution of wages and income resulting in less of a need for redistribution, and an economy with significantly less inflation. While the form of government involvement may differ across these countries, the level of involvement in each far outstrips that of our government. In Japan, for example, government takes an active role in planning and brokering with the private sector. Sweden and Austria, on the other hand, have centralized economic bargaining policies. All attempt to keep wage increases in line with real growth in their economies and thus hold down inflation.

Kuttner argues that it is not the specifics of the policies, nor the particular institutional arrangements that have evolved, that seem to explain the success these countries have had in maintaining full employment and in keeping wage increases in line with real economic growth, but the nature of the relationship between government, the unions, and industry that makes the difference. In each of these countries there appears to have been a conscious movement away from relationships previously driven by conflict and mistrust to one that recognizes that in achieving each party's best interest, the best interests of the other parties are also being achieved.

Underpinning each, Kuttner contends, is the notion of a social bargain through which a

> well organized and powerful labor movement exchanges overt class conflict and militant bargaining over wages for a high employment society with a generous social wage, a state policy commitment to greater equality, and substantial influence for organized workers. (ibid.:148)

While the labor movement in this country has lost much of its influence and many of its members (see Chapter 8 for trends in union membership), the labor movement in these European countries is as powerful as ever. The unions are not only strong, but they are united. When unions enter into collective bargaining, they bargain for all unions—equal pay for all workers doing the same kind of work regardless of the specific industry, and a narrowing of wage differences between low- and high-skill workers and between men and women.

Given this, they are in a position to keep inflation down by "subordinating short-term wage demands to other labor goals, e.g., full employment, egalitarian wage distributions, retraining opportunities, work place enrichment and welfare objectives" (ibid.:142). Kuttner argues, moreover, that it is only when there are strong unions and refined social bargaining machinery that parties will have mutual respect and be willing to look beyond narrowly defined self-interests.

Kuttner concludes that these experiments, whether they are called a social bargain model, a labor corporatism model, or simply collective bargaining, are grounded in refined and expanded Keynesian principles, which assume that the role of government is to pump resources into regions where there is a need for new jobs and/or for the retraining of workers. Moreover, these governments combine training with wage subsidies and job placement services for those workers who have been temporarily displaced.

It is clear from the above that Kuttner gives priority to the value of community in his analysis. In fact, he argues that without this belief in community, there would be no social bargain. Separate unions recognize that they exist in a community of unions, and jointly with government and industry they accept the reality that together they are a community—whether it is called a society or a nation. Furthermore, they reject the idea of a zero sum game since they believe that for each to benefit, they all must benefit.

CHAPTER

10

The Political Economy of Social Welfare:
Promises and Problems

POLICY ANALYSIS AND CRITICAL THEORY

The previous seven chapters have analyzed a number of policy areas, four of which dealt with substantive issues and three others with populations who are the targets of policy initiatives. It should be clear by this point that Boulding's conclusion that "social policy looks like a sticky conglomeration of the ad hoc" (1967:8) is fairly accurate. Although we have developed a framework to provide, in Boulding's formulation, some common threads to unite all social policies and some common denominators to evaluate seemingly heterogeneous policies, (1) the disparity between the rhetoric found in statements of specific policies and the actual policies that are implemented and (2) the glaring contradictions found between and within policies make the policy analysis task extremely difficult.

Still, we believe that the framework offered in the first two chapters of this book is a reasonable attempt to meet Boulding's charge. We began with the argument that to understand this country's social policies is to understand this country's political economy, that all of our social policies are shaped by the needs of our economic system. We then expanded the framework by incorporating first principles such as freedom, equality, and community.

It is this addition that makes this analysis somewhat different. Most analysts, operating within the positivist framework, offer descriptions and explanations of policies but stop short of providing an "understanding" of the policy. This, they argue, goes beyond the purview of the "detached scientist" and enters the realm of the policymaker in that it introduces "values" and preferences. To move beyond the traditional approach is to blend the empirical with the normative.

This latter is the position of Habermas and the current school of critical theory. "The intent of critical theory is to provide us with an accurate depth understanding of our historical situation" (Bernstein 1982:217) and to help us "grasp invariant irregularities of social action as such and when they express ideologically frozen relations of dependence that, in principle, can be transformed" (Habermas 1971:310). As discussed in Chapter 2, Habermas is a major critic of rational planning and rational decision theory. He argues that as each society evolved, some groups gained power and others lost power; that those with power developed mechanisms to maintain that power; and that over time patterns of discrimination and inequality became so ingrained that they are rarely questioned or, if questioned, are quickly displaced. Given this, he concludes that rational decision-makers will only accept courses of action that maintain the status quo, that maintain the existing imbalances. To do otherwise would be "irrational." Rejecting this, Habermas suggests that the analyst has a responsibility to expose these patterns of inequalities and dependence:

> Critical theory aspires to bring the subjects themselves to full self-consciousness of the contradictions implicit in their material existence, to penetrate the ideological mystifications and forms of false consciousness that distort the meaning of existing social conditions . . . where the theoretical understanding of the contradictions inherent in existing society, when appropriated by those who are exploited, becomes constitutive of their very activity to transform society. (Bernstein 1982:182)

Perhaps the most widely recognized theorist and practitioner of this approach in the Americas is Paulo Freire, whose commitment to the idea that empowerment must begin with understanding and insight is captured in the titles of his books, e.g., *Pedagogy of the Oppressed* (1981), *Education for Critical Consciousness* (1982), and *Learning to Question* (1989).

Such is the theoretical background for the particular framework used in this analysis of existing social policies in this country. It is offered as one attempt, and only one attempt, to develop "common threads" and a "common denominator."

SOCIAL POLICY AND SOCIAL ACTION

Policy was described in Chapter 1 as an expression of values and preferences, and therefore policy analysis is as much a normative activity as it is an empirical activity. However, while a specific policy or set of policies may express a statement of what should be done and while these statements may have the power of law or statute, social policy cannot coerce changes in many behaviors or attitudes. It can, nevertheless, create an environment that is supportive to a change in those behaviors or attitudes. For example, Boulding (1967) argues that a major objective of any social policy is to "build community." It is clear that Boulding is concerned with creating environments in which human beings assume responsibilities for the well-being of others, that human exchanges go beyond the dominant rationale of "quid pro quo," and that the rights of the individual do not take precedence over the rights of the community. No social policy, however, can coerce people to do these things, to force them to become integrated in a community, if they do not want to.

Titmuss (1971), though, offers an example of how a policy can support or stimulate a sense of community through his cross-national analysis of blood donors. In countries where individuals are not reimbursed for donating blood, he found virtually no cases of serum hepatitis and few instances in which the supply of blood ran out, compared to countries that allowed individuals to sell their blood or give blood only when they were guaranteed they would receive blood when they needed it. He characterized the former societies as those in which people gave out of a sense of altruism and community. They gave because others needed; they trusted that others, often strangers, would give to them if they were in need. He characterized the latter societies as those in which individuals transacted with others primarily to "maximize" their self-interests. His argument was not that each system shaped the behavior or attitudes of people. Rather, each system was a reflection of dominant attitudes and behaviors and, in part, these attitudes and behaviors reflected the ideology of the existing political economy. He concluded, however, that if a society wants to change these attitudes, policies can support (not cause) the change.

A second example of how government attempts to affect attitudes and behavior is the parenthood insurance policy implemented by the Danish government in the 1970s. Recognizing that most parents found it necessary to work outside the home even when they had young children, the government provided each family a number of days of paid leave—days that were to be used when one of their children was sick and unable to go to school or other forms of child care. The initial policy was carefully drafted so that both fathers and mothers would be encouraged to share the child care functions. In effect, the Danish government was stating through public policy that child rearing, unlike childbearing, was not dependent on the gender of the parent, that fathers had a role in caring for their children. After a few years the government found that in most instances the mother and not the father stayed home when their children were sick. The existing policy was then modified to further encourage fathers to share in these tasks. However, the new policy was more a carrot than a stick. It did not force fathers to participate, e.g., by requiring the father to use a certain percentage of the leave (such a policy could prove harmful to the children and the parents). Rather, it extended the number of covered days but allowed the mother to use only the original number. In this way, the state created an environment that encouraged fathers to share in the parenting of their children.

FIRST PRINCIPLES AND CITIZENSHIP

In Chapter 2, we argued that while social policy is concerned with choosing among multiple, conflicting, and yet desirable goals, there are no scientific rules that help us make these choices. Rein (1976) has suggested that values provide the criteria by which we judge the desirability of a course of action and that each of these needs to be judged within the framework of its value assumptions. However, to be viable, these values need to be relevant; they have to reflect the values of a society, or at least the values some groups in that society hold. This grounding in existing values serves not only as its strength and legitimacy, but also as the root of its problems. Values will always be controversial since very few values are universally agreed upon within a society.

We discussed three such basic values—(1) freedom, (2) equality and (3) community—and suggested that while all three may be desirable organizing principles for social policy formulation since they are espoused by a large number of people in this society, they cannot be simultaneously maximized. The issue becomes one of determining which value is to be given primacy. If we begin with a communitarian first principle, absolute liberty is not possible because social responsibilities take precedence over individual rights. The same happens, of course, if we begin with freedom, with its emphasis on individualism. Finally, while a concern for equality would require some redistribution (at the expense of some individuals' freedom), an egalitarian society is not necessarily one in which a sense of community is strong. We concluded the discussion with the argument that our existing political economy tends to give greater weight to the first principle of freedom with its emphasis on competitive markets, the importance of the individual, and an economic definition of the human person that assumes people interact with others through bilateral, impersonal transactions.

And yet, our emphasis throughout the book has been on the need to balance economic objectives with social objectives, to begin moving away from a system that defines the single purpose of social policies to function as instruments of economic policies, to one that gives greater weight to the first principle of community. Is such a calculation possible? Or is

Friedman (1962) correct when he states that we must start with extending freedom and choice, that anything else is paternalistic and in the long run counterproductive to the economic and social well-being of a society?

Perhaps a way out of this apparent impasse can be found in Marshall's concept of citizenship. One of Marshall's (1965) many contributions to modern social policy is his work on the meaning of citizenship as a criterion for governments to build on when they develop and modify their policies. For Marshall, within modern societies, the rights of individuals are determined by their ability to claim citizenship. Moreover, citizenship itself is a multifaceted status involving different aspects of rights. Finally, Marshall argues that these rights, involving three major categories of citizenship—(1) civil, (2) political, and (3) social—have evolved sequentially over the past 300 years.

As we moved from a feudal economy to a market economy, our practice of allocating rights (including access to goods and services) on the basis of social class began to be questioned. Pressure from a number of fronts to modify the more glaring inequalities found in such a class-driven society grew. These pressures were related in part to the emergence of a middle class that was concerned with both protecting its newly acquired status (and property) and maintaining a reasonably stable work force.

These concerns became the basis for creating the concept of *civil citizenship* in the eighteenth century and for providing the "rights necessary for individual freedom—liberty of the person, freedom of speech, thought and action, the right to own property and to conclude valid contracts, and the right to justice" (ibid.:71). As Marshall points out, these rights are the domain of the judicial system.

The second component—*political citizenship*—only became a reality in the nineteenth century when large numbers of citizens were given the right "to participate in the exercise of political power as a member of a body invested with political authority or as an elector of the members of such a body" (ibid.:72). Marshall points out that while political rights were considered unacceptable in the eighteenth century since they were seen as potentially damaging to the emerging capitalist system, they were now seen as necessary for the growth of modern capitalism. However, these rights were viewed as narrow extensions of civil rights.

The third component—*social citizenship*—has only begun to emerge during the twentieth century. Under this, Marshall includes

[t]he whole range from the right to a modicum of economic welfare and security to the right to share to *the full* in the social heritage and to live the life of a civilized being according to the standards prevailing in that society. The institutions most closely connected with it are the educational system and the social services. (ibid.)

> Citizenship is a status bestowed on those who are full members of a community. All who possess the status are equal with respect to the right and duties with which the status is endowed. There is no universal principle that determines what those rights and duties shall be. . . . [T]he urge forward along the path thus plotted is an urge towards a fuller measure of equality. . . . Social class, on the other hand, is a system of inequality. (ibid:84)

What proves problematic, however, is that the process of defining these "social rights" is open-ended and the list of these social rights is susceptible to change when circumstances of living change. As Dahrendorf (1976) suggests, the right to a minimum wage, to old age pensions, to health care, and to adequate housing and education are merely the beginning of a long and potentially endless list.

While Marshall's first two aspects of citizenship—civil and political—are grounded in law and contract theory, the third—social rights—is not. Rather, it is primarily consensual and rests on the concept of social cohesion and shared social purpose. This again brings us back to the arguments proposed in Chapter 2 and the importance of community as a criterion when developing or analyzing social policies. It also helps us understand more fully why we encounter strong disagreements when we attempt to modify, expand, or add to the existing list of social rights. Donnison recognizes this and points out that we need to be actively involved with "creating and recreating an evolving social consensus" about those measures that will "protect the weak and reduce vulnerability and accompanying disadvantages" (1976:6).

The parallels between these two formulations (i.e., first principles and citizenship) are intriguing:

Freedom   ↔ Civil Citizenship
Equality   ↔ Political Citizenship
Community ↔ Social Citizenship

The language of Milton Friedman as he discusses "freedom" and T. H. Marshall when he discusses "civil citizenship" is quite similar. The major difference is that Friedman, in arguing that freedom, equality, and community are incompatible or at least cannot be viewed as equally important, views freedom as the most important first principle. Marshall, on the other hand, suggests that each is important in its own right and that some are prerequisites to others. The three categories of rights evolved sequentially over the past 300 years. Furthermore, in his view, civil rights (freedom) had to precede political rights (equality) and social rights (community) were only possible after the first two were established. Given this argument, we are not faced with either/or categories but with a continuum—the end point being community. "Citizenship is a status bestowed on those who are full members of a community" (Marshall 1965:84). In Friedman's view we begin and end with the first principle of freedom; in Marshall's formulation, freedom is the first step in the journey to community.

Given this analysis, we would suggest that in this society we have reached a point somewhere between equality and community, between political and social citizenship. We touched on this in Chapter 6 when we discussed various rationales for government intervention into the lives of families. One rationale introduced was that of rights as opposed to other rationales such as need, compassion, or justice. Beginning with Rawls's position based in contract theory and moving on to Rothman's argument that our preoccupation with rights in this country grew out of a profound mistrust of government, we are forced to conclude that we live in an adversarial society, one in which people relate to others as competitors.

To humanize this society, and to protect the rights of citizens, we have established a number of policies that emphasize *equality of opportunity*— that all people should have the same opportunity to achieve their potential, whether they are handicapped children (legislation to mainstream handicapped children in the public school system), minorities (civil rights legislation dealing with school systems, housing, and employment), or the disabled the (the Americans with Disability Act of 1990, which states that disabled persons have the same rights and privileges as nondisabled persons).

We suggested that we would probably locate this society someplace on the continuum between political rights and social rights, between equality and community, because, even though the emphasis in most policies seems to be on equality of opportunity rather than equality of outcome, we do have a number of programs that are expressions of social citizenship or community, e.g., OASDI, Medicare, and public education. The next issue to be dealt with is the extent to which it is possible to evolve even further on the continuum without diminishing our civil and political rights. Is it possible to achieve some balance between economic and social objectives?

ECONOMIC AND SOCIAL MARKETS

In Chapter 1, we pointed out that in our particular form of political economy, we assume that an economic system characterized by perfectly competitive markets provides socially optimal results, i.e., products of the highest quality will be provided at reasonable prices when consumers want them. A corollary to this general proposition is that filtering occurs with economic growth, i.e., benefits will eventually accrue to everyone, even those with the lowest income. A second corollary is that when a particular market is found to be imperfect, government is expected to engage in corrective measures. Government intervention, however, is to be as nonintrusive as possible and should cease as soon as that market becomes competitive once again. Finally, the role of government is to support market theory and principles of free enterprise.

The evidence in the previous chapters would suggest that the theory has failed in a number of areas. We have experienced economic growth over the past 35 years, governments have become involved, and the nature of the involvement has been in support of the workings of those markets. Despite these efforts, significant numbers of people are still poor, unemployed, homeless or living in less than adequate housing, and unable to obtain the medical care they need. Furthermore, if an "invisible hand" does exist, it is both sexist and racist in that women and minorities experience an even higher incidence of these problems.

The housing market has failed to produce the quantity and quality of shelter at reasonable prices needed by millions of people in this country despite the investment of billions of public dollars in that market. The billions of dollars channeled to the medical market have neither produced improved health indicators nor have they controlled rising costs. Tax subsidies and human capital policies have not been able to stimulate the development of meaningful jobs at the level needed.

The issue is not whether a market economy works or not; it clearly does. A more fundamental issue is whether *all* goods and services should be delivered through these economic markets. Is it perhaps more fruitful to think of two separate markets: (1) economic markets and (2) social markets?

In defining the distinguishing characteristics of social services, Titmuss (1968), Rein (1970), and Kahn (1969) question the assumption that social services (broadly defined) are the same as other goods and services. For Rein, social services are "collective interventions which are outside the market place to meet the needs of individuals as well as to serve the corporate interests of the wider community" (1970:43). Kahn makes the same point when he suggests that "social services . . . consist of programs made available by other than market criteria" (1969:179). Titmuss continued the discussion by arguing that while an acceptable objective of an economic market is to maximize profit (to do otherwise would be irrational), it is inconceivable in a caring society that one group is allowed to make a profit from the misery of others, whether that misery is physical illness, inadequate housing, or emotional problems to name just a few, or to charge prices that are out of the reach of people who need the services. None of these theorists are calling for the abolition of the free enterprise system and private markets. All are arguing, however, that in some instances and with certain goods and services, social markets are preferable to the dynamics of economic markets.

One proposed solution would involve following the experiences of a number of European countries, especially those countries that have

1. maintained a market economy,
2. established a number of social markets such as health care and social services, and
3. accepted the notion that industry needs to establish social contracts with employees and government that produce a balance between reasonable profit margins and reasonable wage increases.

These efforts, discussed in the previous chapter, have been successful in keeping inflation within bounds and employment at very high levels. Finally, in these countries, industry has assumed a major responsibility for both the provision and financing of a wide range of health and welfare benefits as part of the costs of doing business. It is not a choice between capitalism or socialism. A robust set of social policies requires a healthy market economy, a free enterprise system tempered or modified by social concerns. Furthermore, the evidence would seem to suggest that in these countries, there is a strong conviction that concerns for the quality of life of all citizens are related to economic growth. As Kuttner argues, competition has been tempered with a sense of community, and that community includes industry, unions, and the government.

This would suggest that if we are able to differentiate between economic and social markets, and if we are able to move away from the deeply held notion that competition is the only way to achieve growth and that to support the dependent is inadvisable in a capitalist society since it invariably retards economic growth, we might begin to move from a society that favors individualism to one that encourages community and a sense of shared responsibility.

BARRIERS TO ACHIEVING COMMUNITY

A major barrier that needs to be addressed is the issue of "interest group politics" (Lowi 1969) and its effect in moving us closer to a "new class war" (Piven and Cloward 1982). We touched on the latter in Chapter 7, on the elderly. As measured by the amount of resources allocated to them, the status of the elderly, relative to other age groups is superior. And yet

[d]espite the general improvement and the increasing reliance on public programs, the distribution of income among the elderly population remains highly skewed, with the bottom group getting a small share not only of total income but of government benefits. (Crystal 1982:30)

The elderly are not a homogeneous group. There are wealthy and middle-class elderly, low-income and poor elderly. This class war became apparent in the passage and repeal of the Catastrophic Illness legislation. As discussed in Chapter 7, a small group of the wealthier elderly was able to mobilize large numbers of elderly to pressure Congress to repeal this legislation, with the argument that the elderly were being unfairly taxed. The reality was that these more affluent elderly (approximately 2 million people) would have had to pay a surcharge to finance part of the costs while the remaining 31 million elderly would have had to pay nothing or a small amount on a monthly basis. This small number already had equivalent coverage through their retirement plans and did not want to pay for duplicate coverage. In countless letters to the editor across the nation, wealthy or upper middle-class retirees argued that it was not "fair" that they be required to support elderly persons who had not made provision for such coverage while they worked. They were being penalized for working hard and achieving success.

The above is a clear example of the absence of a sense of community among the elderly. As long as one group did not benefit more than the other, there was an appearance of community and common need. However once one segment believed that another group was benefiting *at its expense*, community gave way to individual interests. It did not seem to matter that they had more than other elderly persons or that some elderly had greater need. They argued that it was only fair if all elderly were treated the same despite Titmuss's conclusion that such an approach is grossly unfair if some people have greater need. For him, a just system is one that positively discriminates, that gives more to those who need more and less to those who need less.

A second issue is the apparent unwillingness of the elderly to become less parochial (in the sense that they seem to be concerned only with issues affecting the elderly) and to become concerned with the well-being of others. Single-interest politics on the part of the elderly was not only successful in the past but was probably necessary to highlight their needs and acquire resources. There is growing evidence, however, that unless the elderly and their advocates show some interest in broader social concerns, concerns that do not directly deal with aging problems, their future will be shaped by advocates for these other groups. Furthermore, there is a high probability that these other groups will reject the claims of the elderly, who are beginning to be perceived as selfish and unconcerned about other groups.

We see this in communities throughout the nation where elderly citizens aggressively fight against raising property taxes needed to maintain or improve the quality of the local educational system. Their reasoning seems to be that since they no longer have children in school, they should not be expected to pay for the education of those families who do. Again, we see the absence of a sense of community—a sense that the children are important to all and not just their families—that the total community has a responsibility for their upbringing.

The class war, then is not just among the elderly, but between the elderly and other groups. These divisions are critical if we are to resolve the issue of fairness as it relates to the distribution of available social welfare resources. Are resource distribution issues always a "win-lose" situation with some groups being penalized because the elderly are benefiting? As discussed in Chapter 7, the welfare of the elderly has improved significantly in almost every area of social policy since the early 1960s. However, over this same period, the well-being of children has deteriorated. As Figure 10.1 shows, the two poverty lines are almost mirror

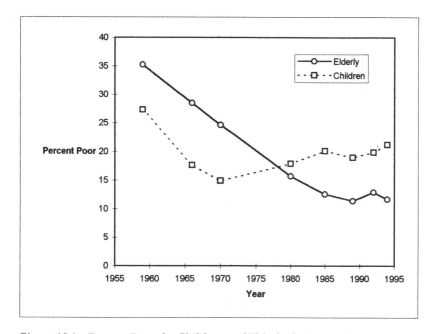

Figure 10.1 Poverty Rates for Children and Elderly. Source: U.S. Bureau of the Census 1996. Statistical Abstracts of the United States. Washington, DC: U.S. Government Printing Office p. 472. Committee on Ways and Means 1994. Where your money goes: The 1994–95 Green Book. Washington, DC: Government Printing Office. p 859–1149. Schmittroth, L. (Editor). Statistical record of children. Washington, DC: Gale Research Inc. p. 615.

images. As the poverty rate for the elderly decreased, the rate for children increased. In 1970, 16% of those under the age of 14 lived in poverty compared with 24% of those 65 years of age and older. By 1982, the situation had been reversed: 23% of children lived in poverty compared to 15% of the elderly. If the cash value of services is factored in (much of it Medicare and Medicaid payments), the percentage of elderly persons living in poverty drops to 4% while the percentage of children drops only to 17% (Preston 1984). By 1995, the percentage of elderly living in poverty continued to decline and the percentage of poor children increased.

Preston also attempted to determine the amount of public expenditures each group received. He notes that Bane's finding that average government expenditures for the elderly in 1960 were three times the expenditures for each child stayed the same through 1979. He also estimates that the allocations for the elderly were six times higher than those for children in 1984. By 1996, expenditures were still four times higher. Moreover, per capita expenditures for the elderly were ten times higher than those for children.

What, if any, is a reasonable rationale for these differences? Do the elderly need more benefits? The data in Chapters 6, 7, and 9 suggest otherwise. The next section will explore a major issue that needs to be dealt with if we are to move beyond these divisive dynamics.

UNIVERSAL SERVICES AND COMMUNITY

In Chapter 2, we discussed the positions of Richard Titmuss and Milton Friedman, articulate advocates for universal and selective provision of social services, respectively. Each of these theorists argues that his position is the "right" course of action given the needs of modern society.

Titmuss reaches his conclusion by applying an analytical framework that gives emphasis to the importance of community, while Friedman concludes the opposite, given his emphasis on the first principle of freedom. The issue, as stated, is clearly that of choosing one over the other.

The historical argument for universal services is basically an argument for community. The underlying assumptions of this approach include:

- A recognition that many of the stresses facing families and individuals are beyond their control. They are victims of broader social and economic forces rather than the cause of their own problems.
- A belief that *all people* are at risk due to external stress and pressure caused by industrialization and urbanization.

- A recognition that because all people experience these risks, we need to respond to these collectively.
- In responding collectively, we believe in notions of common need and shared responsibility.
- Therefore, all people with specific common need should be supported by the larger community and that support should provided through a single system, i.e., they should be treated the same.
- Services should be viewed as entitlements and citizenship should be the primary criterion for eligibility.
- Whereas needs testing builds community, means-testing is divisive and stigmatizing.
- When people believe they have a right to services, they are more likely to use them when needed; when people are made to feel they do not have a right to services, they often go without needed services.
- To respond to needs by providing different levels, types, and amounts of services, and by developing separate systems for different groups of people with common needs, is to reject belief in community.

The traditional argument for selective services is grounded in a different sets of assumptions, all of which are concerned with the rights of the individual:

- Families should be viewed the same way we view economic markets, i.e., they are to be accepted as functioning optimally until proven otherwise.
- Since most of today's families and individuals can meet their own needs, to become involved in their lives would interfere with their right to privacy.
- If we were to become involved in the lives of these families, we would be, in effect, telling them that they are not capable of meeting their own needs without outside help.
- Such a patronizing approach would lead to further weakening of the family, leading inevitably to family deterioration and increased levels of dependency.
- Just as it is appropriate for the state to become involved in markets only when there is clear evidence that a market is imperfect, the state should only become involved with families when there is clear evidence of family pathology or family breakdown.
- When the state becomes involved with imperfect markets, it does so as nonintrusively as possible and for as short a period as possible. To do otherwise would permanently distort that market. So

also with families. Assistance to families should be temporary and families should be encouraged to become self-sufficient and independent.

- It is important, then, to distinguish between those who need public help and those who do not.
- The most philosophically acceptable and administratively feasible way to make these distinctions is through a means-test.
- While a means-test may stigmatize the recipient, it guarantees that only those with need actually receive services.
- To provide services to those who do not need those services or to provide benefits or services to those who could purchase them on their own is inefficient and therefore irrational and inappropriate.

The traditional arguments outlined above force us to think in either/or terms. We choose policies that support interdependence and community or those that support independence and individualism. The problem with this formulation, however, is that as with most dichotomies, both have inherent problems. Whereas universal provision of services clearly supports notions of a more egalitarian society, they are costly. Since the world recession beginning in the early 1970s, a number of European countries with a tradition of universal services have introduced means-testing for some of their benefits. A more relevant question today is not whether we should have universal or selective provision of benefits but whether it is possible to achieve the goals associated with universal services in such a way that the efficiency concerns are also addressed.

First, it is critical that the universal vs. selective argument is put into a historical context. Proponents of universal provision were primarily concerned with the dismantling of the Poor Law with its emphasis on providing assistance only to those who had failed. While pressure in Europe for change in the welfare state began to build in the early years of the twentieth century, it took the traumas of a world depression and a world war actually to achieve it. Unlike this country with its rhetoric of a class-free society, a society in which individuals through hard work could improve their social class, most European societies were still experiencing century-old rigid class distinctions. Furthermore, not only was an individual likely to remain a member of a particular class throughout his or her life, there was little communication between the classes. Middle and upper classes had little understanding of the widespread poverty experienced by large numbers of families.

World War II changed this. First, most of the military were from the working and poorer classes and most of the domestic hardships and deprivations associated with the war were felt by their children and families. The allied countries, one by one, presented their people with a vision of a new order (as Beveridge called it, a blueprint for the future), a more equal order, a fairer society, and a society with fewer class distinctions.

Some of these governments such as the United Kingdom were concerned with the morale of the military during the early days of defeat: in part in recognition that working and poor families were bearing the brunt of the war effort, and in part because more and more middle-class and more affluent families for the first time became aware of the living conditions of the majority of people. Other countries, especially those that were occupied, made similar commitments for the postoccupation era. The war created communities where previously there had been divisions. People suffered in common; they expected to share the future in common. When peace finally did come, society after society in Europe began to tear down the existing Poor Laws and replace them with systems providing universal services. It was a clear expression of the promises made during the war for more egalitarian societies.

However, almost 60 years have passed and many of those who vividly remembered the workhouses and other Poor Law institutions that were operating through the 1930s are now elderly or dead. The majority of the population in most countries was born *after* World War II. Memories, like attitudes, do change over time. What has to be done is to separate out the problems universal provision of services were to correct from the specific structures and mechanisms that were implemented.

The overall problem to be resolved was believed to be the alienation and mistrust experienced by most people living in a divided society. The desired end state was the development of a sense of community and shared responsibility. Specific problems were

- the impact of stigma on the recipient under systems characterized as selective (impacts that were both psychological and behavioral and effected utilization negatively;
- the existence of dual systems—one for the poor and another for the nonpoor;
- an apparent aversion to offer services that would, when possible, prevent problems from occurring (e.g., retraining of workers with obsolete skills) or, when that was not possible, buffer the consequences of those events (e.g., pensions for those unable to work, health insurance for those who are ill); and
- financing mechanisms, especially fee for service, that resulted in many people not receiving services.

Kahn, as early as 1973 and later with his colleague Kamerman (1976, 1987), offered us a systematic and thoughtful critique of this issue. Over 20 years ago he pointed out that even those advocates for selective provision support the need for universal services in some areas of social life, e.g., public health and public education. These areas of public social utilities, in Kahn's terminology, would probably fall under the public interest, externality rationale. For those who identify themselves as selectivists, the task is to limit these to only a minimum number of high-priority areas. At that time, Kahn argued against the notion of a dichotomy, i.e., either universal or selective, and suggested it was more a matter of context, emphasis, and the specific policy.

In his later works with Kamerman, the issue was recast "to reflect a far more complex, subtle and sophisticated elaboration of the options" (1987:277). They accept the need to be more efficient (at least in terms of public expenditures) but they neither discard the concept of universal services, nor do they apparently argue for more selective service provision. First, they cite the work of Garfinkle (1982), who found that means-testing did not produce more efficiency (the argument of the selectivists). Given this, they conclude that universal services would be preferable if the financing problem could be resolved.

Next, they explore the issue of making universal benefits taxable. There is precedence for this not only in this country with our taxing of social security benefits for the more affluent elderly population, but in a number of other countries, especially in the area of pensions and children or family allowances. Every individual or family is treated the same at the point when they qualify for the benefit. Benefits are universal, there is no means-testing, and therefore, in theory, no stigmatization. Every individual or family experiences the same tax process, i.e., they are required to submit data to the Internal Revenue Service or its equivalent. Finally, depending on total family income, which includes the dollar value of the benefit, the tax bracket, and the existing tax rates, some families will have much if not all of the benefit taken back through income taxes; others will have some of the benefit taxed; and still others will keep the total amount.

Not only would this apply to income transfers, but to any benefit, including nongovernmental in-kind benefits such as private health insurance. For example, government could conceivably pay for the health insurance premiums for the unemployed and poor from revenues generated by taxing employee benefits. That portion of benefits paid for by the employer is treated as taxable.

Finally, Kahn and Kamerman extend the analysis by comparing and contrasting "means-testing" and "income-testing" as viable policy instruments. They conclude that means-testing will tend to always stigmatize since, by definition, it involves an assessment of the total worth of the individual. Not just income is examined, but all of the individual's or family's assets must be verified. Income-testing, on the other hand, would be restricted to just that—income—and would be verified through tax returns or wage statements.

This distinction is an interesting parallel to the one made in the nineteenth century between poverty and pauperism as discussed in Chapter 3. Means-testing is compatible with notions of pauperism in that both evaluate the person's eligibility for services or benefits by examining every aspect of that person's life, while income-testing restricts the eligibility to one area of the person's life—the amount of income he or she is able to generate:

> A policy package can be designed to permit income testing without stigma if one can build on a foundation of strong universalism and moves relatively far into the income distribution and to continue universal benefits but control costs by including such benefits as taxable income. (Kamerman and Kahn 1987:280)

This would seem to be as reasonable a way out of the dilemma as possible without radically changing our system of political economy. Government would not provide services but would guarantee to all that these services will be available. Stigma is minimized and, in the context of community, all people have equal access to a single system with each paying according to ability.

This formulation, however, still leaves us with a serious problem that needs to be addressed as we enter the twenty-first century. The traditional dichotomy between institutional and residual models of social welfare and universal and selective provision of services raises other problems. Universal provision has come to mean the application of the same standard to all individuals and an impartial approach to the determination of eligibility and the allocation of resources. This, of course is the perceived value of universal provision. Everyone is treated the same—a prerequisite for community building.

Thompson and Hoggett (1996), representatives of a postmodernist approach to social policy, however, argue that universal provision fails to take into account individual and group differences, the need to value diversity, and the extremely important element of choice. For them, impartiality is confused with uniformity, and equality of treatment with sameness of treatment. Thompson and Hoggett suggest that in building a social welfare system on the principle of universal provision, existing inequalities are ignored and the particular needs of groups such as women and minorities are swept aside under the banner of egalitarianism.

Furthermore, they are equally critical of selective provision as the term has been used—the targeting of services based on a means-test. This approach, in practice, does not address their concern for diversity, choice, and the need to recognize that some groups have different needs. Given this, they argue the need to clarify the terms of the debate and to extend what has become common usage.

First they argue that both terms, universal and selective, are multi-faceted terms that need to be elaborated (see Table 10.1). Universal can be "general" or "specific" and it is the former that proves problematic, i.e., dealing with everyone the same way. Specific universalism is concerned with dealing with the lack of social rights that continues to serve as a barrier to a truly egalitarian society. In practice, they would agree that universal policies that are general are needed to meet the basic needs of everyone, e.g., food, shelter, protection, education, and health care. With Marshall, they argue that citizenship is the basis for these rights. They believe, however, that to stop there will only strengthen existing inequalities in many more areas of social welfare, inequalities that are the product of discrimination. For example, while some might argue the retirement system (OASDI) is gender blind since it calculates benefit levels on the recipients' previous earnings, it is hardly gender neutral in a society in which women have a history of shorter attachment to the labor force given child-rearing demands, and when they do enter the work force, they are paid less than men. To deal with this from a general universal approach ignores the reality of this discrimination.

Thompson and Hoggett next suggest that while negative selectivism is never acceptable (i.e., means-testing) positive selectivism is acceptable in that this strategy moves from uniform benefits to a system that provides different types and amounts of services to those with different types of needs. This position is consistent with Titmuss's (1968) notion of "positive discrimination." Finally, they argue that a combination of approaches—specific universal and positive selectivism—built on a floor of benefits and services to meet basic needs (general universal) not only accepts the notion of diversity but, in extending rights, results in empowerment and does so not by just developing more organizations and agencies to provide services.

The value of this framework is still to be tested in practice. However, given the proposed changes to the Social Security program, e.g., means-testing benefits to keep the number of recipients down, full or partial privatization of the system or raising the tax rate on higher income bene-

Table 10.1. Universal and / or Selective
Provision

| General Universal | Negative Selectivism |
| Specific Universal | Positive Selectivism |

ficiaries would not deal with the concerns raised by Thompson and Hoggett since all elderly are not alike, do not have the same needs, and do not have access to alternative resources.

THE FINAL ISSUE: THE IMPORTANCE OF WORK

The most important single criterion that shapes our system of social welfare has been and continues to be employment. Accepting the political philosophy of Bismarck, we have devised two social welfare approaches over the past 60 years. The first ties benefits to the recipient's work history and tends to be relatively generous. The second provides a basic level of benefits to those who do no have this attachment and are still considered able to work. These benefits are relatively miserly.

It is clear that while we have, in theory, rejected the earlier Poor Laws, we have retained a number of key aspects of those Poor Laws. Social welfare still plays a social control function—a function that includes a concern for maintaining a stable, reliable, and motivated labor force and one that accepts the need to accept authority. As it has evolved over the past two centuries, this system contains elements that reward those who meet these criteria and punish those who do not.

Given this, people in need are still placed in one of two categories. The first group, those who have retired because of age or disability, are rewarded because they have a history of employment and they have contributed to the economy. In the language of the Poor Law, they are the "worthy poor." The second group, those who are not employed and are not disabled or elderly, those who have sporadic employment histories, those who seemingly have no legitimate reason not to work, are punished. They are the "unworthy poor" and their presence is a distinct threat to the economy. By treating them harshly, by giving them less than they need to meet their needs, we are both encouraging them to become a part of the labor force and discouraging those who are working to stop.

Only by applying these concepts can we fully understand why we deal with groups who have the same needs in such different ways. In Chapter 7, we suggested that the state has made a commitment to the elderly, a commitment that it has made to no other group (with the possible exception of veterans though this is experiencing some erosion). Why is it that Congress was willing to pass the Older Americans Act and not the Young Children Act, the Single Parent Act, the Full Employment for Young Adult Act, and so on? Are the ten objectives found in Title 1 of the act only appropriate to the elderly? What if we were to leave out any reference to the elderly?

- An adequate income . . . in accordance with the American standard of living.
- The best possible physical and mental health which science can make available without regard to economic status.
- Suitable housing, independently selected, designed and located with reference to special needs and available at costs . . . can afford.
- Full restorative services for those who require institutional care.
- Opportunity for employment with no discriminatory personnel practices.
- Pursuit of meaningful activity within the widest range of civic, cultural and recreational activities.
- Efficient community services including access to low cost transportation, which provide social assistance in a coordinated manner and which are readily available when needed.
- Immediate benefit from proven research knowledge which can sustain and improve health and happiness.
- Freedom, independence and free exercise of individual initiative in planning and managing their own lives.

It would be difficult to argue that these objectives would not apply to the nonelderly, e.g., to children, to parents (single or otherwise), to young adults, to the disabled. If these are appropriate objectives (or as they have been called, a Bill of Rights for the elderly), why not extend these same objectives and "rights" to all by virtue of need and citizenship? These objectives are an embodiment of the principles one would find in an institutional model built on the principles offered by Titmuss, Marshall, Thompson, and Hoggett. And yet, only the elderly, as a group, are provided benefits within this approach. Other groups, as much in need, receive benefits that tend to be provided within the assumptions of the residual model. Why? The one difference between the elderly and the other groups is the notion that the former have earned these benefits and the others have not. While nine of the ten objectives have been listed above, we purposely left out the sixth objective:

- Retirement in health, honor, dignity, after years of contributions to the economy (U.S. Department of Health, Education and Welfare 1974:2–3).

This is the one statement that is specific to the elderly. In reality, it is not an objective, but a rationale for the other objectives. The elderly are provided these benefits because they worked hard and contributed to the economy. The language is interesting. It does not say that the benefits are provided because they were paid for while working; it states that the benefits are provided because of contributions to the economy while working. The earned rights criterion takes on an subtle but important meaning, best understood within a framework of political economy. The elderly earned these benefits because they were good citizens who were willing to live within acceptable boundaries of what constituted good behavior. Unlike other groups, they were productive.

But who actually pays for these benefits? The OASDI system is a "pay as you earn" system, but each generation of retirees is actually supported by then current workers. Moreover, as discussed in Chapter 3, current beneficiaries are likely to receive significantly more than they contributed. Moreover, the benefits that retirees receive are being paid for by people who are now working.

Another example of who pays for the benefits the elderly receive is in the area of health insurance. While the percentage of general revenue (collected in the form of income taxes) used to support Medicare Part A (Hospital Insurance) is relatively small (approximately 10%), 75% of the funds used for Part B, i.e., physician services, comes from general revenues. In practice this has meant that taxpayers, primarily those in the labor force, are providing an average annual subsidy of $2,400 for each Medicare recipient. What complicates this is the fact that working-age adults were nearly four times as likely as the elderly to have been unable to obtain medical care and were more than three times as likely to have major financial difficulties because of illness.

Arguments such as the above oftentimes are misunderstood. In no way is cutting back on the type and amount of benefits for the elderly offered as an argument. Rather, it is offered as an argument to treat the non-elderly the same as the elderly. If there is a guaranteed income policy for the elderly, there should be one for all people, whether it takes the form of a children's allowance or a negative income tax. If there is value in offering a national health insurance for the elderly, there is value in offering the same coverage for the rest of the population. We base this conclusion on Watson's argument of comparative justice as discussed in Chapter 6. People with similar needs should be treated the same way—the floor we referred to as the general universal upon which specific universal benefits are developed to meet the additional particular needs of different groups.

Is this possible given the size of the national debt and the federal deficit? Yes and no. No, if we expect government alone to provide these benefits. Yes, if we look for more realistic partnerships between industry, government, and citizens. As many European countries have demonstrated, social benefits are a part of the costs of business and therefore should be provided through industry-based mechanisms, whether these take the form of providing pensions, paying for health insurance, or providing services such as day care. We need to deal with the problem of financing retirement benefits not after people retire but while they are working. Too many people who are employed, disproportionately women and minorities, are in jobs that either have no benefits or extremely limited benefits. To wait until they retire and then to supplement minimum social security benefits with SSI is not the long-range solution—it is a bandage that only strengthens existing inequalities. Moreover, strategies that involve the use of taxing benefits or introducing user fees are not, in theory, antithetical to the provision of universal services. It does mean, however, that individuals and families recognize that they live in a community of people with responsibilities for each other, including, as Titmuss argues, strangers. No one is totally independent.

Finally, if recipient groups are to be provided with the level of benefits needed for a reasonable quality of life, divisive strategies will have to be minimized and people will have to recognize that their individual welfare is dependent on everyone's welfare.

Perhaps Shylock's admonition was Shakespeare's attempt to offer a universal warning to societies that pit one group against another, whatever the cause. If we take some liberties with his argument and replace the word *Jew* with any other group, e.g., children, disabled, single mothers, unemployed, or homeless, we end with a disturbing scenario:

> Hath not a . . . eyes? Hath not a . . . hands, organs, dimensions, senses, affections, passions? Fed with the same food, hurt with the same weapons, subject to the same diseases, healed by the same means, warmed and cooled by the same winter and summer as a . . . ? If you prick us, do we not bleed? If you tickle us, do we not laugh? If you poison us, do we not die? And if you wrong us, shall we not revenge? If we are like you in the rest, we are like you in that. If a . . . wrong a . . . what is his humility? Revenge. If a . . . wrong a . . . , what should his sufferance be by example? Why, revenge. The villainy you teach me, I will execute, and it shall go hard but I will better the instruction. *Merchant of Venice* (Act III, Scene 1, 61–76).

If we deny mothers and children today, what guarantee do we have that they will not deny the aged tomorrow? If elderly persons argue that they have no responsibility for children, what argument do they have if the children reject any responsibility for them? If we deny support to the unemployed and homeless, what claim for support do we have if we were to experience unemployment and lose our homes? All of our transfer programs have been built on the principle of trust, as they should be.

A FINAL NOTE

It is clear that, as we move into the twenty-first century, the welfare state that evolved over the twentieth century is experiencing considerable transformation. Moreover, most of the discussion tends to focus on the elements of the transformation—the means—with little dialogue about the purposes or goals we are attempting to achieve. It is almost as if we implicitly believe that there exists a fundamental consensus on these goals and there is no need to debate them. The task is to develop the mechanisms to achieve these "agreed-upon" goals.

First, the role of the federal government is being redefined. Whereas, following the Great Depression, the federal government assumed a very direct role in the lives of individuals through various income maintenance and social welfare programs, this responsibility has been transferred to state and local governments through the development of block grants. While this devolution may achieve the hoped-for goals of effecting needed efficiencies and stimulating state and local governments to develop creative and flexible solutions to long-standing social problems, the potential negative effects need to be addressed. In the 1930s we recognized that many of the problems facing us required national solutions and that the federal government was the level of government capable of doing this. There was a national agenda that superseded the states' more parochial agendas and individuals had rights that should not be allocated on the basis of where one lived but on the basis of their needs. This national agenda involving policy areas such as income maintenance, health care, economic development, and employment is in danger of being lost as devolution continues. What is the likelihood of each of the 50 states passing civil rights legislation, the equivalent of the Americans with Disability Act, or the Social Security Act? Is it possible that the idea of a national identity will become passé or at least eroded? In Donnison's words, who will take responsibility for "creating and recreating an evolving social consensus about those measures that will protect the weak and reduce vulnerability and accompanying disadvantages" (1976:6)?

A second major shift is the move away from entitlements to time-limited benefits in those areas targeting some of these weak and vulnerable people. Welfare reform has replaced a system that guaranteed that the basic needs of children would be met (AFDC) with one that guarantees support, under some conditions, for a very limited period. It is hoped that this new approach will stimulate the dependent to move toward self-sufficiency. Still, this policy in practice assumes that most dependent persons are capable of employment and that jobs that pay a living wage will be available.

While the numbers of individuals and families on welfare have gone down over the past few years, there is little beyond anecdotal data that welfare reform has been the reason. The economy at this time has been healthy and new jobs have been created. However, as discussed in Chapters 8 and 9, this economy moves in cycles. If there is no effort to create new, primary sector jobs, what will happen to these families when the economy cools off? Who will have responsibility for the weak and the vulnerable?

A third issue of concern is the expanding role of the private sector in the provision of social welfare goods and services. The issue is not so much just an expanding role but the significant role being assumed by the for-profit sector. The apparent growing consensus to "privatize" the Social Security system will undoubtedly benefit a segment of the population in that their retirement accounts will far outstrip what they would receive under the current system. But such a system will not be as beneficial to all. There will be losers and winners. The former are likely to be individuals and families with low-income, minimum-wage jobs, minorities, and single parents. The latter are likely to be white, middle-class, and upper-middle-class. Without some safety net, we seem to say that freedom to choose is paramount and if that choice results in future difficulties, the fact that an individual has such a choice is sufficient and superior to a mandatory uniform system.

To some extent, these developments would appear to move us away from a sense of community and shared responsibility—a commitment we have honored, at least in theory, over the past 70 years. This does not mean that notions of freedom and choice are not important. They are, but as we have argued throughout this book, choice is only meaningful when alternatives are available and every one starts from a level playing field.

References

Aaron, H. 1972. *Shelters and Subsidies*. Washington, D.C.: Urban Institute.

Abramovitz, M. 1988. "Regulating the Lives of Women: Social Welfare Policy from Colonial Times to the Present." Boston: South End.

Administration on Aging. 1995. *1995 State Program Report for Titles III and VII of the Older Americans Act*. www.aoa.dhhs.gov/napis/95spr/overview.htm.

Administration on Aging. 1996. *Aging into the 21st Century*. www.pr.aoa.dhhs.gov/aoa/stats/aging21.

Administration on Aging. 1997. *The Growth of America's Older Population*. www.aoa.dhhs. gov/aoa/stats/growth97.html.

Advisory Council on Public Welfare. 1966. *Having the Power, We Have the Duty*. Report to the Secretary of the Department of Health, Education and Welfare. Washington, DC: U.S. Government Printing Office.

Aitkenhead, M. and S. Liff. 1991. "The Effectiveness of Equal Opportunity Policies." Pp. 26–50 in *Women at Work: Psychological and Organizational Perspectives*, edited by J. Firth-Cozens and M. A. West. Philadelphia: Open University.

American Hospital Association. 1994. "Hospital Statistics." *Annual report of the president*.Chicago: Author.

Anderson, H. J. 1978. *Primer of Equal Employment Opportunity*. Washington, DC: Bureau of National Affairs.

Anderson, M. 1971. *Family Structure in Nineteenth Century Lancashire*. Cambridge: Cambridge University Press.

Anderson, O. W. and P. Sheakley. 1959. *Comprehensive Medical Insurance: A Study of Costs, Use and Attitudes under Two Plans*. Research Series No. 9. New York: Health Information Foundation.

Anderson, W. and Locke, H. 1964. "Trickling Down: The Relationship between Economic Growth and the Extent of Poverty among American Families." *Quarterly Journal of Economics* 78(11):511–24.

Annie E. Casey Foundation. 1997. *Kids Count Data Book: State Profiles of Child Well-Being, 1997*. Baltimore, MD: Author.

Arrow, K. 1951. *Social Choice and Individual Values*. New York: Wiley.

Austin, C. D. and M. B. Loeb. 1982. "What Age Is Relevant." Pp. 263–88 in *Age or Need: Public Policies for Older People*, edited by B. Neugarten. Beverly Hills, CA: Sage.

Baldwin, S. 1985. *The Costs of Caring*. London: Routledge and Kegan Paul.

Ball, R. 1971. "United States Policy toward the Elderly." Pp. 1–21 in *Care of the*

Elderly, edited by A. Exton-Smith, J. Evan, and J. Grimely. New York: Academic Press.

Ball, R. 1981. "Employment Created by Construction Expenditures." *Monthly Labor Review* 12:38–44.

Bane, M. 1976. *Here to Stay: American Families in the Twentieth Century.* New York: Basic Books.

Bane, M. and D. Ellwood. 1983. "Slipping into and out of Poverty: The Dynamics of Spells and the Dynamics of Dependence: The Routes to Self Sufficiency." Mimeo, Harvard University, Cambridge, MA.

Banfield, E. 1955. "Notes on a Conceptual Scheme." Pp. 303–29 in *Politics, Planning and the Public Interest,* edited by M. Myerson and F. Banfield. New York: Free Press.

Banfield, F. and J. Q. Wilson. 1963. *City Politics.* Cambridge, MA: Harvard University Press.

Baumheimer, F. and A. Schorr. 1977. "Social Policy." Pp. 1453–1562 in *Encyclopedia of Social Work,* 17th ed., editor-in-chief John B. Turner. Washington, DC: National Association of Social Workers.

Bay, C. 1988. "Freedom as Calamity: The Case of Liberal Individualism in the Western World." Pp. 159–77 in *Democracy, State, and Justice: Critical Perspectives and New Interpretations,* edited by D. Sainsbury. Stockholm: Almqvist & Wiksell International.

Benjamin, R. 1983. "In West Virginia, Recession Is a Mild Word." *Baltimore Sun,* January 30.

Bernstein, R. 1982. *The Restructuring of Social and Political Thought.* Philadelphia: University of Pennsylvania Press.

Beveridge, W. 1942. *Social Insurance and Allied Services.* London: HMSO, Cmd 9663; New York: Macmillan.

Beveridge, W. 1943. *The Pillars of Security.* New York: Macmillan.

Beveridge, W. 1944. *Full Employment in a Free Society.* London: Allen and Unwin.

Bobrow, D. B. and J. S. Dryzek. 1987. *Policy analysis by design.* Pittsburgh: University of Pittsburgh.

Bott, F. 1955. "Urban Families: Conjugal Roles and Social Networks." *Human Relations* 15:346–57.

Boulding, K. 1967. "The Boundaries of Social Policy." *Social Work* 12:3–11.

Bovbjerg, R., and J. Holahan. 1982. *Medicaid in the Reagan Era: Federal Policy and State Choices.* Washington, DC: Urban Institute Press.

Briggs, A. 1967. "Welfare State in Historical Perspective." Pp. 25–45 in *The Welfare State,* edited by C. Schottland. New York: Harper Torchbooks.

Bulmer, M. 1981. "The British Tradition of Social Administration: Moral Concerns at the Expense of Scientific Rigor." Pp. 35–42. Hasting Center Report, New York.

Bureau of Labor Statistics. 1996. *Occupational Outlook Handbook,* 1996–97 edition. Washington, DC: USGPO.

Bureau of Labor Statistics. 1997. *Union Members in 1996.* www.stats.bls.gov/news.release/union2.nws.htm.

Chadwick, B. and T. Heaton. 1992. *Statistical Handbook on the American Family.* Phoenix: Ornz.

Coleman, B. 1997. *Risky Business: Study Finds On-Job Injury Costs High. Phoenix Tribune,* July 28, p. A1.

Coll, B. 1970. *Perspectives in Public Welfare: A History.* Washington, DC: U.S. Department of Health, Education and Welfare, U.S. Government Printing Office.

Committee on Ways and Means. 1992. *Overview of entitlement programs: 1992 Green Book.* Washington, DC: U.S. Government Printing Office.

Committee on Ways and Means. 1994. *Where Your Money Goes: The 1994–95 Green Book.* Washington, DC: Brassey's.

Corbett, T. 1993. "Changing the Culture of Welfare." *Focus* 16:12–22.

Council of Economic Advisors. 1964. "Poverty in America." *Monthly Labor Review* 87:285–91.

Crosland, C. 1970. *The Future of Socialism.* New York: Schocken.

Crystal, S. 1982. *America's Old Age Crisis.* New York: Basic Books.

Dahrendorf, P. 1976. *Inequality: Hope and Progress.* Liverpool: Liverpool University Press.

Danziger, S. and P. Gottschalk. 1995. *America Unequal.* New York: Russell Sage Foundation.

DeAngelis, T. 1997. *Ignorance Plagues Affirmative Action.* www.apa.org/monitor/may95/affirm.html.

deleeuw, F. and N. Ekanem. 1971. "The Supply of Rental Housing." *American Economic Review* 12:214–26.

Demos, J. 1983. "Family Home Care: Historical Notes and Reflections." Pp. 161–75 in *Family Home Care: Critical Issues for Services and Policies,* edited by R. Perlman. New York: Haworth.

Densen, P., E. Balamuth, and F. Shapiro. 1958. *Prepaid Medical Care and Hospital Utilization.* Chicago: American Hospital Association.

Department of Housing and Urban Development. 1974. *Housing in the Seventies.* Washington, DC: U.S. Government Printing Office.

Department of Labor. 1996. *Facts on Working Women.* www.dol.gov/dol/wb/public/wb—pubs/20f96.htm.

Department of Labor. 1997a. *Brief History.* www.dol.gov/dol/asp/public/programs/history/dolchp.

Department of Labor. 1997b. *Value of the Federal Minimum Wage 1954–1996.* www.dol.gov/dol/esa/public/minwage/chart2.htm.

Derthick, M. 1979. *Policymaking for Social Security.* Washington, DC: Brookings Institute.

Devine, J. A. and J. D. Wright. 1993. *The Greatest of Evils: Urban Poverty and the American Underclass.* Hawthorne, NY: Aldine de Gruyter.

Dewey, J. 1939. *Theory of Valuation.* Chicago: University of Chicago Press.

Doeringer, P. and M. J. Piore. 1971. *Internal Labor Markets and Manpower Analysis.* Lexington, MA: Heath.

Dokecki, P., H. Able, K. Alred, B. Beck, W. Donovan, Jr., C. Heflinger, A. Lowitzer, and M. Smith. 1986. "Scholars and Ethics: Towards an Ethically Relevant Agenda for Scholarly Inquiry into Mental Retardation." Pp. 17–37 in *Ethics of Dealing with Persons with Severe Handicaps,* edited by P. Dokecki and R. Zaner. Baltimore: Paul Brookes.

Donnison, D. 1976. "An Approach to Social Policy." *Australian Journal of Social Issues* 11(1):Supplement.

Donzelot, J. 1979. *The Policing of Families.* New York: Pantheon.

Dorfman, D. 1982. "Costs Are Dictating Business Migration from Big Cities." *Washington Post*, September 27.

Dreier, P., and J. Atlas. 1995. "Housing Policy's Moment of Truth." *American Prospect.* 22:68–77.

Dror, Y. 1967. "The Planning Process: A Facet Design." Pp. 93–116 in *Planning-Programming-Budgeting,* edited by F. Lyden and F. Miller. Chicago: Markham.

Dror, Y. 1970. "Prolegomenon to Policy Sciences." *Policy Sciences* 1:135–50.

Dror, Y. 1971. *Design for Policy Sciences.* New York: American Elsevier.

Dubey, S. N. 1991. "A Comparative Analysis of Issues in Affirmative Action Policies in India and the USA." *International Social Work* 34:383–402.

Dudenhefer, P. 1993. "Poverty in Rural United States." *Focus* 15:37–46.

Duke, L. L. 1992. "Career Development and Affirmative Action." Pp. 19–41 in *Women and Men of the States: Public Administrators at the State Level,* edited by M. E. Guy, Armonk, NY: M. E. Sharpe.

Duncan, G., with R. Cole. 1984. *Years of Poverty, Years of Plenty: The Changing Economic Fortunes of American Workers and Families.* Ann Arbor: Survey Research Center, Institute for Social Research, University of Michigan.

Economic Report of the President. 1997. Washington, DC: U.S. Government Printing Office.

Edin, K. J. 1995. "The Myths of Dependence and Self-Sufficiency: Women, Welfare, and Low-Wage Work." *Focus* 2:1–9.

Eggers, W. and R. Ng. 1993. *Social and Health Services Privatization: A Survey of State and County Governments.* Los Angeles: Reason Foundation.

Eller, T. J. 1996. *Dynamics of Economic Well-Being: Poverty, 1992–1993.* www.census.gov/hhes/www/poverty.html.

Ellwood, D. 1987. *Divide and Conquer.* Occasional paper #1, Ford Foundation Project on Social Welfare and the American Future, New York.

Employment Policy Foundation. 1997. *EPI Study Overestimates the Impact of Welfare-to-Work on the Earnings of Low-Wage Workers.* www.epf.org/pr9705206.htm.

Ermisch, J. 1987. *Lone Parents: The Economic Challenge of Changing Family Structures.* Paper presented to the Organization for Economic Cooperation and Development Conference of National Experts on Lone Parents, Paris, December.

Fish, G. 1978. "Housing Policy during the Great Depression." Pp. 129–42 in *The Story of Housing,* edited by G. Fish. New York: Macmillan.

Folsom, J. 1943. *The Family and Democratic Society.* New York: Wiley.

Freidmann, J. and B. Hudson. 1974. "Knowledge and Action: A Guide to Planning Theory." *Journal of the American Institute of Planners* 40:2–14.

Freire, P. 1981. *Pedagogy of the Oppressed.* New York: Continuum.

Freire, P. 1982. *Education for Critical Consciousness.* New York: Continuum.

Freire, P. 1989. *Learning to Question.* New York: Continuum.

Friedman, M. 1962. *Capitalism and Freedom.* Chicago: University of Chicago Press.

Friedman, R. 1968. "Models of Social Welfare." Discussion paper, Institute for Research on Poverty, University of Wisconsin, Madison.

Galbraith, J. 1984. *The Affluent Society.* New York: Penguin.

Garfinkle, I. (ed.). 1982. *Income Tested Transfer Programs: The Case For and Against.* New York: Academic Press.

Garfinkle, I. 1985. "Years of Poverty, Years of Plenty: An Essay Review." *Social Service Review* 59:283–94.

Garreau, J. 1981. *The Nine Nations of North America.* Boston: Houghton Mifflin.

Gil, D. 1973. *Unravelling Social Policy.* Cambridge, MA: Schenkman.

Gilder, G. 1981. *Wealth and Poverty.* New York: Basic Books.

Ginzberg, N. 1979. *Class, Capital and Social Policy.* London: Macmillan.

Ginzberg, E. 1976. *The Purposes of an Economy: Jobs for Americans.* Englewood Cliffs, NJ: Prentice-Hall.

Glazer, N. 1983. *Ethnic Pluralism and Public Policy.* Lexington, MA: Lexington.

Goldman, F. 1948. *Voluntary Medical Care Insurance in the United States.* New York: Columbia University Press.

Goode, W. 1975. *World Revolution and Family Patterns.* Glencoe, IL: Free Press.

Gordon, M. 1973. *The Nuclear Family in Crisis.* New York: Harper and Row.

Gornick, J. 1992. *Handouts for Gender Issues and LIS.* Paper presented at LIS Summer Workshop, Walferdange, Luxembourg.

Gramlich, E. M. and M. Long. 1997. *Growing Income Inequality: Roots and Remedies.* www.urban.org/PERIODCL/pubsect/gramlich.htm.

Gries, J. and J. Ford. 1932. *Housing Objectives and Programs.* Washington, DC: National Capitol Press.

Gronbjerg, K. 1990. "Poverty and Nonprofit Organizational Behavior." *Social Services Review* 62:208–43.

Habermas, J. 1971. *Knowledge and the Human Interest.* Boston: Beacon.

Habermas, J. 1973. *Theory and Practice.* Boston: Beacon.

Habermas, J. 1975. *Legitimation Crisis.* Boston: Beacon.

Haddix, A. C., S. M. Teutsch, P. A. Shaffer, and D. O. Dunet. 1996. *Prevention Effectiveness: A Guide to Decision Analysis and Economic Evaluation.* New York: Oxford University Press.

Hagen, M. 1997. "Insane Rules." *Phoenix Tribune,* September 2, p. A13.

Handler, J. 1972. *Reforming the Poor: Welfare Policy Federalism and Morality.* New York: Basic Books.

Handler, J. 1973. *The Coercive Social Worker.* Chicago: Rand McNally.

Harney, K. 1989. "Nation's Housing." *Washington Post,* January 22.

Harrington, M. 1975. *The Other America.* Baltimore: Penguin.

Harris, A. 1971. *Handicapped and Impaired in Great Britain.* OPCS, Social Survey Division. London: HMSO.

Harris and Associates. 1981. *Aging in the 1980s: Americans in Transition.* Washington, DC: NCOA.

Hart Research Associates, Inc. 1979. *A Nationwide Survey of Attitudes toward Social Security.* Washington, DC: Author.

Hayghe, H. 1994. "Are Women Leaving the Labor Force?" *Monthly Labor Review,* July, Table 1.

Health Care Financing Administration. 1995. "Health Expenditures." www.os. dhhs.gov/news/press/pre1995/930129.txt.

Health Care Financing Administration. 1996. "Managed care in Medicare and Medicaid."www.hcfa.gov/facts/n9609.htm.

Heatherington, E., M. Cox, and R. Cox. 1977. "The Development of Children in Mother Headed Families." Paper presented at the Families in Contemporary America Conference, George Washington University Washington, D.C., June 11.

Heller, W. 1967. *New Dimensions of Political Economy.* New York: Norton.

Hobbs, N., P. Dokecki, K. Dempsey, and R. Moroney. 1984. *Strengthening Families.* San Francisco: Jossey Bass.

Homelessness in America. 1997. www.teleport.com/ronl/homeless.htlm#who is homeless.

Horton, J. 1964. "The Dehumanization of Anomie and Alienation: A Problem in the Ideology of Sociology." *British Journal of Sociology* 15:280–91.

Hoskins, R. 1996. "Social Security in the 90's: the Imperatives of Change." *Social Security Bulletin,* 59:72–78.

Hoyle, K. 1995. *New Survey Reports on Wages and Benefits for Temporary Help Services Workers.* www.stats.bls.gov/pub/news.release/History/occomp.120795. news.

Humphrey, H. 1977. Cited in *Washington Post,* May 13, p.8.

Iatridis, D. 1994. *Social Policy: Institutional Context of Social Development and Human Services.* Pacific Grove, CA: Brooks/Cole.

Job Accommodation Network. 1997. *Facts about the Americans with Disabilities Act.* www.janweb.icdi.wvu.edu/kinder/pages/AOA—facts.html.

Joe, T. and C. Rogers. 1985. *By the Few, for the Few.* Lexington, MA: Lexington.

Johnson, L. 1952. "The Housing Act of 1949." Pp. 194–209 in *Two Thirds of a Nation: A Housing Program,* edited by N. Strauss. New York: Knopf.

Johnston, D. C. 1997. "Executive's Pay Soars More Than Company Profits." *Phoenix Tribune,* September 2, p. B3.

Johnston, G. M. 1995. *The Transformation of American Families: Employment Dislocation and the Growth of Female-Headed Families.* Population Research Institute, Department of Sociology, Penn State University, University Park. www.cpc.unc.edu/pubs/paa—papers/1995/Johnston.html.

Joseph, K. 1974. "Britain: A Decadent Utopia." *Guardian,* October 21.

Kahn, A. 1969. *Theory and Practice of Social Planning.* New York: Russell Sage Foundation.

Kahn, A. 1984. "Why a Modern Society Needs Strong and Sensitive Government." Paper presented at conference Measuring the Impact of Interventions: New Perspectives on Social Work Practice, School of Social Work, Arizona State University, Tempe, May 15.

Kahn, A. and S. Kamerman. 1975. *Not for the Poor Alone: European Social Services.* New York: Harper and Row.

Kamerman, S. and A. Kahn. 1976. *Social Services in the United States.* Philadelphia: Temple University Press.

Kamerman, S. and A. Kahn. 1987. "Universalism and Income Testing in Family Policy: New Perspectives on an Old Debate." *Social Work* 32:277–80.

Kanter, R. 1978. "Work in America." *Daedalus* 107:47–48.

Karger, H. J. and D. Stoesz. 1994. *American Social Welfare Policy: A Pluralist Approach*, 2nd ed. White Plains, NY: Longman.

Keith, N. 1973. *Politics and the Housing Crisis Since 1930*. New York: Universe.

Kettner, P. and L. Martin. 1996. "The Impact of Declining Resources and Purchasing of Service Contracting on Private Non-Profit Agencies." *Administration in Social Work* 20:21–38.

Keynes, J. 1931. *Essays in Persuasion*. New York: Harcourt Brace.

Keynes, J. [1936] 1973. *General Theory of Employment, Interest and Money*. New York: Macmillan.

Knapp, M., E. Robertson, and C. Thompson. 1990. "Public Money, Voluntary Action: Whose Welfare?" In *The Third Sector: Comparative Studies of Nonprofit Organizations*, edited by H. Anheier and W. Seibel. Hawthorne, NY: Aldine de Gruyter.

Kominski, R. 1991. "Does Education Really Pay Off? *Census and You* 26, 8–9.

Kristol, I. 1978. *Two Cheers for Capitalism*. New York: Basic Books.

Kristol, I. 1983. *Reflections of a Conservative*. New York: Basic Books.

Kuttner, R. 1984. *The Economic Illusion*. Boston: Houghton Mifflin.

Kuznets, S. 1953. *Share of Upper Income Groups in Income and Savings*. New York: National Bureau of Economic Research.

Lampman, R. 1984. *Social Welfare Spending: Accounting for Changes from 1950 to 1978*. Orlando, FL: Academic Press.

Lasch, C. 1977. *Haven in a Heartless World: The Family Besieged*. New York: Basic Books.

Laslett, P. 1965. *The World We Have Lost*. London: Methuen.

Lasswell, H. 1951. "The Policy Orientation." Pp. 1–12 in *The Policy Sciences: Recent Developments in Scope and Methods*, edited by D. Lerner and H. Lasswell. Stanford: Stanford University Press.

Lasswell, H. 1970. "The Emerging Conception of the Policy Sciences." *Policy Sciences* 1:3–14.

Lazear, E. P. 1991. "Discrimination in labor markets." Pp. 9–24 in *Essays on the Economics of Discrimination*, edited by E. P. Hoffman. Kalamazoo, MI: W. E. Upjohn Institute.

Lemann, N. 1986. "The Origins of the Underclass." *Atlantic* 257:31–55.

Leonard, J. S. 1991. "The Federal Anti-Bias Effort." Pp. 85–114 in *Essays on the Economics of Discrimination*, edited by E. P. Hoffman. Kalamazoo, MI: W. E. Upjohn Institute.

Levit, K., H. Lazenby, B. Braden, C. Cowan, P. McDonnell, L. Sivarajan, J. Stiller, D. Won, C. Donham, A. Long, and M. Stewart. 1996. "National Health Expenditures, 1995." *Health Care Financing Review* 18:175–98.

Levy, M. 1966. *Modernization and the Structure of Societies*. New Brunswick, NJ: Princeton University Press.

Lowi, T. 1969. *The End of Liberalism: Ideology, Policy and the Crisis of Public Authority*. New York: Norton.

Macbeath, A. 1957. *Can Social Policies Be Rationally Tested?* London: Oxford University Press.

MacIntyre, A. 1981. *After Virtue.* Notre Dame, IN: Notre Dame University Press.

Mannheim, K. 1940. *Man and Society in an Age of Reconstruction.* New York: Harcourt, Brace and World.

Marcus, S. 1979. "Their Brother's Keepers: An Episode from English History." Pp. 41–66 in *Doing Good: The Limits of Benevolence,* edited by W. Gaylin, I. Glasser, S. Marcus, and D. Rothman. New York: Pantheon.

Marlow, C. 1991. "Women, Children and Employment Responses by the United States and Great Britain." *International Social Work* 34:287–97.

Marsh, D. 1970. *The Welfare State.* London: Longman.

Marshall, D. 1969. *The English Poor in the Eighteenth Century.* New York: Kelley.

Marshall, T. 1965. *Class, Citizenship and Social Development.* New York: Anchor.

Marshall, T. 1972. *Social Policy.* London: Hutchinson.

Marshner, C. 1981. "The Pro-Family Movement and Traditional Values." Pp. 148–66 in *What Is Pro-Family Policy?* edited by L. Kagan. New Haven, CT: Yale University Press.

McKinney, E. 1995. "Health Planning." Pp. 1199–1205 in *Encyclopedia of Social Work,* 19th ed. Washington, DC: NASW.

McLanahan, S. and G. Sandefur. 1995. *Growing Up with a Single Parent: What Hurts, What Helps.* Cambridge, MA: Harvard University Press.

McMurtry, S., F. Netting, and P. Kettner. 1991. "How Nonprofits Adapt to a Stringent Environment." *Nonprofit Management and Leadership* 1(3):235–52.

Mead, L. M. 1992. *The New Politics of Poverty: The Nonworking Poor in America.* New York: Basic Books.

Merton, R. 1957. *Social Theory and Social Structure.* Boston: Houghton Mifflin.

Meyerson, M. and E. Banfield. 1955. *Politics, Planning and the Public Interest.* New York: Free Press.

Midgley, J. 1986. *Community Participation, Social Development and the State.* New York: Methuen.

Miller, S. and M. Rein. 1964. "Poverty and Social Change." *American Child* 50:10–15.

Mishra, R. 1981. *Society and Social Policy: Theories and Practice of Welfare,* 2nd ed. Atlantic Highland, NJ: Hunnington.

Moon, M. and J. Mulvey. 1996. *Entitlements and the Elderly: Protecting Promises, Recognizing Reality.* Washington, DC: Urban Institute.

Moon, M. and T. Smeeding. 1989. "Can the Elderly Afford Long-Term Care?" Pp. 137–60 in *The Care of Tomorrow's Elderly,* edited by M. Lewin and S. Sullivan. Washington, DC: American Enterprise Institute for Public Policy Research.

Moreau, J., M. David, W. Cohen, and H. Brager. 1962. *Income and Welfare in the United States.* New York: McGraw-Hill.

Moroney, R. 1976. *The Family and the State: Considerations for Social Policy.* New York: Longmans.

Moroney, R. 1986a. *Shared Responsibility: Families and Social Policy.* Hawthorne, NY: Aldine de Gruyter.

Moroney, R. 1986b. "Family Care: Towards a More Responsive Society." Pp. 139–65 in *Ethics of Dealing with Persons with Severe Handicaps,* edited by P. Dokecki and R. Zaner. Baltimore: Paul Brookes.

Morris, R. 1986. *Rethinking Social Welfare: Why Care for Strangers?* New York: Longmans.

Murray, C. 1984. *The Future of Social Welfare.* New York: Basic Books.

Myerson, M. and F. Banfield (eds.). 1955. *Politics, Planning and the Public Interest.* New York: Free Press.

Myrdal, G. 1940. *Population: A Problem for Democracy,* Godkin Lecture, 1938. Cambridge, MA: Harvard University Press.

Myrdal, G. 1966. *Beyond the Welfare State.* New Haven, CT: Yale University Press.

Nagel, E. 1956. *Logic without Metaphysics.* New York: Oxford University Press.

Naples, N. A. 1991. "Contradictions in the Gender Subtext of the War on Poverty: The Community Work and Resistance of Women from Low Income Communities." *Social Problems* 38:316–32.

National Association of Home Builders. 1985. *Housing America: The Challenges Ahead.* Washington, DC: NAHB.

Nisbet, R. 1967. *The Sociological Tradition.* New York: Basic Books.

Norton, A. and P. Glick. 1976. "Marital Instability: Past, Present and Future." *Journal of Social Issues* 32:8–12.

O'Neill, D. 1967. "Unfinished Business of the Welfare State." Pp. 70–78 in *The Welfare State,* edited by C. Schottland. New York: Harper Torchbooks.

Orshansky, M. 1965a. "Measuring Poverty." In *The Social Welfare Forum.* New York: Columbia University Press.

Orshansky, M. 1965b. "Who's Who among the Poor: A Demographic View of Poverty." *Social Security Bulletin* 28:3–32.

Orshansky, M. 1966. "More about the Poor in 1964." *Social Security Bulletin* 29:3–38.

Osborne, D. and T. Gaebler. 1992. *Reinventing Government.* New York: Plume.

Osterman, P. 1996. *Reforming Employment and Training Policy.* www.urban.org/PERIODCL/pubsect/osterman.htm.

Ozawa, M. 1982. *Income Maintenance and Work: Incentives Towards a Synthesis.* New York: Praeger.

Ozawa, M. 1994. "Women, Children, and Welfare Reform." *Affilia* 4:338–59.

Parsons, T. 1951. "Illness and the Role of the Physician: A Sociological Perspective." *American Journal of Orthopsychiatry* 21:452–60.

Phillips, A. 1958. "The Relation between Unemployment and the Rate of Change of Money Wages." *Economica* 25:283–300.

Pinker, R. 1973. *Social Theory and Social Policy* London: Heinemann.

Piven, F. and R. Cloward. 1971. *Regulating the Poor: The Functions of Public Welfare.* New York: Vintage.

Piven, F. and R. Cloward. 1982. *The New Class War.* New York: Pantheon.

Plotnick, R. 1987. "Income Distribution." Pp. 880–88 in *Encyclopedia of Social Work,* 18th ed., edited by A. Minahan. Silver Spring, MD: NASW.

Plotnik, R. 1995. "Income Distribution." Pp. 1439–1447 in *Encyclopedia of Social Work,* 19th ed., edited by R. Edwards. Silver Spring, MD. NASW.

Poloma, M. 1970. "The Myth of the Egalitarian Family: Familial Roles and the Professionally Employed Wife." Paper presented at the Sixty-Fifth Annual Meeting of the America Sociological Association, Washington, D.C.

Ponsioen, J. 1962. *The Analysis of Social Change Reconsidered: A Sociological Study.* The Hague: s'Gravenhage, Mouton.

Poynter, J. 1969. *Society and Pauperism.* London: Routledge and Kegan Paul.

Preston, S. 1984. "Children and the Elderly in the U.S." *Scientific American* 251:44–48.

Pruger, R. 1973. "Social Policy: Unilateral Transfer or Reciprocal Exchange." *Journal of Social Policy* 2:283–301.

Public Welfare Amendments of 1967. P.L. 90-248. 1968. U.S. Statutes at Large. Washington, DC: U.S. Government Printing Office, Pp. 871–921.

Radner, D. 1989. "Net Worth and Financial Assets of Age Groups in 1984." *Social Security Bulletin* 52:9–14.

Ranney, D. 1969. *Planning and Politics in the Metropolis.* Columbus, OH: Charles E. Merrill.

Rawls, J. 1971. *A Theory of Justice.* Cambridge, MA: Harvard University Press.

Rein, M. 1970. *Social Policy: Issues of Choice and Change.* New York: Random House.

Rein, M. 1976. *Social and Public Policy.* New York: Penguin.

Report of the Poor Law Commission of 1832. 1905. Cd. 2728. London: HMSO.

Report of the Royal Commission on the Poor Laws and the Relief of Distress. 1909. Cd. 4499, Vol. 3. London: HMSO.

Rice, M. 1978. "Housing in the 1960s." Pp. 348–62 in *The Story of Housing,* edited by G. Fish. New York: Macmillan.

Ridley, J. 1968. "Demographic Change and the Role and Status of Women." *Annals of the American Academy of Political and Social Sciences* 375:15–23.

Rimlinger, G. 1971. *Welfare Policy and Industrialization in Europe, America and Russia.* New York: John Wiley.

Robbins, W. 1983. "90% Jobless Rate Grinds West Virginia Coal Town." *New York Times,* April 10.

Roosevelt, J. 1988. "Don't Touch Social Security." *USA Today,* September 28.

Roper and Associates. 1976. *American Families: Changing Attitudes.* Storrs: University of Conecticut.

Rothman, D. 1979. "The State as Parent." Pp. 69–96 in *Doing Good: The Limits of Benevolence,* edited by W. Gaylin, T. Glasser, S. Marcus, and D. Rothman. New York: Pantheon.

Russo, N. F. and B. Green. 1991. *Work and Family roles: Selected Issues.* Unpublished manuscript.

Ryan, W. 1976. *Blaming the Victim.* New York: Vintage.

Schick, F. L. and R. Schick (eds). 1994. *Statistical Handbook on Aging Americans.* Phoenix, AZ: Oryx.

Schmittroth, L. (ed.). 1994. *Statistical Record of Children.* Washington, DC: Gale Research, Inc.

Scholz, J. K. 1993. "Tax Policy and the Working Poor: The Earned Income Tax Credit." *Focus* 3:1–12.

Schorr, A. 1963. *Slums and Social Insecurity.* Washington, DC: U.S. Department of Health, Education and Welfare.

Schottland, C. 1963. *The Social Security Program in the United States.* New York: Appleton-Century-Crofts.

Schottland, C. 1967. *The Welfare State.* New York: Harper Torchbooks.

Schussheim, M. 1974. "Toward a New Housing Policy: The Legacy of the Sixties." CED Paper 29, Washington, D.C.

Schwartz, D., R. Ferlauto, and D. Hoffman. 1988. *A New Housing Policy for America.* Philadelphia: Temple University Press.

Schwartz, J. 1983. *America's Hidden Success.* New York: Norton.

Segre, S. 1975. "Family Stability, Social Classes and Values in Traditional and Industrial Societies." *Journal of Marriage and the Family* 37:431–36.

Sherman, S. 1989. "Public Attitudes toward Social Security." *Social Security Bulletin* 52(12):2–16.

Shogren, E. August 13, 1997. "Clinton: Welfare Reform Is Working." *Phoenix Tribune*, A7.

Shorr, A. and P. Moen. 1977. *Single Parents: Public and Private Image.* Paper prepared for the Task Force on Mental Health and the Family, President's Commission on Mental Health.

Silverman, A. 1971. *User Needs and Social Services.* Report prepared for the House of Representatives, Subcommittee on Housing, Committee on Banking and Currency. Washington, DC: U.S. Government Printing Office.

Singer, B. H. and K. G. Manton. 1993. "How Many Elderly in the Next Generation?" *Focus* 15:1–11.

Slater, C. M. (ed.). 1995. *Business Statistics of the United States, 1995 Edition.* Lanham, MD: Bernham.

Somers, H. and S. Somers. 1965. *Doctors, Patients and Health Insurance.* New York: Doubleday.

Stack, C. and H. Semmel. 1974. "Social Insecurity: Breaking up Poor Families." Pp. 89–105 in *Welfare in America: Controlling the Dangerous Classes,* edited by S. Mandell. Englewood Cliffs, NJ: Prentice-Hall.

Stegman, M. 1970. "The New Mythology of Housing." *Trans-action* 7:55–62.

Steiner, G. 1971. *The State of Welfare.* Washington, DC: Brookings Institute.

Steiner, G. 1976. *The Children's Cause.* Washington, DC: Brookings Institute.

Steiner, G. 1981. *The Futility of Family Policy.* Washington, DC: Brookings Institute.

Stewart, E. M. 1925. "The Cost of American Almhouses." *Labor Statistics Bulletin* 386:1–6.

Stoesz, D. 1985. "The Case for Community Enterprise Zones." *Urban and Social Change Review* 18:20–23.

Strauss, N. 1944. *The Seven Myths of Housing.* New York: Knopf.

Subcommittee on Executive Reorganization, House of Representatives. 1966. Pt. 9, p. 2030; Pt. 11, p. 2837. Washington, DC: U.S. Government Printing Office.

Subcommittee on Housing and Community Development. 1975. *Evolution of the Role of the Federal Government in Housing and Community Development.* Committee on Banking and Currency, House of Representatives, 94th Congress, First Session. Washington, DC: U.S. Government Printing Office.

Summer, L., S. Parrott, and C. Mann. 1997. *Millions of Uninsured and Underinsured Children Are Eligible for Medicaid.* Washington, DC: Center on Budget and Policy Priorities.

Tawney, R. 1961. *The Acquisitive Society.* London: Fontana.

Tawney, R. 1964. *Equality.* London: Allen and Unwin.

Thompson, S. and P. Hoggett. 1996. "Universalism, Selectivism and Particularism: Towards a Postmodern Social Policy." *Critical Social Policy* 46:21–43.

Titmuss, R. 1950. *Problems of Social Policy*. London: HMSO and Longmans.

Titmuss, R. 1958. *Essays on the Welfare State*. London: Allen and Unwin.

Titmuss, R. 1966. "Social Policy and Economic Progress." In *The Social Welfare Forum*. New York: Columbia University Press.

Titmuss, R. 1968. *Commitment to Welfare*. London: Allen and Unwin.

Titmuss, R. 1971. *The Gift Relationship*. London: Allen and Unwin.

Trattner, W. I. 1974. *From Poor Law to Welfare State*. New York: Free Press.

Trattner, W. I. 1989. *From Poor Law to Welfare State: A History of Social Welfare in America*, 4th ed. New York: Free Press.

Tugwell, R. 1934. "Relief and Reconstruction." Pp. 32–48 in Proceedings of the National Conference of Social Work. Chicago: University of Chicago Press.

Tuominen, M. 1992. "Gender, Class, and Motherhood: The Legacy of Federal Child Care Policy." *Affilia* 4:8–25.

U.S. Bureau of the Census. 1977. "Projections on the Population of the United States, 1977 to 2050." *Current Population Reports*. Washington, DC: U.S. Government Printing Office.

U.S. Bureau of the Census. 1984. *Money Income and Poverty: Status of Families and Persons in the U.S. Current Population Reports*, Consumer Income Series, P-60, No.145. Washington, DC: U.S. Government Printing Office.

U.S. Bureau of the Census. 1988. *Statistical Abstract of the United States*. Washington, DC: U.S. Government Printing Office.

U.S. Bureau of the Census. 1989. *Statistical Abstracts of the United States, 1989*. Washington, DC: U.S. Government Printing Office.

U.S. Bureau of the Census. 1995. *Sixty-Five Plus in the United States*. www.census.gov/socdemo/www/agebrief/html.

U.S. Bureau of the Census. 1996a. *Health Insurance Coverage, 1995*. www.census.gov/ftp/pub/hhes/hlthins/cover95/cov95.asc/html.

U.S. Bureau of the Census. 1996b. *Statistical Abstracts of the United States*. Washington, DC: U.S. Government Printing Office.

U.S. Department of Health and Human Services. 1997. *Americans Less Likely to Use Nursing Home Care Today*. www.hhs.gov/news/press/1997press/970123b.html.

U.S. Department of Health, Education and Welfare. 1968. "Health Expenditures Fiscal Years 1929–69 and Calendar Years 1928–68." *Research and Statistics Notes*, No. 18. Washington, DC: U.S. Government Printing Office.

U.S. Department of Health, Education and Welfare. 1974. *Older Americans Act of 1965, as Amended and Related Acts*. Washington, DC: U.S. Government Printing Office.

U.S. Department of Housing and Urban Development. 1974. *Housing in the Seventies: A Report of the National Housing Policy Review*. HUD Publication no. HUD-PDR-64. Washington, DC: U.S. Government Printing Office.

United Nations. 1968. *Statistical Yearbook, 1968*, 20th ed. New York: Statistical Office of the United Nations, Department of Economic and Social Affairs.

USA Today/CNN/Gallup. 1995. Nationwide telephone poll, September 23–25.

Veiller, L. 1910. *Housing Reform: A Handbook for Practical Use in American Cities.* New York: Russell Sage.

Veiller, L. 1914. *A Model Housing Law.* New York: Survey Associates.

Watson, D. 1980. *Caring for Strangers: A Practical Philosophy for Students of Social Administration.* London: Routledge and Kegan Paul.

Wicksell, K. 1958. *Selected Papers on Economic Theory.* London: Macmillan.

Wilensky, H. 1975. *The Welfare State and Equality.* Berkeley: University of California Press.

Wilensky, H. and C. Lebeaux. 1965. *Industrial Society and Social Welfare.* New York: Free Press.

Wilson, A. 1993. "Year of the (Wary) Woman." *Arizona Republic,* January 26, p. C1.

Wood, E. 1919. *The Housing of the Unskilled Worker: America's Next Problem.* New York: Macmillan.

Wood, F. 1939. "The Development of Legislation." Pp. 98–113 in *Public Housing in America,* edited by M. Schnapper. New York: H.H. Wilson.

Woods, J. 1988. "Retirement Age Women and Pensions: Findings from the New Beneficiary Survey." *Social Security Bulletin* 51 (5):3–9.

Woodward, C. 1997. "Work Plentiful for Part-Timers, but Wages Lower." *Phoenix Tribune,* September 1, A9.

Yankelovich, Skelley and White. 1977. *Raising Children in a Changing Society.* General Mills American Family Report. Minneapolis: General Mills.

Yankelovich, Skelley and White. 1985. *A Fifty Year Report Card on the Social Security System: The Attitudes of the American Public.* Washington, DC: NOAC.

Young, M. and R. Wilmott. 1973. *The Symmetrical Family.* London: Routledge and Kegan Paul.

Zimmerman, C. 1974. "Family Influence upon Religion." *Journal of Comparative Family Studies* 5(2):1–16.

Author Index

Subject Index